History Of St. Margaret's Convent, Edinburgh

HISTORY

OF

ST. MARGARET'S CONVENT.

Ballantyne Press
BALLANTYNE, HANSON AND CO.
EDINBURGH AND LONDON

RIGHT REV. JAMES GILLIS, D.D.,

Bishop of Limyra, Vicar Apostolic of the Eastern District of Scotland.

The Revival of Conventual Life in Scotland.

HISTORY

OF

ST. MARGARET'S CONVENT,

EDINBURGH,

THE FIRST RELIGIOUS HOUSE FOUNDED IN SCOTLAND SINCE THE SO-CALLED REFORMATION;

AND

THE AUTOBIOGRAPHY OF THE FIRST RELIGIOUS,

SISTER AGNES XAVIER TRAIL.

WITH A

PREFACE BY THE MOST REV. WILLIAM SMITH, D.D.

ARCHBISHOP OF ST. ANDREWS AND EDINBURGH.

JOHN CHISHOLM,

EDINBURGH, 35 ALBANY STREET.

LONDON, 38 CASTLE STREET, HOLBORN, E.C.

a. m.

Dedicatory Poem

TO

MOTHER MARGARET TERESA

ON

THE OCCASION OF HER JUBILEE, ROSARY SUNDAY, OCTOBER 1883.

BY

REGINALD E. HORSLEY.

A DARK, tempestuous, drear December day!
Behold! an oak does battle with the storm.
An ancient giant, o'er whose plumèd head
The shifting skies of centuries have spread
Alternate canopies of sun and shade.
Full many a triumph has the monarch won
And baffled back the demon of the blast.
Now, once again, the proud old crest is reared
And all day long resists the fierce assault;
Now, bending till the branches lowermost
Are crushed against the bosom of the earth;
Now, like Antæus, from the same broad breast
With freshened strength upspringing from each fall.
At length, at Even when the angry wind—
Its frantic force exhausted all in vain—
With whistling shriek proclaimed itself o'ercome,

And drave the clouds before it to the sea,
The stars looked down upon a world at peace.
Next morn I wandered through the wooded vale,
Came presently beside the stalwart oak,
And stood amazed to note how little ill
The raging hurricane had wrought thereon;
Or, rather, how much good, for all around,
Sad-coloured leaves that owned the garb of death,
And sap-deserted branches lay in heaps,
But not a living bough had fallen down.
So that the storm, intent to slay the tree,
Had only rent its useless parts away
And blessed it with a newer, stronger life.

Then, in the dim recess of far-off years,
My mind, in retrospection, saw a scene
Not all unlike the fight that had been here
And in its issue even as its end.
The oak—the Church—the storm—the nation's strife
That hurled itself upon the spouse of God.
The withered leaves and sapless branches too
All played their part. The leaves th' unstable minds
Throughout the contest lapsing from the arms
In love outstretched, because they could not pierce
The gathered gloom, and see the light of Truth
Behind the mist of temporary sin;
And, so, afraid, fell towards the opposing ranks,
Made "Faith" their watchword, but of faith had none.
The branches, restless spirits, reconciled
Not to the Church which they professed to serve,
But to the ways of infamy and guile:
Who, greedy of the labourer's hire, forgot
To do the labourer's duty, and so fell,
Or not so much did fall, as were cast off
By Mother Church, ashamed of such bad sons.

And then I mused on him * who raised the storm,
Who blew the blast of war about the Church,

* Luther.

In vain attempt to overthrow her sway.
Some good he did, whose only thought was harm,
For Satan never sent an ill on earth
But by the providence of God was found
To fall, a blunted shaft from off the shield
Opposed by Faith to catch it; or to hold
Some element of good within itself
Whereby alone it swayed awhile the world.
So, he reformed thus much, that by his stir
He shook from out the Church those sinful souls
Who would be her undoing. But, he left
The rock-foundationed temple of his God
Unshattered and unharmed, and, furthermore,
This man who first began the mighty strife
Was first to make provision for its end,
But all unconsciously. Like him of Thebes *
Who sowed the dragon's teeth, and straightway saw
A crop of armèd men arise to life
To fall anon upon a bloody death,
He sowed a seed which took quick root and grew,
And spread that crop of sects about the world
Whose first brave deed, discovering that they lived,
Forgetful they were offspring of one sire,
Was to divide, form ranks, take arms and fight;
And this most fair beginning hath so pleased
Their several children, these are fighting still,
And only need a little time to fall,
Merging their dust in that from whence they sprang.

Now, when the seed of that sad fateful plant
Which men call Heresy was broadcast sown,
It fell and flourished in this Scottish land,
Until it loomed a dark, stupendous growth,
That hid the light of God's eternal truth,
And drooped its shadow o'er the nation's heart.
So sat for nearly thrice one hundred years

* Cadmus.

In self-elected darkness those weak men
Who hurled "anathema" upon the Church,
Denying God had sealed her with the right
To guide their souls into the path of peace;
Claiming the guidance of the Holy Ghost
Was theirs alone, and yet uniting not.
Who some by this, and some by that way trod,
And raving all against the Church's sway,
Her spiritual chieftainship—assumed,
And arrogated to themselves command,
Each claiming his alone the right to rule.
Forgetful of the words of Christ the Lord,
"I am the Way! I am the Truth! the Light!"
Sect after sect sowed schism in itself,
And each division ere it yet had grown
To aught that spake of power, cleft again
Until the land was rank with noxious weeds.
But all the while the white pure flower of Faith
Still blossomed, tended by the faithful few.

The Church, meanwhile, reviving from her wounds
Begins to rear her dauntless crest again,
Sends forth a band of earnest souls, who strive
In singleness of mind and life, once more
To sow the long uprooted seed of Truth:
Who, while the hostile camps make mutual war,
Raise up the fallen altars of the Lord.
The which, beholding, for a time the sects
Forget their discord; and uniting all
Fall thick upon their common foe—the Church,
Perceiving either she, or they must die.
For one might fail, and all the rest prevail
Or, all might sink before the might of one,
Which last, and greatest, then might merge the whole;
But if the Church prevailing, should remain,
Full well they knew her truth may slay them all,
Before the world grew old enough to die.
Too late defence! The golden moment gained,

The Church makes good her footing, and at length
The roar of general battle dies away:
A skirmish here, a rally there, and then
The trumpets of the foe ring out retreat
And all their hosts roll backward from the Church,
As from the base of some colossal cliff,
The mighty waves of mighty ocean roll
Stupendous in their rage, but impotent!

And now the need for labourers grew apace,
For, as the tree of heresy succumbed,
Branch after branch shorn by the Spirit's sword,
The too long intercepted Sun of Truth
Shone out and brought the harvest on its beams.
Then one * arose, unrolled, and shook on high
The long neglected banner of the Cross,
And filled with faith espoused the cause of Christ.
Equipped in love, he wandered o'er the soil
Of distant countries, pleading for his own.
His voice, like music soothing after storm,
Made mellow by the orator's sweet craft,
Now rang sonorous as the trenchant tongue
Made war upon the enemy of souls,
Whose wiles so long had kept his land from God;
Now sank to plaintive softness, as he craved
Some means to lighten those who sat in gloom.
What wonder then, that those entrancèd hearts,
Who, while they listened, fed on melody,
Responded eager to his eager call;
Gave of their substance, and because his speech
At once had burned like fire and soothed like balm,
With one consent bestowed on him for name
"John of the Golden Mouth" of latter days.
Then, as the walls of ancient Troas rose
In slow response to hidden harmonies,
So, while his voice made music in the world

* Rev. Dr. Gillis.

In sweet appeal, the sleeping hearts awoke,
And stone by stone the happy earth bestowed,
And stone on stone was reared that sacred pile,*
Meet temple for the priestesses of God!

So this gave gold, and that a gift of land,
Influence and example some would bring;
But one † who sat within her northern home,
Stirred by the power of the preacher's word,
Caught in his golden speech a special call,
A cry that pierced her ever-listening soul,
A summons to the subject from the King:
"Daughter, arise! The harvest now is ripe,
Go forth and gather for me till I come!"
Then bounded every pulse with holy joy,
Throbbed fast her heart with pure ecstatic love;
Each impulse of her ardent will obeyed
In sweet submission, and so murmuring
"O Lord, I come to do Thy will," she brought
Nor gold, nor lands, nor heritage, but this,
The highest, noblest, best of gifts—herself!
What though the pleadings of parental love
Fell sadly for a while upon her ear!
Though passionate devotion wept a space
And strove to quench her holy fire with tears!
What though the glitter of a gilded life
Made effort to enchain her for the world,
She heeded not, because her God had called!
And all her being rapturously rose
In swift spontaneous answer, for she knew
To sacrifice the dearest hopes of life
For vestal years within the courts of God
Was but to forfeit dross, and gain pure gold;
To miss a bauble and acquire a crown;
To lose the trifles of a few short years
And win perfection for Eternity.

* St. Margaret's Convent. † Mother Margaret Teresa.

To kindlier shores she bent her footsteps then,
With one,* like-souled, excelling her in years,
But scarce more skilled to know the voice of Christ;
And, there abiding, for a space she strove
By prayer, and holy living, much retreat,
By contemplation face to face with God
To learn more perfectly the chosen task.
Ere long, moreover, she put on that garb,
Which while it showed her widow to the world
Proclaimed her spouse of Christ. Then set her face
Across the sea, and yearned again for home.
Anon, returned, and with her came a train
Of noble women, careless of themselves
So long as they fulfilled their high behest.
Such souls as theirs, who formed that glorious band
Had in a time of fiercer trouble, sought
To animate the martyrs. So they came.
Ignored at first, then fearfully opposed,
They by their meek but mighty effort razed
The difficult steep hill of human hate,
Sowing all over it the seed of love,
Which burst in blossom by and by, and shed
A sweet forgotten fragrance o'er the land.
So Love began, and Faith made constant prayer,
While Hope sat ever in their steadfast hearts.
Content to toil all through the downcast night,
And drag their nets through seas of unbelief,
Through oceans of intolerance and pride,
Because they knew their Master and the day
Would come together, and their nets be full.

Thereafter, soon the vineyard of the Lord
Was filled with earnest workers, and to-day
The Church that was erst while so sore bested
Has step by step off-shaken all her foes,
And stands resplendent and more glorious—

* Sister Agnes Xavier.

Though men perchance esteem her not so great—
For she has suffered in the cause of God
As hath no other Church before nor since.
And, now, although some wounds are open still,
She fronts her foes most proudly. Ay! and points
To those same wounds as emblems of the love
That Christ her Founder lavishes on her;
Maintaining He has loved her well indeed
Who for His sake hath suffered her to bleed,
And decked her forehead with a martyr's crown,
Undying, even in this dying world.
So looked Sebastian, when the Roman barbs
Made havoc of his life, and did not kill!

The Church, our mother, now gains ever ground,
For every day some wanderers turn again
To her true bosom, yearning to receive,
And every land which cast her off before
Holds now a band of faithful souls, whose cry
Goes up in mighty unison—"How long?"
And not a day but somewhere in the world
The jubilant "Te Deum" swells to Heaven,
While every seraph hymns angelic praise,
Because another lamb has found the fold.

Where better seek to prove this glorious truth
Than here, in this fair land, where active strife
Against the doctrine of the Church hath sunk
To passive sufferance, and undismayed,
Or with a partial discontent at most,
The nation sees the land drift slowly back,
But surely, to her ancient anchorage.

Oh! thou—the only one on earth to-day
Of that bright holy missionary band,
Who set aflame the vestal lamp once more,
Who through the chance and change of fifty years
Hast served like Anna in the house of God,
To thee I bring these thoughts, and offer them
To do thee honour; yet not so much thee
As Him who honours thee Himself to-day
With richer guerdon than my hand can bring.
For I can only weave a wreath of song
And lay it at thy feet—too soon to fade.
But God hath decked thee with another crown,
And its unfading glory shall remain
When mine hath been forgotten. It is well!

CONTENTS.

BIOGRAPHICAL SKETCH OF SISTER AGNES XAVIER (ANN AGNES TRAIL).

ILLUSTRATIONS.

ERRATA.

Page 28, line 16, *for* "heat," *read* "beat."

,, 224, ,, 3, ,, "homum," *read* "bonum."

PREFACE.

To one who has been witness of the vast advance which the Catholic Religion has made in Calvinistic Scotland within the last fifty years, it must prove an interesting study to trace the causes of so remarkable and extensive a development. In that space of time, churches and convents, schools and orphanages, priests and religious, monks and nuns, have multiplied amazingly, and a thousand other active forces of Catholic life have been brought into play; while the freedom now enjoyed by the lately persecuted members of the Church, and the kindly intercourse subsisting between them and their Protestant neighbours, contrast most strikingly with the penal restrictions of old and the once proverbial bigotry of the nation.

Among the factors contributing to such a result, the Convent of St. Margaret's is deservedly numbered. Founded in Edinburgh fifty years ago, it claims the honour of being the first religious house established in Scotland after three hundred years of banishment from a country where the magnificent remains of abbeys, priories, and convents show how flourishing they once had been; and, though far inferior to them in richness, in splendour, and extent, it has rivalled them in good works.

The history, therefore, of such an institution, appears most opportunely at the time when St. Margaret's Convent is keeping her Golden Jubilee, and furnishes a fruitful theme of meditation to the Christian philosopher. For here, as in other cases, he will see how Divine Providence, when it appoints any great work to be done, brings upon the stage, at the right time, the right person in the right place. He will watch with interest the first inspirations, and the gradual fashioning of the young enthusiastic Levite into the compliant instrument of the work; and will mark how, as he developed in power, he was ever looking forward so far in advance of his age, and yet knew so well what suited its wants at the moment.

His genius to conceive, his skill to plan, his labours to realise, his unwearied zeal in consolidating the work of his enthusiasm, are worthily recorded in the following pages, as well as the efforts of the Sisters to correspond with the exertions of the Founder to bring the Convent up to such a state of efficiency as has made it an active instrument in advancing the good cause.

It is a great chapter in the history of the Catholic Church in Scotland, and I heartily recommend its perusal to all who love to study the ways of God in bringing about His designs.

✠ WILLIAM,

Archbishop of St. Andrews and Edinburgh.

22nd July 1886.

INTRODUCTION.

Scotland, at the present day, possesses nearly twenty different Religious Orders or Religious Congregations, co-operating with a zealous priesthood in the work of saving souls, and devoting themselves to all the works of mercy, spiritual and corporal. If we compare this state of things with the religious statistics of fifty years ago, we shall be surprised at the change which so short a space of time has effected, and naturally inquire how it has been brought about.

Perhaps in no country did the so-called Reformation effect its purpose of destruction more completely than in Scotland. For three hundred years scarce a vestige of the ancient faith was to be found in all the length and breadth of the land. Churches, monasteries, charitable institutions of all kinds were swept away; the wealthy Catholics who chose to save their souls at the expense of this world's comfort, went into voluntary exile; the few faithful pastors who escaped death, or who ventured back from the foreign lands to which they had been banished, wandered about from one hiding-place to another, and at the risk of their lives administered the consolations of religion to their scattered flocks.

Doubtless many causes have combined their influence to bring about the comparative prosperity which we now enjoy: our present purpose does not lead us into a search for them; but as Religious Orders have had their share in the merit of the good work, we wish to give the public some account of the circumstances under which these have regained a footing in Scotland, and we publish this little sketch on occasion of their "Golden Jubilee," the fiftieth anniversary of the foundation of St. Margaret's Convent.

Balmez, the learned author of "Protestantism compared with Catholicity," says:—"Religious institutions are one of those points whereon Protestantism and Catholicity are in complete opposition to each other; the one destroys them, the other establishes and encourages them. One of the first acts of Protestantism, wherever it is introduced, is to attack religious institutions by its doctrine and its acts; it labours to destroy them immediately." We have no need to look beyond the boundaries of our own country for proofs of this double assertion; the many ruins that still exist, and the still more numerous traditions, attest the truth of what is said regarding Catholic zeal and Protestant vandalism. It has been said that religion can exist without Monastic Institutions, and this no one will attempt to deny; but because one thing is not essential to the existence of another, it does not follow that the one has not its origin in the other; on the contrary, it may tend to its perfection, as flowers adorn a tree although they are not necessary to its vitality.

DATES OF THE INTRODUCTION TO SCOTLAND OF THE RELIGIOUS ORDERS AND CONGREGATIONS AT PRESENT LABOURING IN THIS COUNTRY.

Women.	*Men.*	*Date.*
Ursulines of Jesus.	...	1834.
Franciscans.	...	1849.
Sisters of Mercy.	...	1849.
Sisters of the Good Shepherd.	...	1851.
... ...	Oblates of Mary Immaculate.	1859.
... ...	Jesuits.	1859.
... ...	Vincentians.	1859.
Sisters of Charity.	...	1860.
... ...	Marist Brothers.	1860.
Little Sisters of the Poor.	...	1862.
Sisters of Nazareth.	...	1862.
Sisters of the Immaculate Conception.	...	1863.
... ...	Passionists.	1865.
... ...	Franciscans.	1868.
... ...	Redemptorists.	1870.
... ...	Benedictines.	1876.
Sisters of St. Joseph.	...	1879.
Servants of the Sacred Heart.	...	1883.
Benedictines of the Perpetual Adoration.	...	1884.

Count Montalembert, in his introductory chapter to "The Monks of the West," writes:—"Wherever the Catholic Church is not the object of open persecution; wherever she is allowed a legitimate portion of liberty, religious houses spring up as of themselves. We have despoiled and proscribed them;—we see them everywhere return, sometimes under new names and appearances, but always with the ancient spirit. They neither reclaim nor regret their former grandeur, they confine themselves to living, and to preaching both by word and example: without wealth, without pomp, without legal rights; but not without friends, and, above all, not without enemies. Friends and enemies are alike interested to know whence they came and whence they draw the secret of a life so tenacious and so fruitful." Three hundred years have passed over Scotland since her hierarchy had been suppressed, and her monks and nuns driven into exile; penal laws had weighed heavily on the exercise of religion, and the little that could be done was accomplished secretly and at the peril of life and liberty. But the watchfulness of the enemy at last began to relax. Before the end of last century many of the penal enactments had ceased to be enforced, and as Catholics became more numerous they also became more courageous.

But yet, only fifty years ago, the glorious ritual

of Catholic ceremonial was comparatively little known, and the service of Sunday was limited, as a rule, to Low Mass and a sermon. God's time had come, however, for the revival of the Church, and He was about to bring back to Scotland the religious habit, so long scorned and abused. The instrument was being prepared for the work, and we shall see in this case, as in many others, how much may be accomplished by one generous soul, devoted to a holy cause, and labouring in absolute dependence upon the guidance of Divine Providence. It was reserved to the deceased Bishop Gillis to restore Religious Orders to Scotland, as likewise much of the external life of the Church in this country.

It would be impossible to give even a sketch of the history of St. Margaret's Convent without constant allusion to the one who was its founder. We shall devote the following chapter to the early life of Bishop Gillis. It is not for us to attempt to write the life of this eminent man—we trust an abler pen will one day accomplish the task. From time to time, however, in the course of this little work, we shall, in his connection with St. Margaret's, bring Dr. Gillis before our readers, and thus in some measure prepare the way for a more detailed biography.

The foundation of a Religious House, destined

to promote the glory of God and the spiritual and temporal good of the sick, the needy, and the ignorant, is at all times an undertaking meritorious in the sight of God, and claiming the gratitude of man. But when we again recall the fact, that for three hundred years not one such establishment had been allowed to exist in Scotland; that the old monastic institutions had been utterly destroyed, and their memory blackened with the foulest calumnies; that these lying tales had been handed down from father to son for generations, and that they were received as gospel truths by the whole Scottish people; we may in some degree measure the difficulties that surrounded the foundation of a Religious House in Edinburgh; and we may all the more "render honour to whom honour is due,"—to the young priest who so bravely faced all the obstacles placed in his way, by Catholics as well as Protestants; the timidity of the former being at times as great a hindrance as the bigotry of the latter.

It is indeed evident that the founding of St. Margaret's meant something more than is implied in the founding of a convent at the present day.

Surely the man who accomplished the resurrection of Religious Orders deserves to be held in everlasting remembrance!

EDINBURGH, 26*th December* 1884.

HISTORY

OF

ST. MARGARET'S CONVENT.

CHAPTER I.

THE REV. JAMES GILLIS.

THIS distinguished prelate was born at Montreal, Canada, 7th April 1802. His father was a Scotchman, who had emigrated in early life, and having acquired a considerable fortune, settled in Montreal, where he married Miss Langley, a native of Kent, then a Protestant Episcopalian. The elder James Gillis belonged to an old Catholic family in Banffshire, and from his childhood stood firm to his faith, although exposed to sneers and petty persecution on the part of his schoolfellows for so doing.

The subject of this memoir was his only son, and it is to be supposed that he instilled the highest Catholic principles into the heart of his beloved child—the seed thus early sown in good ground having borne fruit a hundredfold! When the boy was four years old, he narrowly escaped death. The house adjoining that of Mr. Gillis took fire, and the flames spreading rapidly, it was with difficulty that the child was rescued by his nurse, who carried him from his bed to a place of safety, through the snow of a Canadian winter's night.

At an early age James Gillis was placed by his father at the Sulpician College in Montreal. The priests who conducted this college belonged to the Congregation of St. Sulpice, and had been sent out to Canada by Monsieur Olier, the venerable founder of the congregation, the French Government having giving them the feudal superiority of the island on which Montreal is built. It was, doubtless, owing to his being placed in this college in his childhood that he acquired that proficiency in the French language for which he was afterwards so remarkable; and it was here also that the first germs of his vocation to the ecclesiastical state were fostered and encouraged. It was his delight thus early to erect and decorate miniature altars, and to induce his young companions to join him in performing religious functions and exercises of piety.

The College of Montreal appears to have been in high repute as an educational establishment, many of the youths who pursued their studies at the same time as James Gillis within its walls having been distinguished in after life.

The College Register contains the names of Messrs. Mondelet, M'Cord, Bruneau, and Hippolyte Guy, all eminent at the bar; the Hon. Charles de St. Ours, Conseiller Législatif, and "Son Honneur," Edouard Raymond Fabre, Maire of Montreal, father of Monseigneur Fabre, the present bishop of that city.

In 1816 Mr. Gillis disposed of his property in Montreal and returned to his native land, where, with his wife and son, he settled in the village of Fochabers, and ended his days in peaceful retirement. Mrs. Gillis survived him many years, and in her old age was afflicted with blindness. She had the happiness of being received into the Church some time before her death, which occurred in 1851. In 1817 James Gillis entered the Seminary of Aquhorties as an ecclesiastical student; that institution had then for its Superior the Rev. James Kyle, afterwards Vicar Apostolic of the Northern District of Scotland.

He had not been more than a year in this college when it was determined to send a number of the students to pursue their studies in France; for a considerable portion of the property in Paris belonging to the Scottish Mission, confiscated during the first Revolution, had been restored by the Bourbons, and Bishop Cameron thought it advisable to resume the practice of sending students to that country. Accordingly, after the preliminary arrangements had been made and the more serious difficulties surmounted, Mr. Gillis set out with four companions, 3d December 1818, from Aquhorties. Having sailed from Aberdeen for London on the 8th, they arrived in Paris on the 15th, and on the following day entered the Seminary of St. Nicholas, then the classical institution for the diocese of Paris.

The old "Scots College" of the Scotch Mission still exists in the Rue des Fossés, but the house was too large for the small body of students that could be maintained there; and it was judged more advantageous to let it to a tenant, and place the boys in one of the existing seminaries.

At St. Nicholas, Mr. Gillis distinguished himself, and gained many honours, especially in the school of rhetoric. That he was much beloved by his fellow-students we have a touching proof. On the completion of his course of study, they addressed him in a farewell ode, which expressed their admiration of his talents, and their affectionate esteem for his virtue and amiability. Among his companions was the late Monsignor Surat, Vicar-General of the late Cardinal Morlot, Archbishop of Paris, and one of the victims of the Commune in 1871. After the death of Bishop Gillis, Monsignor Surat recalled the time they had passed together in their early days. He says, "At the Petit Séminaire, he (James Gillis) was always at the head of his class, always had the first places in competitions, the best prizes and highest distinctions in examinations. He worked and studied with indefatigable ardour, even to the prejudice of his health." The same friend testifies to the proficiency of Mr. Gillis, when he passed on to the Grand Séminaire, where he began to give evidence of what he became in after years. "He spoke with remarkable facility and eloquence, and excelled his companions in everything without effort, and with great simplicity. In his conduct he was always extremely exact to rule, pious and edifying." What higher eulogium could be passed on an ecclesiastical student? The late Bishop of Orleans, Monseigneur Dupanloup, was another fellow-student of Mr. Gillis, and in like manner retained through life the greatest esteem and regard for him.

Mr. Gillis left St. Nicholas in October 1823, and entered the Seminary of Issy, a house belonging to the Sulpicians, to study philosophy and theology, but his health gave way, and he was obliged to return to Scotland, which he did in April 1826. In the autumn of that year he was able to resume his studies under the direction of Bishop Scott, in Glasgow. He was ordained priest by Bishop Paterson at Aquhorties, on the 9th of June 1827.

A great part of the first year after his ordination he spent at Blairs with Mr. Menzies of Pitfodels, whose acquaintance he had made in Paris, and whilst revising his studies, he took charge of the Catholics in the neighbourhood.

On the death of Bishop Cameron, 7th February 1828, his successor, Bishop Paterson, took Mr. Gillis with him to Edinburgh, and committed to him the charge of conducting the ceremonial of the deceased prelate's funeral. It was on this occasion that he began to display on a more extended scale that taste for religious ceremonial for which he became so distinguished. His delicate health precluded him from the more arduous duties of a missionary; but his zeal was ever ardent, and he devoted himself with great energy to the duties of preaching and teaching Christian doctrine to the poor Catholic children whom he assembled on Sundays, and to whose instruction he willingly devoted all his ability and earnestness of purpose. He knew the importance of taking hold of the rising generation, and consequently nothing was little in his eyes when the care of children was concerned. He spared no pains to render his catechism attractive to his young flock, and his efforts met with the success he most desired—the increasing number of those who attended his instructions, and their fervent and persevering practice of the duties of religion.

His eloquence in the pulpit now began to attract notice. In 1828 he was deputed by Bishop Paterson to collect money in France for the repairs of St. Mary's Chapel, Broughton Street, Edinburgh. The French archbishops and bishops received the young missionary with the utmost kindness, and furthered his undertaking by their sympathy and recommendations. He raised a considerable sum in Paris and other large towns, and thus enabled the Bishop to make the necessary repairs, to enlarge the Church and adorn the interior. He took advantage of his stay in France to make a spiritual retreat in the Monastery of La Trappe. Far from the scene of his missionary labours, he thought of poor Scotland, grieved over her apostasy, prayed for her return to the ancient faith, and again offered himself to labour with all his strength for the salvation of souls, and the advancement of the Church in that unhappy country where heresy had so long reigned supreme.

The thought occurred to him that if Religious Orders could be restored, much might be accomplished through their instrumentality, and he finally resolved to leave nothing undone to carry this idea into effect. He felt that the inspiration came from God, and that He would provide all that was necessary to its fulfilment. Amongst the ecclesiastics following the exercises of the same retreat was

Monseigneur Soyer, Bishop of Luçon, and to this distinguished prelate Mr. Gillis spoke of his project with all its accompanying hopes and fears. Monseigneur Soyer was a man of large and generous views; and he at once entered warmly into the design laid before him. His own diocese was then just recovering from the devastation caused by the Revolution, and he could well understand the difficulties attending the restoration of religion in Scotland; consequently he was all the more ready to assist Mr. Gillis as far as it lay in his power.

Amongst his priests at Luçon there was a holy man who had done much to repair the evil wrought by the storm of infidel fury,—this was the Rev. Louis Marie Baudouin, now declared "Venerable" by the Church.

Besides seminaries for the education of the priesthood, the Abbé Baudouin had founded a congregation of religious women, called Ursulines of Jesus, devoted chiefly to the instruction of youth. It seemed to Monseigneur Soyer that such a congregation would be admirably adapted to the purposes of Mr. Gillis, and proposed that the latter should make himself personally acquainted with it, promising him, at the same time, all the assistance in his power, when circumstances should favour the execution of his design. Consequently, after the retreat, Mr. Gillis accompanied the Bishop to

Luçon, and was introduced by him to the sisterhood as well as to the saintly founder, the Abbé Baudouin. Some acquaintance with the rules and constitutions of the congregation confirmed the favourable impression it made upon his mind, and Mr. Gillis determined to solicit the consent of his own ecclesiastical superior for leave to establish a house of this order in Edinburgh.

The look of sanctity which shone in the countenance of the Abbé Baudouin made a deep impression on Mr. Gillis, and not less favourable was the opinion formed in the mind of the holy old man regarding the zealous young priest with whom he was now contracting friendship. It would appear that about this time Mr. Gillis had serious thoughts of retiring from missionary duties, and himself entering a religious order. To come to a decision on this important point, he made a spiritual retreat at the Jesuit Noviciate House, Montrouge; his reflections resulted in the determination to devote his life to the service of God and the Church in Scotland. This retreat was made in January 1830. The Revolution of that year breaking out, it was with difficulty that he effected his escape and returned home.

The royal family of France arrived shortly after in Edinburgh. During the sojourn of the royal exiles at Holyrood Palace, Mr. Gillis was much engaged in rendering service to them, and to the members of their suite; this he did gladly, out of gratitude for the kindness with which he had been treated in France. A valuable souvenir of the Bourbon family exists at St. Mary's in the magnificent Monstrance presented by Charles X. on the occasion of the first communion of the Duc de Bordeaux.

In 1831 Mr. Menzies of Pitfodels came to reside permanently in Edinburgh, and he persuaded Bishop Paterson to live with him at his house, 24 York Place. The Bishop took Mr. Gillis with him, as his secretary, and it was probably at this period that the intimacy between Mr. Gillis and Mr. Menzies was contracted, which never flagged during the long years they lived together, and which has borne undying fruit for the good of religion in Scotland.

We have seen that one of the objects dearest to the heart of the zealous priest was the instruction of the young. He felt that unless the rising generation was carefully taught, there would be little hope of improvement in the religious future of the country. He longed to see labourers in the field training the young to the knowledge and practise of piety and virtue. It frequently recurred to his mind that his desires might best be accomplished by a body of Religious, such as he had seen at

Luçon, devoted to teaching, who would show both by word and example how the Christian virtues should be practised. He knew well that prejudice and bigotry, and even the laws of the land, forbade the existence of such an establishment in Scotland. But the penal laws were beginning to be relaxed, and he had no doubt but that all other obstacles would likewise disappear if the true nature of the religious life were better known. He prayed and pondered; he saw the all but insurmountable difficulties of the case. He was a young priest, without influence, experience, or worldly means. He knew the timidity of Catholics, and how even *they* would oppose the introduction of monks and nuns as being rash and impracticable. But, above all, he trusted in the power of God, and he felt that when the time came for the work to be done, God would Himself prepare the way, and send the means. He offered himself, therefore, to the bishop, Dr. Paterson, to take the first step towards the realisation of the project, by again undertaking a tour on the Continent, to collect funds for the establishment of a convent in Edinburgh. The French royal family furnished him with letters of introduction and recommendation, and he set out on a journey through France, Spain, and Italy. The state of France was at that period so disturbed that he had much difficulty in enlisting public sympathy in favour of his mission. In Spain it had not been hitherto the custom to go about soliciting contributions for charitable purposes, and many were the humiliations and rebuffs he received. In Italy, too, he encountered many repulses. Still he returned home with a considerable sum wherewith to begin the work.

During his absence on the Continent he had received the sad news of the death of Bishop Paterson. On the very eve of his death, Dr. Paterson had written him a letter full of affection and encouragement—lines which served to cheer him in many a subsequent trial. This estimable prelate died suddenly on the 30th October 1831, and his demise cast a gloom over the whole of the Eastern District of Scotland.

It would appear that Dr. Paterson had looked forward to having the assistance of Mr. Gillis as his coadjutor. When his papers were examined after his decease a form of postulation was found, in which he petitioned the Holy See for this appointment. The petition, however, was never sent, as the other Vicars Apostolic considered that, notwithstanding the high qualities of Mr. Gillis, he was too young to be intrusted with the burden of so responsible a charge; in little more than a year after, the Rev. Andrew Carruthers was raised to the dignity. Soon after his return to Edinburgh, in 1832, Mr. Gillis undertook the erection of the small building known as the

Cloister Chapel, which has always been a very useful addition to St. Mary's Church, for week-day Masses, Sunday Schools, Instructions, &c.

The consecration of Bishop Carruthers took place on the 13th January 1833. Mr. Gillis exerted himself to make the rite as solemn and imposing as circumstances would allow; he partly conducted the ceremonies and preached the consecration sermon, on the text, "Thou art a priest for ever according to the order of Melchisedech" (Ps. cix.). The consecrating bishop was the Right Rev. Dr. Penswick, V.A., of the Northern District in England; the assisting bishops were Dr. Scott of the Western District, Scotland, and Dr. Kyle of the Northern District. A numerous body of clergy attended on the occasion,—and as we read the honoured names of Macpherson, Keenan, John Gordon, and others (all now gone to their reward), we cannot but thank God for the good work done by those holy and zealous priests, whose remembrance recalls every sacerdotal virtue, and whose lot was cast in times wherein their energies and self-sacrifice must have been taxed to the very utmost. As each one passed away, he might well say, "I have fought the good fight, I have finished my course, and now there is laid up for me a crown of righteousness."

In this year, 1833, the name of Mr. Gillis was on the list of candidates presented to Propaganda as coadjutor to Dr. Macdonell, Bishop of Kingston, Upper Canada.

As soon as the affairs of the Diocese were settled, Mr. Gillis set in earnest about the project he had so long at heart, the foundation of a convent in Edinburgh. The death of Dr. Paterson had retarded its realisation: but Dr. Carruthers willingly sanctioned the undertaking, and Mr. Menzies entered warmly into the project, and promised substantial aid towards its accomplishment.

So great and distinguished a benefactor as Mr. Menzies of Pitfodels deserves more than a passing word, but our space will not allow us to give more than a brief notice of this esteemed gentleman. John Menzies was descended from a very old and opulent family in Aberdeenshire. He was born in 1756, and surviving till 1843, he witnessed nearly a century of Catholic history; and by his exemplary piety and extensive charities he identified himself with religion in every possible way. He was left a widower while still a young man, and this affliction weaned him from the world, and from that time his life was but one continued series of good works.

In 1828 he bestowed on the Catholic clergy of Scotland the extensive estate of Blairs, near Aberdeen, for the foundation and support of a Catholic college, and, as we have seen, came to reside in

Edinburgh in 1831. He was much regretted in Aberdeenshire, where he was beloved and respected by men of all classes and creeds, and of which county he had been unanimously elected Convener in 1810, an office which he held till 1823. He resigned this honourable post on going abroad, and received the thanks of the constituency for his distinguished services. His residing in Edinburgh was an immense gain to religion and to all charitable undertakings.

CHAPTER II.

THE FOUNDRESSES AND THEIR NOVICIATE.

WHILE Mr. Gillis was pondering and praying over his cherished project, Divine Providence was preparing the instruments who were to aid in the undertaking.

Two Scotch ladies, differing as much in age as in other circumstances, and totally unknown to each other, were at the same time being drawn towards the religious life, and were desirous of devoting themselves to Scotland.

One of these was Miss Ann Agnes Trail, daughter of a minister of the Established Church of Scotland. She went to Italy in 1826, in order to cultivate her remarkable talent for painting, and was there converted and received into the Church in Rome, on the 16th June 1828, by His Eminence, Cardinal Odescalchi. During the course of the following year, Miss Trail returned to Scotland, and spent some months with her family; then went to London to consult an eminent oculist, and was invited by the Lady Abbess of the Benedictine Convent at Hammersmith to pay her a visit. It was during this visit that she was introduced to Mr. Gillis, who was passing through London on his way to the Continent, as before stated.

She was delighted to hear from him that the faith was making progress in her native country, and was much impressed by the earnestness and piety of the zealous missionary; his project, too, found a sympathising chord in her heart, and on his return to England she wrote to him, offering herself as a member of his projected Community, being desirous of devoting her talents and her life to the glory of God in her native land. Her resolution was a subject of great joy and thanksgiving to Mr. Gillis.

Miss Trail was so widely known, and her former zeal in the defence of her father's creed had been so edifying to the Protestants, that her conversion to Catholicity naturally attracted a great deal of attention. She possessed a masculine strength of mind, and a highly cultivated intellect. She was credited with having gone to Rome with proselytising intentions, being spoken of as "The lady that went to Rome to convert the Pope." Being about thirty years of age at the time of her conversion, she did not seem a person to be easily influenced against her own convictions; she was, therefore, a very fitting instrument for the work which was expected to be accomplished by the nuns in this Protestant country, and she fulfilled the expectations of those interested in the foundation. At the request of her spiritual director, the Rev. Father Glover, S.J., she wrote an account of her religious experiences from her infancy, and we purpose giving to the public this most interesting history, in a short biography, at the end of this book.

The other lady, Miss Margaret Clapperton, was barely twenty-one years of age, and had always been a Catholic. A native of Fochabers, where Mr. Gillis's parents lived, she had known Mr. Gillis from her earliest years. Moreover, she had long secretly cherished a desire to give herself to the service of God in religion, and when she heard of the proposal to establish a convent at Edinburgh, she at once offered herself and was accepted. Her father opposed her design, fearing that she might not find in the religious life the happiness she anticipated; but being of a very resolute disposition, and firmly believing that her vocation was divine, she withdrew from her home on her own responsibility and joined Miss Trail in London. She still survives, and is an active member of the Community whose first fifty years of existence she now sees completed.

The vocation of these two ladies gave Mr. Gillis

CONVENT OF THE URSULINES OF JESUS, CHAVAGNES.

great encouragement. He saw the finger of God in the wonderful ways that had brought them to him, and he augured good from the circumstances. It was agreed that Miss Trail and Miss Clapperton should proceed to Chavagnes together to commence their noviciate in the Mother House of the Ursulines of Jesus, and there they arrived on the 31st of August 1833.

The Congregation still enjoyed the advantage of being governed and directed by its saintly founder, the Abbé Baudouin. Mother St. Hilaire was the superior-general, and Mother Emmanuel· mistress of novices. The chaplain was the venerable Father Fleurisson, even then universally known and spoken of as "Le bon saint homme." The two Scotch postulants were thus formed to the religious life and to the rules and customs of the Congregation by the holy founder himself, and those whom he had trained. Every attention was paid to them, for the Abbé Baudouin and the other superiors had formed a very high estimate of the virtue and pure intentions of Mr. Gillis, and therefore took a lively interest in his undertaking.

About six weeks were spent in the usual exercises of the first probation, and on Rosary Sunday, the 6th of October, Miss Trail and Miss Clapperton received the long-wished-for habit of religon. Mr.

Gillis repaired to Chavagnes for this occasion, and the Bishop of Luçon, who had arrived on purpose to perform the ceremony, courteously ceded his place to him; it was a truly happy day for him when he gave the veil to the foundresses of St. Margaret's Convent. Miss Trail took the name of Sister Agnes Xavier, and Miss Clapperton that of Sister Margaret Teresa. Rosary Sunday has ever since been commemorated as "foundation-day"—a day of joy and thanksgiving to the Community. The novices remained at Chavagnes till the following summer, being trained by their holy and experienced mistress in all the virtues that should adorn a religious, and gaining all hearts by their simple piety and straightforwardness of character.

Many members of the Community at Chavagnes longed to accompany them to Scotland, and to share in the difficulties as well as in the merit of the new foundation, so interesting in many ways, and offering so wide a field for zeal and self-sacrifice. The Rev. Mother St. Hilaire, whose term of superiority was drawing to a close, offered herself to head the little band, and Mr. Gillis was truly happy to secure the assistance of so distinguished a member of the Congregation. All who offered themselves could not be accepted; those finally chosen were the Rev.

Mother St. Hilaire, Mother St. Paula, Sister St. Damian, Sister Alexis, Sister John Chrysostom, Sister Mary Emily, Sister Angelina, and two lay Sisters—Sister Stephen and Sister Eustelle, who, with the two Scotch Sisters, made a party of eleven.

CHAPTER III.

WHITEHOUSE—LETTER OF THE REV. J. GILLIS TO MISS TRAIL.

WHILE these fervent souls, destined to be the first inmates of the projected convent, were preparing in their peaceful home at Chavagnes for the arduous labours of the future, Mr. Gillis was endeavouring to procure a suitable locality for the convent; which, as may easily be imagined, he did not accomplish without a great deal of difficulty and opposition. At last he succeeded in purchasing a large house and garden, situated in the suburbs to the south of the city. This house was known as "Whitehouse," and gave its name to the shady lane which runs from Bruntsfield Links to the Grange Road; a house not without a certain literary history of its own, for within its walls Principal Robertson wrote his "History of Charles the Fifth," Home his "Douglas," and Dr. Blair his famous "Lectures." It was an old house, part of it being known to have existed long before the Revolution, but it was substantial and well built; and after Mr. Gillis had altered it to suit its future purpose, it assumed a most conventual appearance. About the time that this purchase was effected, Mr. Menzies bought Greenhill Cottage in the same neighbourhood, and fixed his permanent residence there, taking Mr. Gillis to live with him as his private chaplain. This was a providential arrangement for the good of the future Community, for the pious old gentleman, who had furnished the means to purchase Whitehouse, continued till his death a kind and generous benefactor. Mr. Gillis, by living so near the convent, was able to render the Sisters all the spiritual assistance possible, in those days when priests were few.

The interior of the house once prepared for the nuns, Mr. Gillis proceeded to lay the foundation of the chapel, which was designed by Mr. Gillespie Graham, under whose able direction the edifice made rapid progress, and was naturally an object of great curiosity and interest to the many visitors who watched the advance of the work with various feelings. One day while the labourers were employed in digging the foundations of the chapel and excavating for the construction of the vaults, a Catholic gentleman (Colonel Macdonell) entered the grounds to see how they were proceeding. He was much amused by an old Presbyterian minister and his wife, who were gazing down into the excavations with looks of horror. At length one said to the other, "There will be deeds of darkness done here!"

Doubtless the worthy couple were not the only persons who indulged in similar conjectures. On the whole, the amount of Protestant opposition was not great, while many difficulties were raised by timid Catholics, who thought the undertaking rash and premature.

In a letter addressed by Dr. Gillis to Miss Trail at Chavagnes we find the expression of some of his sorrows and consolations. He says: "I have only to say that I have been overwhelmed with labours and difficulties of every kind; but no more about this, for, thank God, the greatest of them are now, I trust, fairly overcome. Now to what will interest you more. We have got a house, and a most excellent one; and I have this day given in the plans for some necessary additions, and for a very neat chapel, which I hope to see finished in the course of the summer. We have a beautiful garden, containing more than an acre and a half of ground, besides back ground, with a range of farm offices, dairy, stables, &c. &c.; and we are about to purchase three additional acres of ground immediately adjoining to our tenement, which will make in all rather more than five acres of ground, so that we shall be quite at home. The name of the place is of happy omen—it is called 'Whitehouse,' the literal translation of the Latin name 'Candida Casa,' the name of the most ancient Christian establishment in Scotland. It is situated at the head of *Bruntsfield Links*, in the most healthy situation about Edinburgh, entirely screened from the easterly winds which are our greatest trial here, and in the immediate vicinity of a tract of land so healthy and agreeably situated that it goes by the name of the *Land of Promise.* It is the spot to which all the invalids are sent for their health. The house, though quite retired, is yet at no great distance from the town, being just fifteen minutes very moderate walking from the new chapel we are now building at the end of Lothian Street, which runs parallel with the south side of the College. Besides Whitehouse, I have likewise, or rather Mr. Menzies has, purchased a nice convenient cottage about a gunshot from the *door of the convent*, where he and I are to live, if God spare us, and which is to be left for the chaplain's dwelling; *but keep this to yourselves.* Lady Carmarthen has promised me all her interest, and she has already begun her begging operations. Do pray for me that I may be enabled to get all things prepared for you, and that Providence may send me wherewith to build our chapel, &c. I have become personally bound for the whole purchase price, which is £3000 for the house, garden, &c., exclusive of the three additional acres we are now thinking of taking. But Providence has been very kind; I am getting new proofs every day that God never abandons us when we rely entirely upon Him. The whole affair, as you may well suppose, is making a dreadful stir among the saints. I am glad of it; it will act as the safety-valve of a steam-engine—the whole will evaporate in noise and smoke; and when you come it will not be possible for them to raise an opposition to it. On the other hand again, the best possible feeling has been evinced by the most respectable Protestants in town, who are disposed to give it every possible support. Oh! you have no idea how fast the whole church machinery is going to pieces here; the incoming General Assembly is expected to be a most stormy one. Dr. Inglis is dead, and Dr. Chalmers is done for; he had a stroke of palsy some time ago, from the effects of which he never will recover so as to be himself again. What do you think he did in one of his last theological lectures at the College here? After a great deal of violent declamation against the Catholics, he maintained that they did not believe in the divinity of Jesus Christ. A Catholic gentleman, a great admirer of his, and one of his particular friends, and who used to attend his lectures regularly, asked him immediately after the lecture how a man of his sense could condescend to repeat such 'abominable nonsense,' and what he must have known full well to be 'abominable falsehood.' 'My good friend,' said Chalmers, 'I had a difficult task to fulfil this morning; very few persons are now disposed to support our Establishment, and the fact is, people must sometimes do the best they can.' I never could have believed that of Chalmers had I not heard it from his friend's own mouth, a gentleman of unimpeachable veracity in any case, but especially in this.

"I called upon Dr. Gordon and gave him your letter and book; he received me very graciously, and we had a long chat about you and France, &c. &c. Since then he has shown the cloven foot likewise. He happens to be a trustee for a bankrupt estate, part of which we purchased for a site of our new chapel in Lothian Street. After selling us the ground, and allowing the chapel to be more than half finished, he thought proper to refuse giving us anything like title-deeds, because, forsooth, he could have no hand in encouraging the erection of a popish chapel; however, he has been forced to give them since. . . . I shall mention to the superior-general, to whom I intend writing immediately, the necessity of having a person at the head of the Sister of Charity department that has already been accustomed to the thing. I can send no more novices from here;

indeed it is now scarcely worth while. . . . Did I tell you that we have got a very valuable addition to our noviciate here in the person of Miss Eliza Witham, a very pious, agreeable, and accomplished young person from the North of England? Her father has the estate of Lartington. I heard the other day from Mrs. Colonel Macdonell, who had it from the Countess Macnamara, that Miss Agnew,[1] a recent convert, a niece of Sir Andrew Agnew, was quite determined to join our establishment of Whitehouse. She is now in Paris with her mother. . . . I have written and sent off a long letter to Cardinal Weld about Whitehouse, and I owe a letter, likewise, to the good Bishop of Luçon. God help me! I have so many irons in the fire, I don't know which to heat first!—Yours very sincerely in Jesus Christ,

"JAS. GILLIS."

[1] Authoress of "Geraldine;" she became a Sister of Mercy.

CHAPTER IV.

JOURNEY TO EDINBURGH—ESTABLISHMENT OF THE COMMUNITY AT ST. MARGARET'S CONVENT, 1834.

THE preparations in Edinburgh being nearly completed, the Sisters began to make arrangements for their journey to Scotland. Sister Agnes Xavier and Sister Alexis went to Paris together some time before the rest, in order to take lessons in lithography; then on the 27th July 1834 the others bade farewell to the home of their happy noviceship, leaving many behind to regret them. It was not generally known in the Community of Chavagnes that the mother-general was really going to Scotland, but it was suspected, and in order to spare both her sisters and herself the pain of saying farewell, Mother St. Hilaire kept her resolution quiet. On the day of her departure she went to the chapel and intoned vespers as usual, but quitted the house before the office was over. The travellers all met in Paris. Sister Agnes Xavier accompanied her companions to Calais, but Sister St. John Chrysostom and Sister

Alexis remained yet for some time, to enable the latter to continue her study of lithography.

When on the point of embarking at Calais, a difficulty presented itself which caused some delay. The French Sisters had omitted to procure from the Minister of the Interior the necessary permission to leave their country. As soon as this was forwarded to them from Paris, they crossed the Channel to Dover and proceeded in two parties to London. The Benedictine Community at Hammersmith received them, and entertained them with more than sisterly kindness and attention until after the Assumption. Mother St. Hilaire and Sister Agnes Xavier travelled to Scotland by stage-coach, the remainder of the party by sea. Captain Anthony Trail kindly saw them on board the steamer, and they had a safe and pleasant voyage, the incidents of which will best be related by a letter which Mr. Gillis addressed to his friend, the Abbé Dubois, and which was published in "L'ami de la Religion" of 20th November 1834: "Thank God, all has hitherto gone well with our religious, and I venture to hope that the more serious difficulties have been overcome. Their journey from Chavagnes to Edinburgh was most prosperous; and from London they were overwhelmed with attention. There were ninety passengers on board. After dinner, the health was proposed of Lord Ponsonby, the Protestant Bishop of Derry, who was on his way to his Diocese in Ireland. After this toast had been honoured, a gentleman rose and proposed the health of the good nuns who were accompanying them to Edinburgh; the toast was most graciously received by every one, including the Protestant bishop. On the second day the religious entered the saloon after dinner had begun; every one rose to beg them to take their places near the head of the table. Since their arrival in Edinburgh, not a single article has appeared in the numerous papers, such as might have been expected from Presbyterian prejudice. Some few bigots look with a jaundiced eye on the new establishment, but do not venture to give open expression to their feelings. Nothing is talked of but the convent; men, women, and children, high and low, rich and poor, ministers of every sort—every one, in short, comes to see it.

"Of our Convent of St. Margaret, at least, no one can say that it contains prisons, dungeons, or any of the horrors related of monasteries. The house is nearly finished, and is really very pretty; all who visit it, except a few Puritans, are delighted with it. An elegant chapel has just been arranged, &c. . . ."

The convent was not completed, however, by

the time the Sisters reached Edinburgh, and they were provided with a comfortable temporary home in the residence of Mr. Stevenson, at Argyle Park. Mr. Stevenson and his sons lived in hired apartments during the four months that the nuns occupied his house, whilst Mrs. Stevenson and her daughters vied with each other in showing their guests the greatest respect and hospitality. A little oratory was fitted up for their use, the simplicity of which may be inferred from the fact that a chest of drawers served for the altar; the first Mass there was said by Mr. Strain, afterwards Vicar Apostolic, and finally Archbishop of St. Andrews and Edinburgh. Many of the Edinburgh Catholics called during this period to make acquaintance with the nuns, and amongst the first came Mrs. Colonel Hutchison, who will never be forgotten at St. Margaret's, of which she was a constant and true friend. Bishop Carruthers called on the day after their arrival, with the Rev. Stephen Keenan and the Rev. M. Griffin; Mr. Menzies and his cousin Miss Maxwell, Lady Gordon, Colonel O'Reilly, Colonel and Mrs. Macdonell were early visitors, and they all remained staunch friends of the Community as long as they lived.

The few months spent by the Sisters at Argyle Park were not idle ones, for many necessary preliminaries had to be seen to before going into the convent. Household linen was prepared, and the costume of the Sisters remodelled; Mr. Gillis did not think the cap worn at Chavagnes sufficiently distinguished from the ordinary secular dress, and he wished this first Community in Scotland to wear a dress more strictly conventual. Patterns were accordingly procured by Lady Wellesley from several convents in England and Ireland, and at length the present coif and veil were approved of as the costume of the religious of St. Margaret's. It was hoped that the convent would be ready for occupation before Christmas, but the inclemency of the weather had retarded the progress of the workmen, and it was not until St. Stephen's Day, December 26, 1834, that the Community took possession of its long-desired convent-home. Mother St. Hilaire and Sister Agnes Xavier were the first to enter it; the others followed in the course of the day, their number being increased by the addition of their first postulant, Miss Witham of Lartington. The house presented a bare appearance at first; but, thanks to the generous donations of kind friends, it did not remain long empty. The most necessary articles were quickly provided, and after two days' hard work, cheerfully accomplished, there was an oratory ready for the celebration of the Holy Mass.

On the Feast of Holy Innocents, which was a Sunday that year, Bishop Carruthers said the first Mass, in the apartment, which served afterwards as the pupils' drawing class-room. Many friends of the Community assisted at this Mass, rejoicing together, and uniting in thanksgiving to God for the consolation He gave them in this event. After Mass the guests sat down with the bishop and priests to an elegant *déjeûner*, provided by the orders of good old Mr. Menzies. No time was lost by Mr. Gillis and the religious in completing all the arrangements. The various offices were filled; Mother St. Hilaire was nominated superior, and Sister St. John Chrysostom first mistress of the boarding-school. The regular exercises of the religious life began to be followed out, and Scotland possessed once more the blessing of a monastic institution, from whose humble walls a constant service of prayer and praise ascended to the throne of the Most High.

CHAPTER V.

THE CONGREGATION OF THE URSULINES OF JESUS.

THE Community, destined by Divine Providence to be the first in the field in this country, does not belong to the old Order of Ursulines, as many erroneously imagine, but to a Congregation founded in France immediately after the Revolution, and adapted to the difficulties of the times.

The nuns belonging to a *religious Order* are generally confined within the precincts of their own establishment, and are said to be *cloistered.* There they devote their lives to the sanctifying of their own souls, spend much of their time in prayer and in praising God, and for the rest, usually practise some kind of manual work, or teach girls, who live as boarders within the cloister. This was the only kind of nuns known for many years; but as time goes on, and outward circumstances change, the Church finds that she, too, has new wants, and it is beautiful to see what variety is compatible with her immutability; she has always found religious Orders ready to assist in the necessities of the time, and adapt themselves to its circumstances.

A glance at the history of the Church, and at the origin of the military Orders, the Orders for the redemption of captives, the preaching and teaching Orders, will testify the truth of this remark. To meet the various wants that occur as time goes on, religious bodies uniting contemplation with active duties have been introduced, and to these we give the name of *Congregations*. The members of every religious congregation are bound to devote a considerable part of their time to the direct worship and praise of God, so as to fulfil a duty binding upon every rational creature, a duty which many neglect whilst engaged in the turmoil of worldly pursuits.

The Congregation of the Ursulines of Jesus, which Mr. Gillis chose as the one most likely to suit the requirements of this country, was founded in 1802 by a holy priest of Luçon, the Venerable Louis Marie Baudouin. The rule is that of St. Augustine, with the constitutions of St. Ignatius. All the establishments of this Congregation in France, as well as two in South Wales and one in Spain, are subject to the Bishop of Luçon and the superiors at Chavagnes; but the house in Edinburgh is independent of the French superiors. The Institute is devoted to teaching, first, young ladies of the upper and middle classes, then the poor, and lastly, women of every condition, who come to be instructed in the houses connected with the Institute. Ladies' retreats are also given at stated times, in the houses of the Order, and individual ladies may generally find in them accommodation and every facility for making spiritual retreats at any time. The Sisters visit the sick in their homes, and carry consolation as well as corporal relief to the poor and suffering. The Sisters at St. Joseph's Convent, Perth (a filiation from St. Margaret's), regularly visit a large public prison, Perth Penitentiary, to give instruction to the Catholic female prisoners detained there. The name of "Ursulines," or more correctly, "Ursulines of Jesus," was attached to this Congregation by the following circumstance. When Monsieur l'Abbé Baudouin returned from exile after the reign of terror, he gathered together a few faithful and zealous ladies, some of whom had been trained to the religious life in convents before the Revolution; his object being to collect together and instruct in religion the young girls of all classes who had no means of learning the science of salvation; and as no religious Order was sanctioned by the French Government of those days, except that of the Ursulines, this Congregation applied for the official approbation under the name of "Ursulines of Jesus." In France, where the houses of this Order are very numerous, the nuns are usually called "Dames de Chavagnes," from the name of the town in which the Mother House is situated; they are also occasionally spoken of as Nuns of the Incarnation, because their chief object is to imitate the Incarnate Word of God, "poor, chaste, obedient and teaching."

At St. Margaret's Convent, arrangements had been made for the reception of young lady boarders, whose education should be the principal work of the Sisters; but it was deemed desirable to undertake some more ostensible work of charity, in the midst of the city, and there the field provided ample scope for such a purpose. This was also the most likely means of bringing down the blessing of God upon the whole undertaking: for has He not promised to reward even a cup of cold water given in His name?

As a beginning to this latter enterprise, a small house was rented in Reid's Court, and Mother St. Paula, Sister St. Damian, and Sister Margaret Teresa formed a little Community there, where they were known as "Sisters of Charity." When it was agreed to give them charge of the Catholic poor schools, the nuns took a larger house, which Mr. Gillis also managed to buy for the purpose. This was "Milton House," the property of a Lord of Session of that name, and in it the

Sisters began their labours in May 1835. They likewise took charge of a small dispensary, and distributed medicines to the poor *gratis*, while Dr. Strain, brother to the late Archbishop, kindly gave the benefit of his medical skill to the poor applicants.

This establishment was mainly supported by subscriptions, and the Sisters were enabled by the same means to distribute bread, potatoes, &c., three times a week. Their time was fully occupied; for, in addition to all this, the sick poor were visited in their own homes, and a small number of orphans were received into the house. The day-school was well attended, and in course of time the Sisters opened a school for day-boarders of the middle class.

The small number of priests in Edinburgh rendered it impossible to appoint a chaplain to the establishment, and the Sisters were under the necessity of attending the public services in St. Mary's Church, Broughton Street. Thither they conducted their pupils, and on Sunday evenings Mr. Gillis used to give them instructions in the cloister chapel adjoining the church. Many persons of the congregation resorted to these instructions, in order to benefit by his words; even when the instructions were given in Milton House, as happened occasionally, they were always numerously attended.

But let us return to St. Margaret's, where we left the Sisters organising their work and the boarding-school. The first pupil who presented herself was Miss Helen Grant, afterwards mainly instrumental in founding St. Catherine's Convent of Mercy, Edinburgh; she was soon joined by Miss Dorothy Maxwell, Miss Agnes Kirsopp, Miss Flora Grant, Miss Jane Grant, and others. Several postulants were also received during the early part of the year 1835. Miss Harriet M'Nab and Miss Elizabeth Martin, choir Sisters; Hannah Edgar and Helen Ingram, lay Sisters.

ST. MARGARET'S CONVENT, EDINBURGH, IN 1835.

CHAPTER VI.

OPENING OF THE CONVENT CHAPEL—CEREMONIAL OF GIVING THE RELIGIOUS HABIT—BISHOP MURDOCH'S SERMON. 1835.

IN 1835 the Feast of St. Margaret was kept on the 16th of June; the chapel was finished, and the opening of it was to be celebrated at the same time as the reception of the postulants. A most impressive service was arranged, and successfully carried out, and many were moved to tears at the sight of the ceremonial, now revived after so many years of oblivion in Scotland.

An impartial and very detailed description of the ceremony was written by a Protestant eye-witness, and published in the *Edinburgh Observer* of June 19, 1835. It would be a pity to alter or curtail this account, and therefore we quote it in full, with the beautiful discourse pronounced by Dr. Murdoch on the occasion.

"The times have changed—some may perhaps think that they are out of joint—when in Presbyterian Scotland, from whose soil the fury of the Reformation had swept away every monastic and conventual establishment, leaving scarcely one stone upon another of the edifices, which Catholic piety had reared as retreats from the cares and concerns of the world, one of these proscribed institutions has at length, at the distance of three centuries, ventured to rear its head, in all the security afforded by the tolerant spirit of a more enlightened and beneficent age. This event, which will no doubt be viewed with very opposite feelings and sentiments, was, on Tuesday last, signalised by the solemn dedication of St. Margaret's, where, in its beautiful Saxon chapel, the *chef d'œuvre* of Gillespie Graham, was at the same time performed the interesting and affecting ceremony of admitting three young persons, who then entered their noviciate into the Community of the Sisters of Charity. The company present was not numerous but select, and the scene, which was singularly touching throughout, appeared to make the deepest impression upon all who witnessed it. Many were affected even to tears, and none, we will venture to say, remained insensible to the interest created partly by the ceremonial itself, but still more by the spectacle of young persons, in the flower of their age, voluntarily renouncing the world, and dedicating, not the dregs or lees of an exhausted and weary existence, but the first fruits of their years to the service of their God. The Roman Catholic ritual, generally considered, is gorgeous and imposing; but of all the ceremonies of the Catholic Church, there is none, perhaps, so simple, so beautiful, so expressive, and, at the same time, so affecting, as that which, after the lapse of three hundred years, was, on Tuesday last, performed in the Chapel of St. Margaret's. It seemed to us, we confess, the very poetry of religion; a visible representation, if we may so express it, of the finest and the purest images; a living picture painted in all those divine colours which Holy Writ supplies for completing such a delineation. In the foreground were observed youth, and purity, and piety, devoutly kneeling, or lowly prostrate before the altar of sacrifice; then appeared the willing victims, wearing the white emblems of innocence and truth, and crowned with garlands of flowers, betokening their espousal to the Great Head of the Church; and lastly, were beheld these youthful novices casting their crowns upon the altar—receiving the sacred badge of the Cross, with the other ensigns of their vocation as Sisters of Charity—renouncing the world with all its ties, whether of blood or of affection—and dedicating themselves to the service of religion, and the continual practice of that Divine virtue which forms the distinguishing mark of genuine Christianity. The whole scene, indeed, spoke to the heart, and spoke not in vain.; the impression made by it was both deep and powerful; the feelings were addressed in a manner which irresistibly called forth the sympathetic response of 'a few natural tears;' and even some who had supposed themselves armed in proof against the access of any such emotions, were subdued and melted under its softening influence. We abstain from touching upon points of polemical disputation; we have no opinion to give on the long agitated question as to the nature and tendency of conventual institutions; our only object is to describe what we know, by visible signs, many felt on the occasion, and to state, as a fact, that the general effect produced by the ceremonial was, in the highest degree, softening and impressive. We may add, however, that the bitterest enemies of such establishments as St. Margaret's, have invariably made an exception in favour of the Sisters of Charity, whose services in the cause of suffering humanity have secured them the admiration of those who abhor their religion, and who would willingly lend a helping hand to pull down that Church which considers them as amongst its purest and brightest ornaments. Of these heroic women, indeed, whom neither pestilence nor death can discourage or repel in prosecuting their labours of charity, it may with truth be said, in the eloquent language which Burke applied to Howard, that they make it their business 'To dive into the depths of dungeons; to plunge into the infection of hospitals; to survey the mansions of sorrow and pain; to take the gauge and dimensions of misery, depression, and contempt; to remember the forgotten; to attend to the neglected; to visit the forsaken;' and not merely to compare or collate distresses, but, as far as lies in their power, to relieve them. 'Their plan, in short, is original; and it is as full of genius as it is of humanity.'

"When the procession entered the chapel, and the bishops reached the altar, the choir performed the *Asperges*, during which the Right Reverend Dr. Carruthers sprinkled the chapel with holy water; and this, upon the return of his lordship to the foot of the altar, was followed by *Sanctus Deus.* Mr. Gillis then gave out the *Veni Creator*, which was performed thrice, with a soft voluntary, until the bishop had done reading the prayers at the side of the altar. Next came the sermon, which was delivered by Bishop Murdoch of Glasgow, from the front of the altar. In eloquent and powerful language, the right reverend preacher alluded to the havoc which the Reformation had made in the Catholic institutions of this country, and also to the fiery bigotry which, even in recent times, had consigned to the flames the only Catholic chapel in Edinburgh; and whilst he contrasted the persecuting fury of former times with the enlightened and tolerant spirit of the present, he at the same time earnestly disclaimed alluding to these things as matters of reproach to Protestants. He adverted to them merely as facts in history, and proceeded to describe, in animated terms, the progress which, in spite of all obstacles and difficulties, the Catholic religion was making in every part of the country, rearing up temples which adorned the spots where they were placed, and giving promise of that ultimate triumph which, he felt assured, their religion would one day obtain. With respect to the Institution of St. Margaret's, he said he was willing that it should be tried by its merits and judged by its fruits. He then shortly described the objects for which it was founded, more especially as a place of education for Catholic females, and concluded a powerful discourse with a most impressive prayer for the prosperity of the Institution.

"The sermon was followed by the ceremony of the Clothing, which we have already attempted to describe though in very feeble and inadequate terms. Those who witnessed it were alone in a condition to judge of the impression which it produced; but to convey any just conception of it in words would be entirely hopeless. The novices kneeling or prostrate before the altar,—the deep interest with which they were regarded,—the solemnity of the service, heightened by an imposing array of clergy robed in splendid vestments,—the beautiful, expressive, and highly poetical character of the ceremonial, which was not lessened by its novelty,—the effect produced by Bishop Murdoch's excellent discourse,—and the air of tranquil, settled, yet almost sublime devotion in the countenances of those young persons who were preparing to set the seal to their own separation from the world,—formed altogether a scene which the imagination may picture to itself, but which our feeble pen would in vain essay to describe. The novices were presented to the bishop by the Reverend Mr. Gillis, who humbly requested that his Lordship would allow them to enter the religious state. 'Do you know them to be worthy of that holy state?' inquired his Lordship. 'As far as human frailty will allow me to judge, I believe them to be so, and present them as such to your Lordship,' replied Mr. Gillis. A series of questions were then put by Mr. Gillis to one of the novices, by whom they were answered with a dignified distinctness, blended with that grace and delicacy which form the peculiar ornaments of the female sex. These questions, about which the public may not unreasonably feel some curiosity, were, as nearly as we could collect, substantially as follow:—

"'What object have you in view in wishing to be received as a member of this religious society? To take upon myself the obligations, and to share in the advantages of a religious life.—Will you endeavour to walk in a manner worthy of your vocation? It is my desire to do so.—Is it of *your own free will* that you present yourself here, or *have you been in any way forced to this step?* I come *of my own accord,* without either *inducement or compulsion.*—Are you disposed to renounce the things of the world according to the precept of Jesus Christ? With the help of God, I do renounce them.—Will you persevere in this resolution, and promise to obey the rule of St. Augustin, of which the Church has approved? With the help of God, I do promise to obey it.—Are your ecclesiastical superiors to understand that you are willing to make choice of a single life, and that you will endeavour to sanctify it by the daily practice of temperance and piety? Yes; I make that choice of my own free will, and with God's assistance I hope to persevere in the practice of those virtues which are most likely to render it acceptable in His divine sight.—Are you ready, then, to promise obedience to the superiors of this religious institution? I am; and my most earnest desire is to make that promise irrevocable.—Are you prepared to encounter the hardships of a religious life, to submit to the contingencies of voluntary poverty, and to suffer persecution and contempt for the kingdom of heaven? With God's assistance, I will rejoice with the apostle at being accounted worthy to suffer reproach for the name of Jesus.—Are you willing, then, to renounce all things for the sake of Christ, to bid adieu to your father and mother, to your brothers and sisters, to your relations and friends, to all the pursuits, and vanities, and illusions of the world? I am, with God's help; my most earnest desire is to live henceforward for God alone. —Are you ready even to renounce yourself, to take up your cross, and to follow Jesus Christ in the path of His divine counsels? I am, with the assistance of His grace.'—All the novices were then asked, 'But are you, my dear children, in the same dispositions; do you concur in the sentiments that have here been expressed, and do you ratify the promises that have just now been made? We do, to their fullest extent, and with all our hearts.' On receiving the cross they were addressed in these words:—'Receive the sign of your redemption, wear it as a seal upon your heart, and remember that your love for Christ should be as strong as death.' Mr. Gillis then said, 'Think seriously, my dear children in Jesus Christ, of the obligations which you are now so anxious to take upon yourselves; the angels who rejoice in heaven over the perseverance of the just, as well as over the conversion of the sinner, are witnesses to your sincerity, and you will have to answer at the day of judgment for the step you are now preparing to take.'

"They then received the other emblems of their vocation, and on their heads, covered with white veils, were placed crowns of flowers, which they afterwards deposited on the altar, in token of their complete renunciation of all the ornaments, as well as the pursuits of life, and their exclusive dedication to the service of religion. Mass followed with some variations suited to the occasion; and at the offertory, the novices, with lit tapers in their hands, approached the altar, in front of which sat Bishop Carruthers, to whom they were formally presented. Mass then proceeded as usual, and when the officiating priest, Mr. Gillis, commenced the last gospel, the choir performed the *Magnificat* and *Finale.* The whole of this imposing ceremonial, so new in Scotland, occupied nearly three hours; but it was regarded throughout with undiminished interest and attention by all present, amongst whom were a considerable number of Protestants.

"After the service, several distinguished persons who had been attracted thither, examined the interior arrangements and accommodations provided in St. Margaret's, with a view to its principal destination as a place of education for young ladies of the Catholic persuasion, and with all of which they expressed themselves highly gratified. These, indeed, are of the most complete and admirable description, with a view to health and comfort, as well as to education. The situation is one of the finest which could have been selected, in one of the most beautiful spots in the vicinity of Edinburgh; the grounds are extensive and tastefully laid out; and the retired nature of the place secures it a complete immunity from all those spectacles which, in spite of every precaution, are obtruded on the sight of young females in a great city; whilst the means which have been provided for the cultivation of the mind, the formation of the taste and manners, and the education of the heart, which is by far the most important of all, are such as can scarcely fail to recommend St. Margaret's, in a pre-eminent degree, to Catholic parents in all parts of the country.

"To prevent misconception, it is proper to add, that although all the ladies connected with St. Margaret's belong to the same Order, and are under the same superior, those who act as Sisters of Charity inhabit a different residence, and form a separate establishment from that of St. Margaret's, which, as already mentioned, is exclusively a seminary of education for the female branches of respectable Catholic families."

Sermon preached at the opening of the Chapel of St. Margaret's Convent, by the RIGHT REVEREND JAMES MURDOCH, *Coadjutor of the Western District of Scotland.*

"The earth, Christians, is filled with the presence of God: immensity is one of His essential attributes. "In Him," says the Apostle, "we live, and move, and have our being" (Acts xvii. 28). Wherever we are, we are surrounded by the Deity. As the air encompasses the bird in its flight, as the water encircles the fish while it swims through the ocean, so does the presence of the Godhead environ us at all times, and in all places. Whithersoever we go, our God is with us. We cannot escape from His hand nor from His eye. All this is beautifully expressed by the Royal Prophet in one of his Psalms: "Whither," says he, "shall I go from Thy Spirit? or whither shall I flee from Thy face? If I ascend into heaven Thou art there, if I descend into hell Thou art present; if I take my wings early in the morning, and dwell in the uttermost parts of the sea, even there also Thy hand shall lead me, and Thy right hand shall hold me. And I said, perhaps darkness shall cover me, and night shall be my light in my pleasures; but darkness shall not be dark to Thee, and night shall be light as the day. The darkness and the light thereof are alike to Thee" (Ps. cxxxviii. 7–12). Thus the universe ought to be looked upon as one great temple of the Almighty. At all times, during the day and during the night, in light and in darkness, in the fields and in our dwelling-houses, at home and abroad, asleep and awake, we ought to consider ourselves in the immediate presence of our Creator; we ought to conduct ourselves as under this conviction; our appearance should be suitable to the great Being in whose company we are; our thoughts should be pure in the sight of Him who is holiness itself; our words should be fitted for the hearing of the God of sanctity; our actions should each one declare that the Lord is nigh to us; and our whole deportment proclaim that we are, and look upon ourselves, as the children of the Most High. Such, my brethren, should be our feelings, and such our conduct, in all circumstances. With what sentiments, then, of respect and awe should we enter those places that are immediately set apart and consecrated to the worship of the Almighty! Though by His immensity He is everywhere, though He fills the vast expanse between earth and heaven, though His essence cannot be confined within the precincts of material walls, yet we find that from the beginning He has chosen to dwell, as it were, and to manifest Himself particularly in certain places. The greater part of the earth which we inhabit is contaminated with vice; crime stalks wide over the face of the globe, and in a manner pollutes the air we breathe. Hence has it been deemed proper to select certain spots, and to consecrate them to the special worship of the Deity, as if to express our sense of His immaculate holiness, and our desire to escape from the contagion of the world. Solomon was the first to build a house to the true God; and the Almighty, on the day of its solemn dedication to His service, showed, in the presence of all the people, how agreeable to Him was the erection of the Temple. When all the holocausts were ready, He sent down fire from heaven to consume them, and at the same time filled the house with a cloud of His glory. Afterwards, appearing to Solomon, He said, 'I have sanctified this house which thou hast built, to put my name there for ever, and my eyes and my heart shall be there always' (2 Chron. vii. 16). Justly, then, did the Israelites respect the Temple of Solomon; justly did they venerate its sanctity; justly did they flock to it from all quarters, to present their petitions to the Most High, to tender their homages, to offer their gifts and sacrifices; justly did they, when removed far from it, in their captivity, open their windows, turn their faces towards Jerusalem, where it stood, and, at the risk of their lives, worship their God, as we find recorded of the Prophet Daniel. Yet the Temple of Jerusalem was only a type, a figure of our Christian Temples. It only contained the Ark of the Covenant,—our Churches contain the Tabernacle in which the Son of God resides truly and really in the adorable sacrament of the Eucharist. In the Temple of Solomon was offered to God only the blood of animal victims; on our altars is offered up to heaven, in a mystical manner, the blood of Him who died upon the cross for the redemption of the world. In the Jewish Temple was expounded the law of Moses,—in our Churches are explained and inculcated the laws and maxims taught and promulgated by the Eternal Son of God Himself. What reverence, then, ought we to manifest in the House of God! With what respect ought we to cross its threshold! With what feelings of awe ought we to come into the presence of the Great Creator of the Universe! With what humility ought we, like the publican, far from the altar, to bow ourselves down, to strike our breasts, and acknowledge our unworthiness! With what purity ought we to enter the sanctuary of Him who cannot endure the sight of iniquity! In the Temple of Jerusalem the people were, by various barriers, kept back from the more holy places; the priests were obliged to go through several purifications before they were allowed to advance to the altar, to discharge their functions; the Holy of Holies, where God had chosen His special residence, was entirely removed from the view of the crowd,—the High Priest alone was permitted to set his foot there, and he only once in the course of every year, and that after the most solemn oblations. It was, my brethren, for our instruction, that all these ordinances were made in the old law; it was for our instruction that the Almighty commanded such respect to be shown to the Temple of Jerusalem. Far more venerable and holy are our Temples, Christians! They are indeed the houses of God; for in them the Divinity may be said truly to dwell. They may, with truth, be styled not merely the gates of heaven, but the new heavens upon earth foretold by the Prophet. Here are not merely the Tables of the Law enclosed in the Ark, but the great Author of the Law, Jesus Christ. Here is not merely the manna that fell from the clouds, and fed the Israelites in the desert, but the true bread that came down from heaven,—the body and blood of Jesus Christ, that nourish our souls to life eternal. Here is not merely the rod of Aaron, the emblem of his priesthood, but the 'Priest for ever, according to the order of Melchisedec' (Heb. v. 6). Here is offered not the flesh of oxen, and of other animals, but the Lamb without spot that taketh away the sins of the world. Here is daily erected, as it were, on the altar, the Cross of Calvary, and the Eternal Son of God presented to His Heavenly Father under the form of death, for our sakes. Here is daily immolated, in a mystical manner, Him at whose expiry on the tree of ignominy the sun withdrew his light, the rocks were rent asunder, and the earth was shaken to its centre. Here lies daily on the altar He whom in heaven millions of angels and archangels adore,—He before whom the cherubim and seraphim cover their faces with their wings, through awe of his Divine Majesty,—He in whose presence the powers of heaven tremble. Here may every penitent sinner approach to the foot of the altar, to be sprinkled, not with the blood of animals, but with that of the Son of God made man. Here is our crucified Saviour to be daily found a victim of propitiation for every repenting criminal. Here does the God of goodness daily place His throne, and sit ready to receive and grant the petitions of His creatures. Here does He scatter abroad the riches of His bounties. Here, in fine, does He "delight," as He Himself says, "to dwell in the midst of the children of men" (Prov. viii. 31). The faithful are no longer, like the Jews, kept at a distance from the altar; Jesus Christ has broken down every wall of separation, and invites all to come to Him and to be refreshed. Every Christian is now permitted to draw nigh to the Holy of Holies, and to take his stand among the angels and archangels at the foot of the throne of the Most High God.

"Cold and heartless, my beloved brethren, nay, utterly undeserving the name of Catholic, is he who can witness the dedication of a church to the God of Heaven, without feelings of joy and exultation. Feebly does the fire of zeal or love for the heavenly religion of Jesus Christ burn in the bosom of him who does not rejoice to hear of its advancement in distant countries; but no spark slumbers in the breast of the man who is not gladdened by the sight of its progress in the land which gave him birth. Boundless, then, my Catholic brethren, ought to be our gratitude to the God of goodness for His bounties towards us. Since the period of the Reformation there was a time when but one solitary Catholic priest wandered over the length and breadth of this kingdom, and he skulking in disguise, as if he had been some wretch who had imbrued his hands in the blood of a fellow-creature. Now, the ministers of your holy religion are to be found in town and country, and proceed to the discharge of their sacred functions without the fear of molestation. There was a time when your forefathers might be truly said to be without temple, without altar, and thought themselves happy when they could assist at the adorable mysteries, in some secluded spot or unsuspected barn;—two-thirds of a century have scarce yet elapsed since the only Catholic chapel in this city was burnt to ashes. Now, your places of worship adorn the cities of the land, and are widely scattered over the surface of the country,—now, you walk with safety to the house of prayer, and at noon-day worship the Almighty with almost all the splendour and solemnity of Catholic times and Catholic countries. Scarce now does the year roll over in which several edifices are not reared and dedicated to the service of God, according to the form and faith of the Catholic Church. Once more, then, I proclaim it, my Christian brethren, your bosoms ought to be filled with the warmest gratitude for the many mercies that have been bestowed upon you.

"But there is something in this day's solemnity that ought to make your hearts superabound with joy. The Temple which to-day is consecrated to the God of Heaven, and in which, for the first time, is offered up to the Eternal Father the dread sacrifice of the altar, has an association which renders the day of its opening a day of special jubilation. You sit assembled, my friends, in the first Conventual Chapel that has dared to raise its head in this kingdom since the days of the Reformation. Once Scotland vied with other countries in the number of her monastic establishments, where learning was cultivated, where piety flourished, where the voice of Divine praise night and day was seldom hushed, where the virgin gave her undivided heart and chaste affections to her heavenly Spouse; where the mortified follower of Jesus Christ crucified never eased his shoulders of the burden of the cross; where the ardent lover of God strove daily to add new fuel to the fire of Divine charity in his bosom; where the world was despised; where honours, riches, dignities, and beauty were looked upon as empty trifles; where the path of self-denial was unceasingly trodden; where the whole Community so often fell prostrate before the throne of God, and sent up to heaven a loud cry for mercy on a sinful world; where also the hungry were fed, the naked were clothed, the houseless were sheltered, the orphan was provided for, the widow was solaced; where, in fine, the stranger always found an open door, and where hospitality was ever ready to welcome and refresh the traveller. Yes, Scotland was once happy in her numerous monasteries and convents, from whence issued a sweet odour of virtue that attracted multitudes around to the faithful service of the world's Creator; but a misguided zeal declared a war of extermination against them. Now, history can scarce show the spots where many of them stood, while the majestic but mouldering ruins of others, weeping, as it were, still point to heaven, and bid us think of the many faithful souls which they sent up to the mansions of everlasting bliss.

"If I have alluded to their destruction, believe me, my friends, I have done so not in anger, nor in reproach. Ah! no; there is not room in my breast for one drop of bitterness, on this day when everything around me carries me, in imagination, back to the times of St. Margaret, the glorious patroness of this temple and its adjoining convent. Often have I adored in silence the judgments of God, and sorrowed at the causes that brought about the expulsion of my religion and its institutions from the land of my birth. But away, sorrow, on this joyful occasion, when opens a new era in the history of the Scottish Mission; when I am about to behold a spectacle for three hundred years unwitnessed amongst us; when, at the foot of the altar, three tender females are on the point of renouncing all to follow Christ, of putting on the humble habit of spouses of Jesus, and of bidding farewell to this world and all its delusive charms and false allurements. Thrice happy daughters! who have been chosen by the Almighty to set to your countrywomen the noble example of leaving father and mother, brothers and sisters, in order wholly to consecrate yourselves to His love! Once again, away from my breast every feeling but that of joy on this day, when, in the name of the Catholics of Scotland, I hail the appearance among us of these venerable Sisters, who have courageously and cheerfully abandoned their native land, and come to spend their days in a country where they knew the name of a nun has hitherto been held in scorn and contempt. But fear not, little flock, let me address you in the words of Jesus Christ to His apostles; fear not, for you are under the protection of your Divine Spouse. As it pleased the Almighty to give the apostles a kingdom here, in the conversion of the world to Christianity, and a kingdom of bliss hereafter, as the reward of their labours; so, I trust, it will please your Eternal Father to give to you, in this world, a rich harvest of happy fruits in the good you are about to accomplish, and in a future world crowns of never-fading glory, in recompense of your charity. If at present you are only the grain of mustard seed, be comforted when you reflect, that that small grain grew into a goodly tree, so that the birds of the air came and dwelt in the branches thereof. Yes, my fellow-Catholics, if to-day St. Margaret's stands alone, the time may not be far distant when the increase of similar institutions may be proclaimed with as much joy as I at this moment experience in alluding to its solitary existence. Great, I am sure, must have been the difficulties encountered in the completion of this establishment; the heavier, then, is the debt of gratitude which the Catholics of Scotland owe to those who, trusting in God, commenced, and relying on His assistance, and disheartened by no obstacle, have finished the work. I stand not, however, here the panegyrist of these latter persons. No; I leave future generations to extol and bless them, and the God of Heaven to reward them. Neither does time permit me to expatiate on the happy fruits which this institution is calcuated to produce, and I make no doubt will produce amongst us. If here present there be any person who expects me to enter on a defence of the monastic Orders of the Catholic Church, to such a person I have only to say, that addressing myself to them who call themselves the followers of Jesus Christ, I should conceive that I grossly insulted them, if I deemed it necessary to offer to them any apology for the profession and practice of Christianity in its perfection,—for the practice of the most holy and sublime maxims and virtues taught by the religion of Jesus,—for the practice of humility and self-denial inculcated almost in every page of the Gospel, —for the practice of poverty of spirit and estrangement from everything earthly, so strongly recommended in the Divine oracles,—for the practice of angelic chastity, which in some degree raises mortals above the sphere of their nature, and places them on a level with the celestial spirits—for the practice, in fine, of Divine charity, in both its branches, which makes men in some measure partakers of the Divinity. What more excellent objects, I would ask, can be considered, than those of this establishment? Its inmates renounce all to follow Christ, and solemnly and irrevocably consecrate themselves to the service of their God. Here, in their retirement, to act the part of Moses praying on the mount, with uplifted hands, during the conflict of the Israelites with their enemies,—to present themselves before the throne of the Almighty God, and to send up to Him their most fervent supplications for aid to their fellow-mortals living in the midst of a corrupted world, and unceasingly exposed to violent attacks from cunning, powerful, and indefatigable foes, is to form one of their frequent occupations. Some of them are to dedicate themselves to the instruction of youth; of these it will be the task to plant deeply in the breasts of young females the seeds of early, unaffected, and enlightened piety; to impart to them an education grounded upon and blended with religion; to adorn their minds, to refine their manners, and thus to send them back to the world, ornaments to their sex, an honour to their religion, and models of virtue to their neighbours. Others of these devout Sisters are destined to devote themselves to the exercise of the most heroic charity; to fly at all hours to the abode of distress, to take their station beside the bed of sickness, to administer to the temporal and spiritual wants of the dying, to solace and support them under their pains, to dispose them for a worthy reception of the last sacraments, to inspire them with confidence in the God of mercy, to fill their hearts with sentiments of the deepest sorrow for past guilt, and, angels of consolation, to stand by till they deliver the departing Christian soul into the hands of celestial spirits, to be conducted by them, through the perils of death, to the presence of its God. These courageous Sisters, neither the squalid appearance of the most wretched hovel, nor the loathsomeness of disease, nor the fear of infection, nor the dread of death, shall drive from the field of their operations, nor deter from their labours of love. But I must content myself with this brief allusion to the ends which the Community of St. Margaret's has in view. Their utility, their excellence, are surely unquestionable. I am not afraid, then, to rest the fate of the Institution upon its own merits. Nay, I entertain not a doubt, that the prejudices at present existing against such establishments in the minds of many of our Protestant brethren, will gradually die away, and in numerous instances give place even to admiration. But this, my beloved brethren, must be the work of Him in whose omnipotent hands are the minds and hearts of men, and to whom alone it belongs to prosper the efforts of His servants.

"Unto Thee, then, do we appeal, O God of majesty! Sanctify this house which we consecrate to Thy honour, as on the day of its dedication Thou didst fill the Temple of Jerusalem with a cloud of Thy glory. God of Charity, take this infant Community under Thy special protection; guard it as the apple of Thine eye; bless and prosper its operations of love! God of Purity, lover of chastity, receive the hearts and affections of Thy three devout servants, who this day consecrate themselves to Thee as to their only Spouse! God of Goodness, shower down Thy grace upon us all, enable us to pass through this world as travellers on our way to our true and everlasting home,—enable us ever to distinguish ourselves as Thy disciples by the badge of charity, that loving Thee, and loving one another in this world, we may be overwhelmed in the joys of love in the next!"

CHAPTER VII.

BENEFACTORS—PRESENTATION OF THE SANCTUARY LAMP —RELICS OF ST. CRESCENTIA, V.M.—DEPARTURE OF THE REV. MOTHER ST. HILAIRE—LETTER OF THE REV. JAMES GILLIS. 1835-1837.

WITH the solemn opening of the chapel, the convent may be considered fairly established. The Sisters had spent six busy months before this event receiving pupils into the boarding-school and postulants to the noviceship; setting their house in order, and organising all their work. They had much to be thankful for in their intercourse with the outer world, for they were generally well received and respectfully treated by those with whom they had to deal. It is true the convent windows were broken more than once by those whose ignorance and bigotry could find no more dignified mode of expression, but better informed Protestants were indignant at such outrages, and publicly expressed their indignation by the pen of the late Dr. William Chambers, who was always an ardent admirer of Bishop Gillis.

Those who appreciated the labours of the religious were both generous and thoughtful in supplying many a useful article. The Countess de Senfft Pilsach, wife of the Austrian ambassador, sent a beautiful embroidered preaching stole; Mrs. Gandolfi gave a complete set of vestments; Mr. Menzies presented another set; and Mrs. Englefield, with many other things, presented a valuable collection of books for the convent library. Sir George Warrender, Bart., of Lochend, although a Protestant, was an early benefactor to the Community, for it was he who suggested the substitution of an open railing for the stone wall that separated his own grounds from the convent garden; and he placed in it a door of communication by which the Sisters and their pupils might have free access to the Warrender parks, for the purpose of air and recreation.

On Friday the 6th January 1837, a magnificent silver lamp, intended for the service of the convent chapel, was formally presented to Mr. Gillis, in presence of Bishop Carruthers and a number of friends of the Institution, who had assembled for the occasion in the large schoolroom of the convent. The lamp was executed from a design of Mr. Gillespie Graham, the architect of the convent, by Messrs. Cross & Carruthers of Elm Row; and is considered by persons of good taste and judgment in such matters, as unrivalled by anything of the kind to be met with in this country.

On the evening referred to, the schoolroom was tastefully decorated, and the lamp suspended amidst handsome drapery. The subscribers to the presentation assembled, the Community and pupils being also present. Lieutenant-Colonel Macdonell, C.B., who had been unanimously requested to present the testimonial to the Rev. Mr. Gillis, proceeded to fulfil this pleasing duty in an eloquent speech, in which he set forth the services rendered to religion by Mr. Gillis, and the many ways in which he had won the esteem, admiration, and love of his flock. After referring to the sorrows through which the Church in Scotland passed, during the gloomy time of the so-called Reformation, the destruction of churches and religious houses, and the consequent want of instruction to the ignorant and relief to the poor and needy, Colonel Macdonell proceeded to draw a happy augury for the future from the establishment of the convent, in which they were now met together, and which, he trusted, was the foundation-stone of many similar institutions which would ere long restore to Scotland her ancient faith, hope, and charity. Before concluding his address, Colonel Macdonell read the inscription on the lamp, which was follows:—

"THIS LAMP,

intended to serve as a visible emblem of that Divine Light of Faith and Charity which has burned in the Catholic Church from the beginning, and which will continue to diffuse its radiance with unquenchable brightness to the end, is presented to the Rev. James Gillis, Founder of St. Margaret's Convent, Edinburgh, by a number of his personal friends, in testimony of their respect for his character as a clergyman, their admiration of his talents and eloquence as a preacher, and their deep sense of that fervent and holy zeal with which he has laboured to promote the interests of true religion, to re-establish one of its beneficent institutions, and to extend the practical influence of that charity without which Christianity is but an empty name."

EDINBURGH, ST. MARGARET'S DAY,
10*th June* 1836.

Mr. Gillis was deeply touched by this proof of regard and esteem, and feelingly expressed his gratitude to all concerned in the presentation of the lamp, not only for the costly gift, but for the kind sentiments of which Colonel Macdonell had been the interpreter. Referring to the inscription on the lamp, Mr. Gillis said:—"One complimentary expression, however, in that inscription, I must beg leave in a very great measure to decline. I am there called the *Founder* of St. Margaret's—Sir, that title belongs much more truly to one whose venerated head now lies mouldering in the grave; to the zealous and disinterested prelate who lately presided over this district, *Bishop Paterson.* Had it not been, sir, for the last words that he ever wrote in this world, penned, as it turned out, on the very eve of his death—I acknowledge it here—I would have shrunk from the difficulties which this establishment then presented to me. Since then, another fatherly hand has been stretched forth to support it, but for which any exertions of mine, however great, must have proved unavailing. That it may long continue to be uplifted to Heaven in behalf of this establishment, and of us all, is, I am sure, sir, yours as well as my most earnest prayer."

When Mr. Gillis had concluded his reply, Bishop Carruthers addressed the company, and then all present proceeded to the chapel, where solemn vespers were sung and benediction was given, the bishop being assisted by the Rev. Mr. Gillis and the Rev. Mr. Malcolm.

The lamp, after the usual benediction, was suspended in the chapel and lighted for the first time, and there it still burns, to the glory of God and "*Ob rei memoriam.*"

Mrs. Colonel Hutchison will ever be remembered in the annals of St. Margaret's Convent as a most liberal and constant benefactress; to her generosity and good taste the chapel owes the handsome carved oak screen which surrounds the choir, where a simple iron railing had originally been placed. Mrs. Hutchison loved to identify herself with everything pious and useful, and was always ready to come to the aid of the nuns, bóth at St. Margaret's and at Milton House. It was she who enriched the convent with the precious relics that now lie under the high altar, the body of St. Crescentia, Virgin and Martyr.

In 1842 Mrs. Hutchison visited Rome, and was presented to Pope Gregory XVI. as "a convert from Protestantism." His Holiness received her most graciously, and desired her to ask some favour which it might be in his power to grant; she at once asked for the relics of a saint as a gift for her eldest daughter. When she explained that her "eldest daughter" was the newly founded convent in Edinburgh, her request was readily granted, and the body of St. Crescentia, along with the necessary authentication, was confided to her care to be conveyed to Scotland.

She returned home in company with the Right Rev. Dr. Ullathorne, then Vicar Apostolic of the Midland District in England, and now Bishop of Birmingham. The journey was not accomplished without many interesting adventures, and amongst others, the arrest of Mrs. Hutchison at Leghorn, where she was mistaken for a person of the same name who had assisted in the escape of Lavalette in 1816. After reaching London Dr. Ullathorne drew up a statement of the case and presented it to

Lord Aberdeen, by the hands of Lord Cunningham, Mrs. Hutchison's brother. Lord Aberdeen brought the affair under the notice of Prince Metternich, and in due course came an apology, with which the matter ended.

One good result of this misadventure was, that the long list of "contraband individuals" kept on the frontier of the Lombard territory was cancelled; and whereas, previous to this time, many English travellers had been stopped and turned back, an end was now put to this nuisance. The case of relics which the good lady guarded with jealous care, added greatly to her solicitude on this memorable journey; but she contrived by many an artifice to conceal "the box of bones" from those who would have treated it with contemptuous disrespect, and had great joy in presenting it to the Community as soon as she reached Edinburgh. The elegant shrine in which the relics now repose was designed by Mr. Pugin, and executed by Messrs. Bonnar & Carfrae, under the superintendence of Bishop Gillis. By special permission of the Holy Father, the feast of St. Crescentia is kept on the 10th October, and the relics are exposed during the octave.

Of Mrs. Hutchison's journey home, Dr. Ullathorne wrote many years afterwards:—"Mrs. Hutchison, however harassed, and though labouring under the difficulty of not knowing the language, bore herself admirably through all her anxieties and fatigues. She went every morning to communion, and even though travelling early and late, she went invariably at whatever time we stopped before 12 o'clock, to receive the Blessed Sacrament at the nearest church. When, however, we reached London, her strength completely broke down, and she required some days to recover herself."

It was to be expected that many persons would feel curiosity to see the interior of the convent; and with a view to dispelling prejudices and enlightening the minds of Protestants, visitors were permitted to see the chapel, class-rooms, and dormitories. Some amusement was afforded by the expressions of astonishment elicited by the cheerful appearance of both Sisters and pupils, as it was generally believed that the inmates of a convent could not be otherwise than miserable.

One day a carriage full of ladies stopped at the gate; the card taken to the reverend Mother was that of the Duchess of St. Albans, who was conducted through the establishment by Sister Agnes Xavier. In the schoolroom the party of visitors found the children engaged with Mother St. John Chrysostom, who was giving a lesson in making artificial flowers, an accomplishment in which she excelled. A table covered with those that were finished attracted the admiration of the Duchess, who, without further ceremony, swept them all into an embroidered apron which she wore, after the fashion of the day. Turning to her *dame de compagnie*, she said, "Leave a ten pound note." The flowers were willingly relinquished on such liberal terms.

Mother St. John Chrysostom was a perfect mistress of all kinds of needlework, and many beautiful specimens of her skill remain at St. Margaret's in the vestments which she and her pupils embroidered. The drawing-class was conducted by Sister Agnes Xavier, whose reputation as an artist had been widespread long before she entered religion. Even in the convent she was frequently requested to paint miniatures by those who remembered her fame as the first lady artist of the day. She brought to St. Margaret's some of the paintings she had executed in Italy, and they are unrivalled in their purity of tone and exquisite finish.

It was a great advantage to the school to possess mistresses so eminently qualified for the work of teaching. The frequent visits of Dr. Carruthers, Mr. Gillis, and other friends interested in the convent school, were a constant stimulus to exertion. The venerable bishop regularly assisted at the examinations, and himself interrogated the children;

when absent or unable to be present, Mr. Gillis, or some other ecclesiastic, took his place.

The religious and their pupils were frequently reminded that a stamp of perfection should be apparent in all their work, of whatever kind—that they should strive to excel; and this not from motives of worldly pride, but for the honour of the Catholic Church and the glory of God.

As time went on, and the question of education became one of the leading topics both of Church and State, it became still more necessary that Catholic schools should be able to hold their own, and accordingly we shall find that renewed efforts were made, and a higher standard attained, which effectually destroys the old-fashioned theory that the Church is the enemy of advanced education.

In the midst of many consolations, however, the Community were not exempted from the common rule, that those who follow our Lord must carry the cross. In the spring of 1837 the health of the venerable superior, Mother St. Hilaire, gave way, and her children saw with sorrow that she must return to her native country. The French superiors recalled her (for they retained jurisdiction over the subjects whom they had lent to Scotland); and her departure was the first great trial that fell upon the young Community. Mother St. Hilaire was universally esteemed and loved; her subjects were accustomed to lean upon her as their guide and support on every occasion, and some were so deeply attached to her that they could not endure the thought of separation. One of them, Miss Laing Meason, actually accompanied her to France and never returned to Edinburgh. The loss of their beloved Mother was all the more keenly felt by the Sisters that Mr. Gillis was absent at the time of her departure. He was in very delicate health, and had been ordered by the physicians to try the mineral waters at Strathpeffer.

On this, as on many other occasions, when he was far away from his little flock, he endeavoured to sustain their courage and animate their zeal by the beautiful fatherly letters which he addressed to them. His letter of condolence may here be inserted in full, for it contains a well-merited eulogium of the good Mother who had left her native land in order to assist in the foundation of this Community. He wrote from Strathpeffer on 16th July 1837:—

"MY DEAR CHILDREN IN JESUS CHRIST,—I feel more than I can express in words the privation to which the unavoidable circumstance of my absence from Edinburgh subjects me at this moment, and I will not disguise from you that my mind would be wretched in its thoughts and apprehensions were I not convinced, *intimately* convinced, that now, more than at any other time, I can safely rely on your fervour in the accomplishment of all your duties; on your unlimited confidence in the guidance of Divine Providence, on your simple and silent submission to the adorable will of God; and I am sure I can add,—on your attachment to your ecclesiastical superiors both in this country and in that which several of you have left, to obey, like Abraham, the call of our common Master. You are now, for a time, my dear children in Christ, *a motherless family;* but you are not without that Father of us all who is in heaven, and who is never nearer to us than when we are in tribulation and distress. Fear not then, ye little flock, He will not leave you orphans. Beg of Him daily to grant to your superiors that spirit of wisdom and counsel which they now stand in particular need of for your good; and beseech Him likewise to bestow upon you *all* that simple, docile, charitable spirit that will free you from all pernicious solicitude and disquiet of mind, and dispose you for listening with that confidence of children to the voice of Almighty God, in that of those whom He has placed over you. Both your superiors in France and those of this country will have concurred in their views respecting the administration of both our little Communities, ere any permanent arrangement is made known to you relative to the future government of

St. Margaret's and Milton House. Meanwhile, the prudence of our worthy Bishop will suggest to him what temporary measures are most fit, and with them you will comply, *as if they had been written in the Rule*, till such time as everything be finally settled.

"To her that has left us, my dear children in Christ, we owe a debt of gratitude which it would ill become me to forget while addressing you on the present occasion; the readiness — nay, the eagerness, with which she endeavoured to forward, in its earliest infancy, the work that God has called you to partake in; the disinterested manner in which, at an advanced period of life, she abandoned her own country, while in a delicate state of health, to trust herself to the severities of a foreign climate, and to the privations of a land of which she knew not even the language; relying upon God alone, and the word of a stranger— shall never be obliterated from the heart of him whom religion has since taught her to call her Father. To you, my dear children in Christ, the recollection of her many amiable qualities, the purity of her intentions, and the sincerity of her affection for you, will long, I trust, render dear to you the name and remembrance of your late Mother.

"She could not have undertaken to return alone

to France. Her departure, then, has necessarily deprived us of another Sister, and, I grieve to add, that the health of a third has made it necessary for her to avail herself of this opportunity of repairing to a milder climate. But though separated outwardly, they will ever remain united with us in thought, in affection, and in prayer; let this spiritual union be mutual.

"In order to draw down the blessing of Almighty God, both upon those who have left us, and upon those who remain, you will recite daily the Litany of the Blessed Virgin, preceded by the usual invocation of the Holy Spirit—'*Come, Holy Ghost, replenish the hearts of Thy servants*,' with its versicles and prayers, and followed by the aspiration, '*Most Sacred Heart of Jesus, have mercy on us!*' three times repeated. The object of these prayers is to obtain for us all the respective graces we require at this particular juncture, and God's blessing and protection for your Mother and her travelling companions.

"These prayers will be continued daily till further intimation be given respecting them. My last recommendation to you all is *Charity! Silence! Obedience! Prayer!* and may the God of all consolation comfort, strengthen, and protect you.—Your unworthy but devoted friend and Father in Jesus Christ, JAMES GILLIS."

The paternal advice of Mr. Gillis was carefully followed, and fervent daily prayers were offered to God for the Mother to whom so much gratitude was due, as well as for guidance in the choice of those who were to fill the most important posts in the Community.

CHAPTER VIII.

CONSECRATION OF BISHOP GILLIS—HIS LABOURS FOR SCOTLAND—LETTER TO THE COMMUNITY OF ST. MARGARET'S—HE VISITS CHAVAGNES. 1838.

THE year 1838 was destined to be a memorable one in the annals, not only of St. Margaret's, but of the Eastern District of Scotland. The venerable Bishop Carruthers, feeling the weight of advancing years, presented a postulation to the Holy See for the nomination of Mr. Gillis as his coadjutor. The application was favourably received, and the Bulls appointing him Bishop of Limyra, and Coadjutor of the Eastern District of Scotland, with right of succession, were issued on 18th July of the previous year. Owing, however, to a verbal error in these documents, the consecration did not take place till Sunday, 22d July 1838. The ceremony was an imposing one, and was witnessed by an immense concourse of people, both Catholic and Protestant, drawn together, less by the novelty of the spectacle, than by the high reputation of the Bishop-Elect. Needless to say with what joy the inmates of St Margaret's assisted at the ceremony. The house was, for once, left in charge of one French Lay-Sister, Sister Stephen. She felt a little nervous at being alone; and as a precautionary measure, she rang the Community bell at the usual hours, that the neighbourhood might not suspect her solitary condition. Nothing disastrous occurred, and the Sisters were much amused at the device of Sister Stephen, which was long remembered as a joke against her.

St. Mary's had been decorated for the auspicious occasion with much taste and elegance. The Gothic pulpit, hung with crimson cloth, displayed the armorial bearings of the Right Rev. Dr. Carruthers. The passages were carpeted, and lined on each side with the school-girls of Milton House, dressed in white, and gentlemen vergers were stationed at intervals along the aisles, having in their hands white rods tipped with gold. But these secondary matters only diverted the eye for an instant from the sanctuary, which naturally formed the principal object of attraction. Nothing had been left undone that could enhance the beauty of the arrangements and decorations. The platform of the sanctuary, which had been enlarged to nearly the full breadth of the chapel, was carpeted with crimson cloth; and at either extremity of the Gospel and Epistle side respectively, were two small altars, each bearing a large gilt crucifix and candlesticks, above which appeared the armorial bearings of the bishop-elect. On one of these was displayed the episcopal insignia of the new bishop, consisting of crozier, mitre, gloves, ring, &c. The faldistorium for the consecrator stood at the Epistle side of the altar, while facing each other, at either side, were the chairs for the presiding bishop, Dr. Carruthers, and the assisting prelates with their chaplains.

The consecrating prelate was Bishop Baines, Vicar-Apostolic of the Western District of England, assisted by Bishops Scott and Kyle, Vicars-Apostolic of the Western and Northern Districts of Scotland. Bishop Murdoch, of Glasgow, preached the consecration sermon. The ceremonial was performed with all the accustomed solemnities. Upon the enthronisation of the new bishop, the consecrators intoned the "Te Deum." A contemporary witness says, "At this moment the scene was unspeakably grand, solemn, and imposing, the bishops and clergy having arranged themselves on both sides in the form of a coronal, to which the variety and splendour of their vestments gave the most picturesque effect, whilst the centre figure of the group, arrayed in full pontificals, appeared in all the mild dignity of his high office, as if he had descended from a higher sphere to minister and rule in the Church on earth."

While the choir was still pealing forth Graun's magnificent composition, in a harmonious burst of praise and thanksgiving, the newly consecrated bishop was led pontifically through the chapel, and in his progress blessed the people, all of whom were deeply affected by this touching part of the ceremony. Returning to the sanctuary, he chanted the episcopal form of benediction. During the last gospel the anthem for the Queen, "*Domine salvam fac Reginam*," was sung, the concluding prayer being chanted by Dr. Baines. The choir performed Beethoven's "Alleluia Chorus," while the clergy retired to the vestry.

Notwithstanding the length of the ceremony, which began at eleven o'clock and did not terminate till nearly four, no symptom of weariness or inattention manifested itself; and even Protestants, of whom there were several hundreds present, appeared to take almost as deep an interest in it as Catholics. It is almost superfluous to add, for it is a natural consequence of what has just been stated, that the most perfect order and decorum prevailed throughout the whole service; and although considerable discomfort must have been experienced by many persons owing to the crowded state of the chapel, no one evinced the slightest uneasiness or impatience.

Our space will not permit us to insert the whole

of the eloquent discourse delivered by Bishop Murdoch on this occasion; but we cannot withhold from our readers the concluding portion. After a brief sketch of the foundation and progress of the Catholic Church, the preacher proved the succession and mission of her bishops from the apostles, and their jurisdiction from the Roman Pontiff, the direct successor of St. Peter,—then turning to the occasion of the day, he thus addressed his hearers:—

"Gratifying, my Catholic brethren of Edinburgh, gratifying in the extreme must be to you the imposing ceremony which you are now witnessing. With hearts full of joy, I doubt not, you have this day all hurried to the temple of God, to behold the consecration of him whom Divine Providence has destined to preside over you as your bishop;—and justly do you rejoice and feel glad. I am aware that the pulpit is not the place, and the celebration of the Divine mysteries is not the occasion, for the effusion of flattery; and I know also that the lips of God's ministers ought never to utter the language of adulation. But surely I may, without impropriety, briefly congratulate you upon the choice which your venerable bishop has made of a coadjutor. From what you all know he has been as a priest, I think you cannot doubt what he will be as a bishop. It is necessary, says St. Paul, that a bishop should be blameless; that he should have a good testimony from them that are without; that he should be able to exhort in sound doctrine, and to convince gainsayers. By these tests of the apostle I fearlessly leave him who is this day raised to the Episcopacy to be tried. I boldly challenge any man to step forth and before God charge him with any delinquency. And if an ardent zeal for the glory of God, for the honour of religion, and for the salvation of souls redeemed by the blood of Jesus Christ, be another recommendation to the Episcopal office, has he not already given proof that this holy virtue devours his soul? Whilst, like the Prophet Jeremiah, he might yet style himself but a child in the ministry, did he not enter on and carry through an undertaking which, considering the time, the place, the circumstances, and his means, well might and certainly would have appalled any one but the man who was determined to yield to no obstacle in promoting the glory of God, and who felt in his heart that no one ever trusted in the Almighty and was confounded? Is there not in the vicinity of your city an establishment which will hand down his name in benediction to posterity as that of the man who had the courage to revive those holy and charitable institutions which once adorned our [illegible], but which the hand of misguided zeal three hundred years ago had laid in smouldering ruins? Yes, in St. Margaret's Convent he has raised to himself a monument, on the front of which might be inscribed these words—'What man dare for the glory of God, I dare.'"

In the event of that 22d July there was a consoling proof that the reign of error and of prejudice was approaching its term. A new era had risen for Scotland; the day had dawned, and the shadows began to depart. On the following Sunday, Dr. Gillis celebrated his first pontifical mass in St. Mary's Chapel, Broughton Street. Dr. Baines preached. The chapel was again crowded.

In the course of the previous week it had been resolved to pay some tribute of respect to Dr. Baines, who, during his short stay in Edinburgh, had won the regard of all; and with this view it was decided to present him with an address, expressive of the deep sense which the Catholic body here entertained of his services, and their admiration of the manner in which these had been performed on an occasion to them so interesting and important. An address embodying these sentiments was accordingly prepared; and, by previous arrangement, it was agreed that it should be presented immediately after mass in the cloister chapel.

The leading members of the congregation assembled accordingly, when the address, signed by Sir Charles Gordon of Drimnin, on behalf of the Catholic body in Edinburgh, was read by Dr. Browne.

In his reply, Dr. Baines, after returning thanks for the high compliment paid him, said, "To assist, when requested, at the consecration of a brother bishop, I regarded, I assure you, as an obligation of charity; whilst to officiate at the consecration of a valued and intimate friend, was to me a positive pleasure. But, to consecrate Dr. Gillis was *more* than these, it was a *great honour;* and I feel confident that my name, when it would otherwise have been forgotten, will live in the recollection of my having been selected to impose hands on a prelate of such distinguished merit."

Another proof of the estimation in which the new bishop was held is furnished by the gifts offered on the occasion of his consecration. His crozier was presented by Mrs. Colonel Hutchison; altar service by the pupils of St. Margaret's; magnificent vestments by the Abbé Fréyer, who had been his professor at St. Sulpice, and who was a cousin of Napoleon I. The letter which accompanied this gift was signed thus, "Aujourdhui votre Père,—demain, votre fils.—Fréyer."

Very shortly after his consecration, Bishop Gillis was deputed by the Scotch bishops to inquire into the state of such property as belonged to the Scottish Mission in France; and to obtain aid from the Society for the Propagation of the Faith. This society having been founded for the purpose of assisting missions in countries beyond the limits of Europe, declined to come to the aid of Scotland and other countries where Catholicity was once more reviving, and where assistance was greatly needed. As nothing would induce the council of the Society for the Propagation of the Faith to revoke its decision, Dr. Gillis determined to obtain the required help by means of another channel, and with this view (supported by the Archbishop of Paris, Monseigneur de Quelen, and other influential persons) he set on foot a society for affording relief to European missionary countries.

He succeeded beyond his most sanguine expectations. The new institution was entitled "L'Œuvre du Catholicisme en Europe," and its central council was established in Paris. It was so warmly supported that it bid fair to endanger the prosperity of the older society; and eventually the whole case was referred to the Holy See. It was decided that rather than have two societies whose ends were in reality so similar, and which yet might prove injurious to one another by reason of their interests clashing, they should be amalgamated, and that all missionary countries, whether European or otherwise, should receive aid in proportion to their necessities, and the resources at command.

Though the work begun so prosperously was given up, Scotland has much reason to be thankful for the aid received for so many years past, from the Association for the Propagation of the Faith, owing to the exertions of Bishop Gillis.

The following letter was written by Dr. Gillis to the Community of St. Margaret's while he was in Paris :—

"PARIS, *16th January* 1839.

"MY DEAR CHILDREN IN JESUS CHRIST,—A letter should reach Edinburgh to-day in which a promise is conveyed to you that you are soon to receive through the Embassy a literary bundle containing special answers to all your epistles; but as I find that my best resolutions are too often frustrated by the unforeseen avocations that cast up for me every day, many of which, unfortunately, I cannot always cast off, I must again beseech my creditors to take a shilling in the pound rather than lose all; and to accept as an instalment one letter instead of twenty, till I can make out twenty times as much leisure as I have just now, to repay them in full; which I do solemnly here declare to be my *bona fide* intention. 'Je vous l'avais bien dit,' some of you will be saying, 'que notre père ne tiendrait pas parole, pour son retour. Nous voici presque à la fin de Janvier, et il n'a pas encore quitté Paris.' Yes, my dear children, but if you only knew what detains me here, I am sure you would not find fault with me were I to spend here the whole twelve months. Don't startle at this, however; I am not going to put your patience to such a trial. When I arrived here, I found the state of our affairs different from what we had supposed it to be; and *that*, together with the unsettled state of the French Ministry (the fate of which is not yet quite decided), has obliged me to remain much longer in Paris than I had otherwise any idea of doing. I am glad, however, to be able to say, that my time has not been altogether lost. I have succeeded in getting possession of the Library of the Scotch College here, the books of which are now undergoing a regular sorting with a view to obtain a correct catalogue of them, and to complete such works as have been partly pillaged; after which operation I shall have them, please God, transferred to Scotland. I am also getting a search made in the public Archives, where, I am convinced, several interesting and important documents may be recovered which belonged to us previous to the first French revolution. Several highly important title-deeds of our properties here, have in the meantime been mislaid in the Bureaux of the different Ministries, which I have also been promised the recovery of, and which I must endeavour to have immediately effected. They have also agreed to name me administrator of the Scotch colleges and properties in France, in the name of the Scotch bishops; and I am waiting every day for the *ordonnance* to that effect. But Divine Providence has, moreover, thrown in my way a charitable undertaking, the ultimate results of which, if it succeeds, it would be difficult to define. It is this. To establish an association on a plan somewhat similar to that of the *Propagation de la Foi*, for the support and advancement of Catholicism in Europe; that of the *Propagation de la Foi* being exclusively for the benefit of missionary countries *out* of Europe. I have neither time nor space at present to enter into a detailed statement as to the high importance of such an undertaking, further than that it will prove, I trust, truly beneficial to Scotland among other countries, and that as to its organisation several great difficulties have already been overcome, and that with the assent and concurrence of the good Archbishop of Paris, I am to begin it, please God, in the beginning of February, by one or more charity sermons on behalf of Scotland and of those other countries in Europe where our holy religion is yet in the minority. Pray for me, my dear children in Jesus Christ, that my own unworthiness may not present an obstacle to the success of so desirable an undertaking; and depend upon it God will not allow you to be the sufferers from my absence, whilst I remain here thus employed for His greater glory, as well, I hope, as for your future happiness and the ultimate prosperity of our establishments in Edinburgh. My health, thank God, continues as good as I can expect it to be. I don't expect to become a Hercules in strength for some time yet, but as long as I hang together, I have reason to be thankful, and you likewise, after the Saturday, 4th March. If God spares me to see that day again, I shall probably be saying a Mass of thanksgiving at Chavagnes on my way home, as I am determined not to delay anywhere unnecessarily the moment I can quit Paris, nor make out any other visits than those of Luçon and Chavagnes, except at Bourbon-Vendée, which is on my way. I can assure you, you cannot be more anxious to have me back than I am myself to see home once more, but I cannot possibly leave at the present moment for the reasons above mentioned. Meantime, my dear children, continue united among yourselves, and apply yourselves with renewed zeal and fervour to the faithful accomplishment of your various duties,—'tis the surest way of making time ***short*** in this world, as well as for ensuring elsewhere that happiness which awaits us when time shall be no longer. God for ever bless, support, and comfort you all, is the daily and fervent prayer of your ever devoted and affectionate Father and friend in Jesus Christ,

✠ JAS. GILLIS.

"*P.S.*—I would bid you sing, '*Il reviendra à Pâques,*' if I were not afraid that some of you would be wicked enough to add, '*ou à la Trinité,*' but I do positively assure you I intend to be with you '*avant Pâques,*' so let the sacristan have all things ready for Holy Week as usual. God bless you all!"

He spent Christmas in Paris fulfilling the immediate end of his mission, and then availing himself of a short interval of leisure, he went to Chavagnes in Vendée to renew his acquaintance with the Religious Congregation at the Mother House. There he spent the Feast of the Purification. The Annual Letter, sent from the Superioress General to all the houses of the Institute, contains a notice (which we here subjoin) of this visit, which was highly appreciated:—"During the days which Dr. Gillis spent here he was never disengaged. So far from resting himself, his Lordship preached at the seminary, opened a retreat at the parish church, and presided at a ceremony of Clothing and Professions at the convent. Nor were the hours of recreation less occupied, for then, with his usual kindness, he gave pleasure to every one, his conversation was so charming, so edifying, and the anecdotes he related so interesting! On the Feast of the Purification I expressed to his Lordship the pleasure we enjoyed in his company; he sighed as he replied: 'Your Sisters at St. Margaret's have not had Mass this morning; they have much to suffer. . . . I shall not be able to return to them before Passion Sunday.'" He did not return even then; for he spent Holy Week and Easter in Paris; and knowing how much his absence was felt by the Community, he wrote some beautiful letters to the Superiors of both houses, giving them valuable instructions and all the encouragement in his power.

CHAPTER IX.

MOTHER ST. JOHN CHRYSOSTOM RETURNS TO FRANCE—HER MIRACULOUS CURE—DEATHS OF ST. MARY PHILOMENA KIRSOPP AND SR. ANGELA WITHAM. 1839-1844.

Mother St. John Chrysostom was obliged to leave Scotland about this time; her health was completely broken down, and she was recalled to France. With Sister Alexis as her travelling companion, she got as far as London, and on reaching the Benedictine Convent at Hammersmith became so ill that her life was despaired of. However, God had still a great deal of work for this zealous religious to do, and He vouchsafed a favourable answer to the earnest prayers offered for her recovery. On the 16th November, after the physicians had given up all hopes of recovery, and she seemed at the last extremity, she was suddenly and completely cured on the application of some moss from St. Wulstan's Well. Her restoration to health was as complete as it was instantaneous, and caused no little surprise both to the house doctor and the consulting physician whom he had called in; they declined to attribute it to any miraculous interposition, but at the same time declared themselves quite unable to account for it by natural causes. She continued her journey to Chavagnes, and wrote the details of her cure to her beloved Sisters and children in Edinburgh, where the news gave great joy to all who had the privilege of knowing the good Mother.

The year 1840 was rendered memorable in the annals of St. Margaret's by the funeral of the venerable Bishop of Kingston, the Honourable and Right Rev. Bishop Macdonell, who had died suddenly in Dumfries, and whose remains were laid in the convent vaults until the wishes of his people in Canada should be ascertained. So remarkable had been the career of this illustrious prelate, and so much good had been effected by his zeal in the interests of the Catholic Highlanders, that Dr. Gillis resolved that he should be buried with honour.[1] He brought the body to Edinburgh and

[1] The Honourable Alexander Macdonell devoted his whole life to the relief and improvement of the Highlanders. When at the end of the last century the Highland proprietors thought to improve their estates by removing the tenants of small holdings and substituting farmers of a wealthier class, Mr. Macdonell, then a missionary priest in Inverness-shire, constituted himself the apostle and guardian angel of his dispossessed countrymen. At first his influence obtained work for hundreds of them in the factories of Glasgow and Greenock; but the depression of trade, consequent upon the Continental Wars, threw the Highlanders out of employment, and the zealous priest conceived the idea of getting them embodied as a *Catholic corps* in his Majesty's service, which was accomplished, with Macdonell of Glengarry, chief of the clan, as colonel, and the Rev. Alexander Macdonell as

caused the obsequies to be performed with extraordinary pomp at St. Mary's, after which the coffin was placed in the vaults under the convent chapel. It lay there till 1861, when, as we shall see, the Bishop of Kingston, Dr. Horan, came to remove it to Canada.

On the Feast of St. Andrew, 1840, Sister Agnes Xavier Trail and Sister Margaret Teresa Clapperton, with two French Sisters, made their vows, which bound them to the Society for life; this being the first solemn profession of religious for centuries, it excited considerable curiosity, and was witnessed by nearly 400 people in the convent chapel.

The first death that occurs in a Community is always a deeply felt sorrow. As years pass by they rob us of many who are dear to us, and who will never be forgotten; but probably the first death

chaplain. When the regiment was disbanded in 1802, he accompanied a great number of the men into Canada, and there spent himself in the midst of them for more than thirty years, working wonders for their spiritual and temporal welfare. The mission that brought him across the ocean at the advanced age of 79, was still the same that had prompted his labours in youth. He left a flourishing Church in Canada, and now he returned to see the condition of those who had remained behind. He visited various parts of the Highlands, crossed over to Ireland, and finally returned to Scotland, arriving at Dumfries on the 11th of January 1840. Next day he said Mass as usual, but on the 14th he called his servant and complained of cold; the servant asked if he felt unwell, and receiving no reply, quickly summoned the Rev. Mr. Reid, who administered Extreme Unction and the last Blessing, and the noble old man passed into eternity without a moan. He may truly be said to have "fallen asleep in the Lord." He was then eighty years of age.

makes more impression than any which follow. On the 13th of April 1842 the Community mourned the decease of Sister Mary Philomena Kirsopp. This amiable young Sister had been one of the first pupils in the convent school. On the completion of her education she spent a short time with her family at the Spital, Hexham, and then begged to be admitted to devote her life to God in religion. She caught cold on the journey to Scotland, and was so evidently delicate that her health seemed to render her stay at St. Margaret's unadvisable. Many prayers were offered, and St. Philomena was particularly invoked to obtain the restoration to health of the fervent postulant. She became so much better that she received the habit, and—in gratitude for the intercession of the saint—the name of *Philomena*.

The recovery was, however, not permanent, rapid consumption set in, and the end approached only too quickly. On her deathbed Sister Mary Philomena pronounced her vows, and overflowing with happiness and gratitude gave up her soul to God. Her sorrowing Sisters felt that they had indeed lost one most dear to them on earth, but they had gained an intercessor in heaven.

The first postulant who joined the Community, as we have seen, was Miss Eliza Witham, of Lartington, called in religious Sister Angela; she took a prominent part in the care of the young ladies at St. Margaret's, being highly qualified for this charge by her refinement of manner and cultivated mind. She was both beloved and revered by her pupils, to whom she was perfectly devoted. One evening it was observed that she left the schoolroom hurriedly, and that her handkerchief was stained with blood. The illness increased, and Sister Angela was the second nun of St. Margaret's who passed away from earth to heaven. She expired with a smile on her lips, on Holy Saturday, 6th of April 1844.

CHAPTER X.

LABOURS OF BISHOP GILLIS FOR THE ADVANCEMENT OF RELIGION — FIRST VISIT OF HER MAJESTY QUEEN VICTORIA AND THE PRINCE CONSORT TO EDINBURGH. 1842.

For the first few years after his consecration, Dr. Gillis was chiefly occupied in labouring for the Church in Scotland by his foreign negotiations for pecuniary aid and by preaching. We may easily understand that he devoted such leisure as remained to him to the Community at St. Margaret's, and to the instructions which he gave with such success on Sunday evenings in the cloister chapel at St. Mary's, and afterwards in the oratory at Milton House. He was now called to take a more active part in the direction of the Diocese. Dr. Carruthers felt the effects of advancing age, and determined to retire to Blairs College; and while retaining the administration of the vicariate in his own hands, he resigned the charge of Edinburgh to his coadjutor.

Dr. Gillis then carried into effect some alterations and improvements in the church and presbytery in Broughton Street. A new altar, pulpit, and bishop's throne were erected, and the sanctuary was enclosed by a carved oak screen. The residence of the clergy was likewise arranged with a view to their greater comfort and convenience.

The services rendered by Dr. Gillis to religion were recognised by the Catholic body, and found expression on the 14th July 1841, when a large and influential meeting was held in the Waterloo Rooms, Edinburgh, Sir William Drummond Stewart of Murthly being in the chair. On this occasion the bishop was presented with a magnificent clock, surmounted by a planetarium or orrery. Inside the glass case were two hundred guineas, intended for the purchase of a carriage. Sir William Stewart briefly stated the object of the meeting, and called on Mr. Stodart Macdonald to read the address, which set forth the feelings of admiration, respect, and affection which had actuated the subscribers, and which they desired to express to the bishop, and at the same time to beg his acceptance of the testimonial which was presented to him. The bishop made an appropriate reply to the address, returning thanks to his friends for their kind feelings towards him, and for the gifts that had been offered. We need scarcely add that the "two hundred guineas" were expended on ecclesiastical purposes.

The week following this meeting Dr. Gillis

celebrated Pontifical High Mass and administered Confirmation in the newly-restored chapel of Murthly Castle, Perthshire, the seat of Sir William Stewart. This chapel had existed prior to the so-called Reformation; and the conversion of Sir William Stewart to the Catholic faith was the happy occasion of the ancient edifice being again used for its original purpose. Alas! it has once more fallen into Protestant hands, by default of Catholic heirs. May angels still guard it for the ancient faith till brighter days dawn again!

About this time the bishop founded a Catholic Friendly Society, under the name of the "Holy Guild of St. Joseph." Its object was to provide assistance for the members in time of sickness and old age, and to defray funeral expenses. This society did good service for many years; but when deprived of the protecting hand that had fostered its existence, it was dissolved, and its place has been taken by various other confraternities annexed to the different parish churches.

It was on Quinquagesima Sunday, 1842, that Bishop Gillis opened for the first time in Edinburgh the devotion of the Quarant' Ore, and the convent chapel was the privileged sanctuary in which it was inaugurated. We can easily imagine the joy and alacrity with which the religious undertook to prepare the throne where our Blessed Lord was to give audience to His loving children, and bestow His blessing upon them. They spared no pains to adorn the sanctuary for the occasion, and the three days during which the exposition lasted were a happy carnival for them. It was a consolation to them also to witness the fervour of the people, who came in great numbers to pay their homage of love and reparation; and earnestly did they pray that this devotion might soon be known and practised throughout the land.

The bishop never lost an opportunity of advancing the interests of religion, and he knew well that many of the beautiful devotions encouraged by the Church, but not practised in this country, needed only to be known in order to be appreciated. He ventured further than any of his predecessors, indeed it was a characteristic of his, which did not escape the notice of those who had known him from his earliest years. To him we owe the introduction of the Living Rosary which he established at Milton House, amongst the pious Catholics who frequented the Sunday evening instructions there.

Let us turn for a moment from our humble annals to recall an event which awoke the loyal enthusiasm of the whole country—the first visit of Her Majesty Queen Victoria and the Prince Consort to the northern portion of Great Britain. This occurrence brought joy to the Catholics of Edinburgh, no less than to their Protestant neighbours, and Dr. Gillis did all in his power to animate his flock with the heartfelt loyalty for which he was himself conspicuous. The royal yacht left Woolwich on Monday, 29th August, and after a prosperous voyage arrived in the Firth of Forth on the evening of Wednesday the 31st. An officer on board one of the vessels of the squadron published a few interesting details of the advance of the ships up the Firth. "When off Dunbar, besides the illumination of the town, a royal salute from the battery, the magnificent sight burst upon us of beacon fires lighted on all the conspicuous Scottish hills. The night was quite dark but clear; astern were all the lights of the steamers, bending like a crescent round the royal yacht in the centre; while on the coast around in East Lothian, Mid-Lothian, in Linlithgow, Fife, and Clackmannan, bonfires blazed on all the remarkable heights, all announcing the cordial welcome that awaited her Majesty from her Scottish subjects, while to the east of Edinburgh the summit of Arthur's Seat seemed a blaze of fire, shedding a flood of light over the surrounding heights and the valley below, and giving an aspect of wild grandeur to the surrounding scenery.

"It has been my lot to witness beautiful illuminations in various parts of the world . . . but I never remember anything that made so deep an impression as our passage up the Firth of Forth on that occasion. The beautiful expanse of water, the brilliant lights around, the rapid speed of the vessels, the recollection of the precious freight intrusted to our charge, and the feeling that through the merciful providence of God we had been enabled to bring our voyage to a happy end, all combined to render the scene one of thrilling interest, far beyond my powers of expression."

Her Majesty's early landing at Granton Pier on the morning of Thursday, the tardy arrival of the Lord Provost of Edinburgh, and the general mismanagement of the pre-arranged ceremonial, were long remembered.

The royal party were entertained at Dalkeith Palace by the Duke and Duchess of Buccleuch, and paid their first visit to Edinburgh on Saturday, September 3d. They entered the Queen's Park by Parson's Green, where an immense crowd had assembled, all manifesting by loud cheers the enthusiasm with which they were animated. The cortege proceeded up the Canongate, and here, we may be sure, the bishop had not forgotten the little orphans of Milton House. The Sisters had managed to provide the children with white frocks and neat blue bonnets. Each child was provided with a basket of choice flowers, and all were placed on a platform the height of the garden wall. As the royal carriage passed, they rendered their homage to the Queen by showering down their bouquets on her and the Prince. Her Majesty smiled graciously, and expressed the gratification which this simple and touching welcome afforded her. Prince Albert fastened one of the flowers in his button-hole, and the royal pair bowed repeatedly in acknowledgment of the tribute of loyalty offered them.

CHAPTER XI.

DEATH AND OBSEQUIES OF MR. MENZIES OF PITFODELS —VISIT OF HIS ROYAL HIGHNESS THE DUC DE BORDEAUX TO ST. MARGARET'S CONVENT. 1843.

BUSINESS connected with the interests of the Scottish Benedictine Monastery at Ratisbonne took Dr. Gillis abroad in August 1843. He did not proceed direct to Bavaria, and when at length he arrived in Munich, a letter awaited him announcing the death of his dear friend and benefactor, Mr. Menzies. At once he hurried home in order to direct the funeral obsequies and attend to the affairs which this death would render immediately imperative upon himself. In Mr. Menzies the inmates of the convent lost a valuable friend, and one whose fatherly kindness had adopted them as his own family. His sudden death was a great shock to them, and was all the more keenly felt as the Bishop was absent at the time. They prepared, as they knew Dr. Gillis would wish, to receive the remains of the venerable old man with all the reverence due to his great virtue and benevolence. The chapel was draped in black, and a large catafalque erected in the centre of the choir

JOHN MENZIES, ESQ., OF PITFODELS.

surrounded with lights. The body lay there awaiting the instructions of the Bishop, from the 12th of October till the Feast of All Saints, on the evening of which it was conveyed to St. Mary's Church for the solemn Requiem Mass.

Meantime Dr. Gillis returned, and on Sunday the 28th of October he issued a beautiful Pastoral Letter, eulogising the departed gentleman, bewailing his loss to the Church and to all works of charity, and finally giving directions for the funeral, which was to take place on Thursday the 2d November, the Feast of All Souls. No one was better at organising a grand ceremony than Dr. Gillis; he not only conceived the ideas, but he had the necessary talent for carrying them into effect.

Nothing was ever forgotten that could add to *the moral effect* which he strove to produce, and certainly the funeral that took place on the 2d of November was such as left a lasting impression upon all who witnessed it. St. Mary's Church was beautifully decorated for the solemn occasion; the windows darkened, the paintings covered with mourning; the gallery and pulpit draped, and ornamented with the escutcheon of the deceased; a splendid catafalque in the centre of the church, with pillars supporting a canopy of black cloth and ermine surmounted with plumes, &c. From the centre a large burnished crucifix rose above all the rest, and was the most conspicuous object there. In the absence of Bishop Carruthers, the Requiem was sung by Bishop Kyle, assisted by the Rev. Stephen Keenan, deacon, and the Rev. W. Bennett of Stirling, subdeacon; Bishop Murdoch preached, while Bishop Gillis took his place as chief mourner at the head of the bier, all the priests who could possibly attend were present, and the solemn music of Mozart's Requiem Mass added to the impressiveness of the function. Probably Scotland never witnessed such an imposing funeral ceremony, even in the days of Catholicity. The procession which passed through the streets, carrying the precious remains to rest in the crypt at St. Margaret's, was such as Edinburgh never saw equalled. At the close of the service in St. Mary's the procession was formed :—

Two Mutes on Horseback;
Twelve Baton-men;
The men of the Congregation, all in deep mourning;
The Standard-Bearers and Standard;
The Council of the Holy Guild of St. Joseph;
The Members of the Guild;
THE FUNERAL CAR,
drawn by six beautiful horses led by grooms, and bearing the Sarcophagus containing the body of the deceased, surmounted by the large burnished crucifix, rising above the plumes, and flanked by three members of the Holy Guild carrying lamps of most elegant design on handsome shafts;

The Deceased's Private Carriage,
followed by twenty-five poor men who had been clothed
at Mr. Menzies' expense, bearing torches;
The private carriage of the Right Rev. Dr. Gillis, with his
Lordship as Chief Mourner;
The Bishops and Clergy in mourning carriages each
drawn by four horses;
The Trustees of the Deceased;
The Pall-Bearers,
And the private friends of the deceased, all in carriages.

In this order the procession passed along York Place, St. Andrew's Street and Princes Street, down Lothian Road and across Bruntsfield Links to the convent, extending to half a mile in length. It is believed that not fewer than 50,000 of the inhabitants turned out to see the imposing spectacle, the large crucifix towering over all, the symbol of faith and salvation, being the chief object of attention. The body was laid before the altar in the convent chapel, surrounded by a group of simple but sincere mourners—the nuns and their pupils, the Sisters from Milton House, and the orphans; the *Miserere* was chanted and the *De Profundis*, then the Community formed with the children a procession through the convent garden to the crypt below the sanctuary, where the mortal remains of their revered friend and benefactor were laid beside those of the good and great Bishop Macdonell of Canada. One hundred poor people were clothed at the expense of the deceased, fifty Catholics and fifty Protestants; the male portion of the Catholic poor alone attended the funeral.

Towards the end of October the nuns were honoured by a visit from the young Duc de Bordeaux, the representative of the dethroned branch of the Bourbon family. This visit was especially appreciated by the French religious, who retained all their Vendéan loyalty, and who rejoiced at having so favourable an occasion of giving expression to their sentiments towards him whom they styled Henri V.

There were many in Edinburgh who remembered the Prince as a boy at Holyrood, and who gave him a cordial welcome to Scotland; but we must confine ourselves to his reception at St. Margaret's, which was indeed a great event to the inmates of the quiet enclosure. In the absence of the bishop, Mr. Malcolm, the senior priest at St. Mary's, did the honours, and the rooms of the convent were tastefully decorated for the reception of the royal visitor. The refectory, drawing-room, and school-room, forming a suite that communicated with each other by large folding-doors, were thrown into one, and at the upper end, in the large oriel window, a throne was erected with a neat daïs of crimson velvet surmounted by a crown and the *fleur-de-lis*, with the initial letter *H* in gold beneath it. Opposite the throne, and at the further end, standing against a crimson background, was a bust of his Royal Highness, taken when last in Edinburgh. On the left of the throne stood the Sisters, and on the right the pupils of the boarding-school, dressed in white with green sashes; the pupils of Milton House, and a few lay friends. Lady Dorothea Leslie, sister of the Earl of Newburgh; Mrs. Colonel Hutchison, Mrs. Hamilton Colt of Gartsherrie, and her daughter, Mrs. Osborne; Mrs. Keith, Mrs. Collingwood of Lillburn Towers, and her two nieces, the daughters of Sir Thomas Haggerston; Mrs. M'Kenzie, Colonel Leslie, Mr. Turnbull, advocate; Mr. Alexander Fletcher, and several priests.

About half-past twelve the Duke arrived, and, preceded by Mr. Malcolm, entered the school-room, and took his place on the seat of honour, whilst Miss Kyle of Binghill, one of the pupils at the piano, played "Henri Quatre," as an *entrée*.

The eldest of the young lady pupils at the time, Miss Kyan, being presented to His Highness by the reverend Mother, read the following address:—

"To His Royal Highness the Duke of Bordeaux.

"*May it please your Royal Highness,—*

"We, the pupils of St. Margaret's Convent and the orphans of Milton House, most respectfully, and with the cordial feelings of dutiful and grateful hearts, welcome your Royal Highness within the hallowed precincts of St. Margaret's. We proudly avail ourselves of this auspicious occasion to express all the happiness we feel in seeing you in Scotland. When you were last in Edinburgh, illustrious Prince, St. Margaret's was merely thought of; but now in its beauty and usefulness it teaches us to think of and imitate those whose piety and zeal, while advancing the interests of truth, have reared in our behalf this thrice happy home; and while recurring to this past, we have been taught affectionately to remember your illustrious sister, one whom we love, Prince, as yourself; and whose hearts, when they were young as ours, first communicated with God at the sanctuary of St. Mary's Church in Edinburgh.

"We bitterly regret the absence on this happy morning of our beloved Father, the Right Rev. James Gillis, Bishop of Limyra; and we still weep for the loss of a good man and a devoted friend of your Royal Highness, whose cherished and venerable remains, honoured with merits and the sanctity of years, now rest upon a bier, and whose marble lips, could they but speak, would breathe a blessing on Henry of France. But we do not on this account hail with less joy your visit to St. Margaret's; we know that your Royal Highness is familiar with sorrow, and the circumstance, whilst reminding us of the presence this day at St. Margaret's of a noble scion of the Lilies, will teach us through life a useful lesson, that true pleasure, like the flower of the cemetery, never 'grows more luxuriant than in the neighbourhood of death.'

"Led by our studies to a knowledge of the history and virtues of your Royal House, and instructed in the language, and sharing in the affectionate loyalty of our dear superiors, we fervently pray that every good and perfect gift may be granted and secured to

"HENRY OF FRANCE.

"Signed in the name of the pupils of St. Margaret's Convent and the orphans of Milton House.

"PHILLIS KYAN."

ST. MARGARET'S CONVENT, EDINBURGH,
20th October 1843.

To this address the Duke replied, that it gave him the greatest pleasure to revisit Scotland, which was associated with many of his earliest thoughts, and not the weakest, those that were connected with religion. Since his return to Scotland all classes had shown him the greatest attention, and while gratified by all, he certainly felt the greatest delight in those that were combined with, or flowed from religion, for therein lay the secret of individual as of national happiness.

He felt greatly pleased with the allusion to his sister. She, too, had not forgotten Scotland, and one of her latest requests to him was that when in Edinburgh he would inquire after several young ladies whose names had been given to him, and who had been receiving lessons with his sister's masters.

The Lady Superior then presented the inmates of the convent and of Milton House to the Duke, whose respectful attentions to them and the pupils gave great satisfaction. He was afterwards conducted through the garden, stopping at every point from which the city was to be seen, and when he said adieu at the convent gate, the party he left breathed a prayer for his safety and prosperity.

Passing by the bust of himself which was conspicuously placed in the hall of reception, he smiled and remarked, "Ah, j'étais bien jeune alors." On the following Sunday he heard Mass in St. Mary's, where Mr. Malcolm had prepared a pew in the centre, ornamented with the crown and *fleur-de-lis*. Every mark of respectful attention was paid to him by the leading Catholics in Edinburgh, and he duly appreciated it all, having a kind word for everybody; however, he paid the nuns this compliment, with which they were much pleased: he told Mr. Malcolm, "De toutes les fêtes que j'ai eu en Ecosse, il n'en est point qui m'aient été au cœur comme celle à Ste. Marguérite." Leaving the city, he secured for himself the blessing of the poor, by leaving a large sum of money to be distributed in charity by Mr. Malcolm.

CHAPTER XII.

MILTON HOUSE—DAY SCHOOLS—CONVERTS.

THE establishment at Milton House, which had done so much good in the city, and been so warmly supported at first, was now beginning to feel that the charm of novelty had worn off, and that people were less ready to pay their subscriptions than they had been at first; the work was not of a self-remunerating nature, and an existence that depends entirely or even mainly upon the benevolence of others is always precarious; the superiors felt the burden of supporting the poor and the orphans to be quite beyond their means, and it was at length resolved to break up the establishment. The orphans were dispersed to other institutions of the same kind in Great Britain and Ireland, and the pupil boarders transferred to Pentland House, which was rented for the purpose and used as a second-class boarding-school.

From the books kept at Milton House, we find that

the average number of poor children attending the school during the nine years was	380
Those who came to Sunday-school .	500
The first communions made	704
Protestant children instructed by their parents' desire	69
Converts instructed	307
Adults instructed	987
Abjurations made at Milton House, .	87
Indigent families visited and assisted .	1640
Poor relieved at the Dispensary . .	4300

The boarding-school was afterwards removed to more suitable premises in George Square, and ultimately to Lochrin House; but when the last lease of Lochrin House expired in 1858, the superiors decided upon giving up the boarding-school as being disadvantageous to the convent; and after a short interval they opened at No. 4 Nicolson Square a day-school, under the name of St. Ann's Seminary; this school has succeeded admirably, and is now carried on in a handsome building erected by the religious on their own property in Strathearn Road.

After the death of Mr. Menzies, Dr. Gillis continued to reside at Greenhill, and to superintend the two Edinburgh congregations. He frequently celebrated Pontifical High Mass, and delivered courses of controversial lectures at St. Mary's. These last bore abundant fruit, by enlightening the minds of the many Protestants who went to hear him, at first merely out of curiosity, or admiration of his eloquence, and who in many cases were drawn to study the Catholic doctrine, and to submit to the Church. Dr. Gillis took the greatest pains with the converts who consulted him. He never hurried them into the Church; their reception was delayed until both he and they were perfectly satisfied with their convictions of the truths of religion and with instruction. He began by recommending a careful study of the "Penny Catechism," and then as each point required elucidation, he applied his whole attention to the subject, and never left any point until it had been thoroughly explained and accepted. He also acted with the greatest prudence and kindness towards the Protestant relatives of his converts, and in many cases won whole families to the Church by dealing thus gently with their prejudices, and never missing an opportunity of placing the truth, with all its beauty, before their minds. Many eminent men consulted him by letter, and received replies which contained exhaustive information on the point at issue. It was indeed a red-letter day for the Bishop when he could welcome a wandering sheep to the fold!

He usually received his converts into the Church at St. Margaret's, where he said Mass, and administered Holy Communion and Confirmation to his neophytes. No one who had the happiness of being received into the Church by Bishop Gillis could ever forget his joy, or his paternal kindness. He was indeed a "good shepherd," rejoicing to open the fold to those "other sheep" who had heard the Master's voice and followed it. The first convert received by Dr. Gillis into the Church at St. Margaret's was the late Mrs. Glassford Bell of Glasgow. A long list of names which swell the number of "Rome's recruits" as years went by, include among others those of Mrs. Monteith of Carstairs, Mrs. Edgar, her son and several daughters, Mr. and Mrs. Gerard of Rochsoles, Mrs. Pittar, Viscount and Viscountess Feilding, the Very Rev. Henry Rawes, Mr. and Mrs. Leslie and their family, Lord Ralph Kerr, Lord John Kerr, Captain Miller of Glenlee, &c. &c. These and many others look back to the quiet chapel at the convent as the cradle of their faith, and venerate the memory of him who first broke for them within its walls the bread of angels. In preparing converts for reception into the Church, Dr. Gillis naturally employed the nuns to assist in giving the necessary instructions; and in this work Sister Agnes Xavier was a valuable aid. She had gone over the ground herself, and knew its difficulties. She had studied every phase of Protestant doctrine, and the refutation of every one of its many fallacies. Moreover, her love for the faith, and her ardent zeal for souls, led her to spare no pains in smoothing the way for those who were striving to find the truth.

In September 1844 Dr. Gillis purchased the parks at Greenhill, hoping to be able to erect on that site a cathedral and a college for the education of young men for the priesthood. With the co-operation of the gentlemen of Edinburgh he also established the brotherhood of St. Vincent de Paul, so widely known for its charity to the poor, and which continues its labours, having considerably developed and prospered since its foundation. In the first days of the society, after having had a conference at Greenhill, the members were in the habit of resorting to the convent chapel where benediction was given by the Bishop.

CHAPTER XIII.

FATHER O'DONNELL—DR. GILLIS GOES ABROAD—HIS LETTER TO THE COMMUNITY OF ST. MARGARET'S—PLANS FOR A CATHEDRAL IN EDINBURGH. 1847-1849.

ON the Feast of St. Margaret, 10th of June 1846, Mass was said in the convent chapel by the Rev. Alexander O'Donnell, who on that day was appointed chaplain to the Community, in place of the Rev. Æneas Dawson. Father O'Donnell was chosen for this position by Bishop Carruthers, who held him in the highest esteem. He lived at St. Mary's, Broughton Street, during the first nine years of his chaplaincy; but, notwithstanding the distance he had to walk, Father O'Donnell never failed to be at the convent in good time for the early Mass, and never (except when laid up by a dangerous illness,) did he disappoint the Sisters by failing to offer the Holy Sacrifice. He would even forego a few days of vacation rather than put the Community to the smallest inconvenience.

His devotedness to the interests of the Community during a period of nearly thirty years is beyond all praise; and the religious justly look upon him as the best friend they have ever known, after Bishop Gillis.

In the spring of 1847 Dr. Gillis set out for the Continent, where he visited Ratisbon, Munich, Vienna, Venice, and Rome. The chief object of the journey was to inquire into matters connected with the monastery in Ratisbon, which it was desired to convert into a seminary for the education of ecclesiastical students for the Scottish Mission.

While in Rome he obtained a Brief from Pius IX. approving of the erection of a cathedral in Edinburgh. This Brief was published by Bishop Carruthers in a Pastoral Letter on Easter Sunday 1849.

In July [illegible] Dr. Gillis returned to Bavaria, with ample powers from the Vicars-Apostolic to conclude the business of the monastery at Ratisbon, on the best terms he could obtain. He made every possible effort with the Bavarian Government, and had recourse also to Lord Palmerston, then Foreign Secretary, to prevent the property being taken out of the hands of the Scottish Mission, to be given over to the Benedictine Order in Bavaria. The British Government made a representation through their envoy at Munich, and the measure was suspended, and finally [illegible] to the [illegible] of the Holy See.

The following letter from Dr. Gillis to the Community at St. Margaret's will give some idea of his stay in Germany, at a time when there was a good deal of excitement on the Continent. It will also prove how closely he was united in thought and memory with those he left in their quiet convent home.

"SWITZERLAND, ST. GALL,
16th October 1848.

"MY VERY DEAR CHILDREN IN CHRIST,—Three months have now elapsed since I left London for the Continent; they have swept past me, like most of my existence for the last twenty years, with the rapidity of lightning. With much to think of, much to write, and much to do, I have travelled since I left you some thousands of miles in anything but good health; and those among you who know how different the outward appearances are which a Catholic bishop is obliged to assume abroad from those of *presbyterian* simplicity in honour throughout Scotland, will easily understand that my leisure moments cannot have been much increased in number from being obliged constantly to pack and unpack, to dress and undress, to be one day a layman and another day a bishop, to run here and run there for every single thing I wanted—to be, in a word, my own chaplain, my own secretary, my own servant, my own paymaster, my own everything.

"Without wasting more words, then, in endeavouring to describe my protean existence since the month of July last, let me assure at once every inmate of St. Margaret's that *not a single day* has passed since I crossed the British Channel in which I have not re-crossed it in thought and prayer in all the earnestness of my heart for those whom I now address as my own children. I have knelt at many a holy shrine since I last bade you farewell, but I have never done so without making your spiritual and temporal welfare the special object of my unworthy prayer. My last petitions have been offered to-day in the cathedral (once the old Abbatial) church of the Monks of St. Gall. This celebrated old Benedictine abbey was founded by a Scottish hermit of the name of Gall in the beginning of the seventh century, and the town of St. Gall owes its origin to the abbey. The abbey was once the nursery of learning throughout the whole of Europe, and the remnants of its library still contain manuscripts of the highest value. I reached this yesterday on my return from Lyons; and to-day being the Festival of St. Gall, and still kept here with the greatest solemnity, I had the happiness of offering up the Pontifical High Mass, the first which a Scotch bishop ever celebrated here since the period of the Reformation, and, in so far as tradition goes, for many a long year, if not century, before.

"*Munich*, 31*st October*.—Another fortnight has elapsed since I was obliged to break off the above and since then my time has been entirely swallowed up with travelling, or with the business I have here on hand, and which, considering the difficulties with which it is beset, has required my whole leisure and attention. I cannot, however, allow this month to close without endeavouring to bring likewise to its termination a letter that long ere this time should have found its way to Edinburgh. To give you then some general idea of my wanderings since the end of July, I found on arriving at Frankfort that the Bishop of Ratisbon, whom I required to see in the first instance, was not at Ratisbon, but in Bohemia, and to Bohemia consequently I was obliged to go. I returned with the Bishop to Ratisbon, which we reached on the eve of the Assumption, and on the following day I officiated pontifically morning and afternoon in the cathedral church, one of the finest old Gothic churches in Germany.

"After spending a fortnight at Ratisbon, making myself master of the history of the old monastery and of the various documents to which I required to refer in treating with the Government here, a study that was rendered rather difficult from the circumstance of my not understanding German, and having as my only translators persons who had almost completely forgotten their English, and after drawing out my memorial to the King and getting it translated into German for the Government, I set out for Munich, which I reached on the 29th August. Here thirteen days more were spent running first after one person and then after another; writing, talking, trying to persuade a set of *Germans* against their will, which is no very easy matter—in a word, one day went after another like so many hours. The King gave me very fair promises, and if he will only stand by them, I have carried my point; but I very much fear the advice he has received since from his precious ministry is very little in my favour. To give them time to prepare the advice in question, I was coldly informed would take them two months or so, and they have kept their word. The first German that ever was hatched must have come out of a snail shell. You may naturally suppose I was not going to spend all that time here doing nothing but counting my fingers, so I determined to turn it to account by running through Switzerland to Lyons, whither I ought to have gone long ago, but never could get it done. You may here very properly stop me, I own, by the question, but why did you not write to us *before you started for Lyons?* Ah! well, to be sure I might have done *that;* and in as far as I did *not* do it, and did omit doing so without any good and sufficient cause, I have only now to throw myself on your all merciful forgiveness. However, I do sincerely believe that what made me anxious to start without a day's delay at the time, was the information I had received from the Bishop of Milwaukie, that the distribution of the Propagation of the Faith funds was to take place at Lyons in September, and it was the 13th of September before I could leave Munich. Eleven days of constant travelling, except two spent at Geneva, but very well filled up, took me to Lyons. There I really did intend to write to you, but there again I was rendered altogether useless for two or three days by the dreadfully bad weather; and during the rest of the ten days I spent there, my time was taken up preparing a memorial for the Council of the Propagation of the Faith. I met these gentlemen at last, and addressed them for nearly three whole hours. I hope my time was not altogether lost. It was of the greatest importance at the present moment to secure the continuation of the usual annual grants to Scotland, and which were in very great jeopardy from the sudden depression in the general funds because of the troubled state of France and of most of Europe. Should the times get better, however, I have every reason to believe we shall be more largely helped than before. I did not forget to plead the cause of George Square, but I regret to say that owing to the utter uncertainty of public events, the Board could not in common prudence undertake any new burdens this year. I left Lyons on the 3d of this month, while the cavalry was flying at full gallop through the streets to suppress an insurrection of the *Gardes Mobiles*, a set of harum-scarum brainless young gentlemen, who had been kept quiet for half a twelvemonth by putting a military coat upon their back, but who on being disbanded had chosen to smash all the windows and furniture of their barracks (some few months before, the convent of the poor Sisters of the Sacred Heart, who had been expelled) and were now proceeding to besiege the prefecture, and had already made a prisoner of the chief magistrate himself. *Vive la république!*

On Sunday the 8th inst. I preached in French at Geneva to induce the Catholics of that *Protestant Rome*, as they call it, to set to and build a new church. The following days I spent partly at *Annecy*, where I went on a pilgrimage to the tombs of St. Francis of Sales and of St. Jane de Chantal. I had the happiness of saying Mass there on the 10th. The next day I went to see that poor persecuted Bishop of Lausanne and Geneva, whom I find they have since expelled from Friburg—and the men who do this call themselves Catholics! Thank Providence, my dear children, that you are where you are. Had you witnessed the state of the Continent, as I have been doing for the last three months, you would fall upon your knees and thank Heaven from your inmost heart that to you has been given so peaceful a retreat at St. Margaret's; had you been in the inside of the poor convent of Capuchin nuns which I visited along with the good old Bishop of St. Gall, and which really is *Bethlehem* in all its bareness, and heard these poor persecuted creatures sigh after a home of any kind in any country in which they could be allowed to exist in peace, you would be ashamed of the luxury of comfort that surrounds you in Edinburgh. I don't, of course, include the *cholera*, but that I trust will not come your way. Catholicism in Germany is in a very poor condition, and Switzerland still worse. I have now again returned to Munich, as I find, quite in time for the rate at which German business habits travel, and am now in daily expectation of another audience from the King, when I trust something may be come to in the shape of a decision; provided we are not again thrown here as everywhere else in Germany into some new revolutionary movement and confusion. In consequence of what is now going on at Vienna a hundred thousand men have been battering that unfortunate capital with grape shot since Thursday last—what the result may be, God only knows. Whatever way matters go, I own I am prepared for a desperate attempt on the part of the rebellious spirits of the Continent, so that it is a very probable case I may be obliged to return to England at very short warning. I trust, however, it may be otherwise. We had here the other day a row among the *Beer Barrels.* Beer to a Bavarian is the greatest enjoyment of life. He sits over it, he talks over it, he sings over it, smokes over it, snores over it, drinks it like a fish; but when made to pay too dear for it, fights for it like a tiger. Private property was here for three hours last week at the complete mercy of the mob, the soldiers standing by and looking on—for *they* drink too. Two of the most remarkable persons I have had occasion to see since I have been in this country are in the Diocese of Ratisbon. I went with the Bishop to see them—one is a woman of about one or two and thirty, bedridden for several years past, and a very great, and apparently a very patient, sufferer. She bears the *Stigmata* very plainly marked. We found her lying in a garret room, with everything about her very poor, but very clean. It was on a Friday—and it seems that on Fridays she loses her voice and cannot speak above her breath. She seems during all that day to be absorbed in meditation on the Passion of our Blessed Lord. She assured us that there was nothing to fear for the Church from all the present disturbances, that there would be no war—in a word, that God had none but views of mercy for us all. *If it really turns out so*, I shall believe her to be a prophetess. Last year about Easter the famous Abbess of Minsk assured me that in *two years* from thence there would not be a Protestant left in England —may be so; but in that case there is a great deal to do in the way of conversion before Easter next. The other person to whom I have alluded, whom I also went to visit in company with the Bishop of Ratisbon, is a young girl of thirteen—she likewise is bedridden, and has for the last two years taken neither meat nor drink of any kind—at least, in solid nourishment, for the last two twelvemonths, and no liquid for the last eighteen months. The Holy Communion is her only food. She is the daughter of very pious and simple peasants. We found her lying with her eyes bandaged, as she cannot well bear the light—the curtains of her bed were half-closed, and her head was resting on her right hand, with the rosary beads between her first finger and thumb. Her mother took off the bandage that I might see her face; she is a very pleasing looking child, and extremely simple in her manner. I felt her pulse—it was neither weak nor strong; but her hands and her feet, which her mother uncovered, were as plump as those of a person in perfect health. She is carried every other Sunday or so to church, and it takes three women to carry her. She, too, suffers acutely on Fridays, and during all Lent till the morning of Easter Sunday, when all suffering leaves her and she becomes of a sudden gay and playful. The venerable Nich[illegible] de Vanderflue, they say, lived eighteen years wi[illegible] out eating or drinking. On the principle of [illegible] *que le premier pas qui coûte*, I can see no [illegible] why a person who has continued to fast [illegible] years shouldn't fast for two hundred. [illegible] all kinds of prophecies going on the [illegible] now, and there is a singular agreement [illegible] them. One says that the present [illegible] to be the last sovereign of that [illegible] enough that the other day [illegible] he should no longer reign [illegible] Now, if he is only to re[illegible] Parliament, his reign may [illegible] there is another reason, in my view of things, apart altogether from prophecy, which numbers the days of the Prussian monarchy, it is the pure creation of Protestantism, and along with it, it must fall. Another prophetic saying, quite common throughout Germany for many a long year is, 'I would not be a fruiterer in 1847, nor a king in 1848, nor a soldier in 1849, nor a gravedigger in 1850, but anything you like in 1851." The fruit was so abundant in Germany in 1847 that it brought nothing in the market. In Switzerland I found the same saying in other words—'All the difficulties of Europe are to be settled between 1848 and 1850.'

"When the Bishop of Trèves was in London at the opening of St. George's, he told us that two years ago one of his priests brought him an old book from his library, on the blank page of which was written, in a very old hand, a Latin sentence saying that in 1848 many kings and princes would cease to reign because of their incapacity to govern their kingdoms. And it is curious enough that in running my eye over an old book on judicial astrology, which I got sight of here from the University Library, I found the following announcement, 'In the year 1840, or thereabouts, the kings of Europe will begin to show their incapacity to reign, and their kingdoms shall pass out of their hands.' The book was printed at Frankfort (which is now making mincemeat of all the princes of Germany) in 1665. We certainly live in very strange times, and stranger ones still are yet at hand, or I am much mistaken; and yet here am I striving to set up a college in the midst of this political Babel, and in the very heart of it too. Really, I seem to have been destined to try my hand at odd doings, I was going to say from St. Margaret's downwards. But I will not say that, for I hope, my dear children, that St. Margaret's will also weather the storm that has beset it for more than twelve years now in one way or another, and that there are days before us all, when we shall not regret the occasional blasts we may have suffered from, individually, from time to time, but rejoice in feeling our bark ride safe at last on a calm and friendly sea. In as far as I am concerned for the present, I am sure you will be glad to hear me say that for some weeks past I am much better in health than I have been for very many months back.

"*All Saints.*—To-day I have officiated pontifically here in the Church of St. Louis, a very costly edifice built by the ex-King Louis; and this afternoon I have visited the great cemetery of Munich. It is really a very singular and beautiful sight. Every tomb is most tastefully decorated with crowns garlands, and flowers of every sort and in wondrous profusion, and throughout the whole, thousands of coloured lamps are burning; at the foot of each grave is placed a holy water vat, many of a permanent nature and of very elegant construction. The crowd is immense, and every one is expected to sprinkle the grave of his relations or friends. There are large reservoirs of water in different parts of the ground, and they are all blessed for the purpose, so that there is no lack of holy water. What a singular world this is! The crowds who lie buried in that cemetery once thronged its walks on similar occasions, to deck the graves of previous generations; to-day we look down upon theirs; to-morrow, others will look down upon ours. How many who last week were full of life and spirit in Vienna who now are carried in cartloads to a common grave! Vienna surrendered on Sunday, after sustaining a most fearful bombardment of balls, shells, and Congreve rockets, that must have been productive of fearful loss of life. The town was, they say, on fire in many directions. God help the innocent! As for the demons in human shape who have forced on this dreadful catastrophe, God in His mercy forgive them, but I hope they have been sufficiently punished to teach them to behave themselves a little better for the future. By far the most important part of the business is yet to come. Will the victors find out at last that there is no doing without religion, and that the Church must be freed from the shameful fetters it has worn in Austria for so many long years past? If so, there is yet hope. If not, the late siege is but the forerunner of still more fearful disasters.

"God bless you all, my dear Children in Christ, prays your most truly in our Lord,

"✠ JAS. GILLIS.

"*P.S.*—I have not time to read over. The paper is so very bad here, and my eyesight is now, I fear, getting habitually so confused at night, that I doubt whether this epistle will be at all legible. As I write to you all, I need scarcely add, remember me most kindly to the whole Community, but let some one convey my best wishes and blessing to the children of both houses. I pray for them daily with all my heart, and I long to tell them something of my adventures since we last parted.

"Patrick and Mary[1] I still imagine most edifying in their respective departments, the one offer-

[1] Patrick Fegan, for many years the faithful gardener and valued friend of the Community. He only quitted St. Margaret's to assist his brother in the management of a small farm in Ireland. While hearing Mass he was struck by paralysis, and expired after a short illness.

Mary Keenan was the convent portress. and held that employment till the increased number of Sisters admitted the appointment of a member of the Community to take charge of the gate.

ing up her rheumatisms for the sins of the house, and the other smiling upon the daisies, or piously nodding assent to Mr. O'Donnell's moralities. Everything kind to Mr. O'Donnell."

On the return of Bishop Gillis in 1849, he turned his mind to the fulfilment of his ardent desire to erect a cathedral and a college on the ground purchased some years previously at Greenhill. He engaged Mr. Welby Pugin, the celebrated ecclesiastical architect, to furnish designs, and to test the quality of the stone on the proposed site.

The plans were exhibited to the public in 1850 and were greatly admired. Want of funds to raise these costly structures obliged the Bishop to relinquish the accomplishment of this undertaking. He received many fair promises of aid; but as they were not substantiated, it was impossible to proceed with the work. It was objected that the situation was too far removed from the city to make the church practically useful. To this the Bishop replied, that the tendency to build on the south side of Edinburgh would soon bring the city out to Greenhill. The experience of the last twenty years has gone far to prove the correctness of his prevision.

At the Exhibition of Architectural Drawings in

Edinburgh in 1881 the designs of Mr. Pugin for "St. Margaret's Cathedral" were much admired.

Perhaps at some not very distant period the cherished hope of Dr. Gillis may be realised, and we may yet see a Catholic cathedral worthy of our holy faith and of the beautiful city of Edinburgh.

CHAPTER XIV.

CORPUS CHRISTI PROCESSION—VISIT OF THE EX-QUEEN OF THE FRENCH—THE DOWAGER-MARCHIONESS OF LOTHIAN—DEATH OF BISHOP CARRUTHERS—BILL FOR THE INSPECTION OF CONVENTS—DEFINITION OF THE DOGMA OF THE IMMACULATE CONCEPTION. 1850–54.

WE have repeatedly alluded to the zeal of Bishop Gillis in promoting the beauty of Church ceremonial. He thus strove to enkindle in the hearts of his flock a more ardent love of our holy religion, by rendering it attractive even to the outward senses; while he deepened that love by directing it to rise from the seen to the unseen—from earth to heaven.

Accustomed as he had been from youth to the magnificent ceremonies of the Church in Catholic countries, he endeavoured, as far as circumstances would permit, to carry out in Scotland the heart-stirring functions with which he had been so long familiar. In this he found a willing and able co-operator in Father O'Donnell, who, like the Bishop, claimed St. Sulpice as his *Alma Mater*, and having been trained in the same school, in nothing did he and the Bishop work more heartily together than in the celebration of the festivals as they came round. The approach of *Corpus Christi* inspired Father O'Donnell with the idea that a solemn procession of the Blessed Sacrament might take place in the convent grounds. He proposed it to Dr. Gillis, who eagerly adopted the suggestion, and spared no pains to render it imposing, to honour the God of the Holy Eucharist.

This first procession of the Blessed Sacrament round the garden took place in 1850; the venerable Bishop Carruthers himself officiated; a large body of priests assembled, the "Body Guard of the Hidden God;" and an immense crowd of people, who were admitted to the grounds by ticket. Dr. Gillis preached a magnificent sermon, and the emotion was indescribable as the procession emerged from the chapel to wend its way round the garden. First came the cross-bearer and acolytes; then the pupils of the schools dressed in white, with long muslin veils; then the Sisters, each group carrying an appropriate banner; then the clergy.

Behind the clergy walked Bishop Gillis, immediately in front of the canopy, under which Bishop Carruthers was bearing the Holy of Holies. The canopy was borne, as it has been ever since, by members of the Brotherhood of St. Vincent of Paul

All who witnessed that procession were struck by the appearance of the saintly Bishop, who reminded them of the holy old man Simeon bearing the infant God in his arms; he looked so venerable, and so rapt in devotion, as he proceeded round the grounds from one altar of repose to another. The effect produced was deep and lasting; and to this day the spectators of that first procession remember the feelings of consolation with which they assisted at the solemn act of faith, reparation, and love offered to Him whose sacramental presence had been long ignored in Scotland.

The singing of the Litany of Loretto every Saturday evening in the convent chapel, was begun by Bishop Gillis after a visit to the Holy House at Loretto, where he made the promise, that in his convent in Scotland the nuns and children would pay that act of homage to our Lady, in union of prayer with those who sing it in the Holy House itself. This devotion had been carried on at St. Margaret's for more than thirty years before Lady Herries obtained from the Holy See the indulgence granted to those who assist at the Saturday evening Litany.

The devotions of the Month of Mary were likewise inaugurated here, and in 1853 was established a weekly procession of the Blessed Sacrament round the interior of the chapel, on the Thursdays in May.

A visit from the ex-Queen of the French, Marie Amélie, and the Duchess of Orleans, caused a little excitement in the convent, when, on the 13th of July 1851, a Requiem Mass was celebrated for the soul of the Duke of Orleans. The ex-Royal family were received by the Bishop with that gracious courtesy for which he was so remarkable; and were conducted by him to the refectory, where the Sisters were assembled to meet them. The Queen spoke with the most unaffected piety of the nothingness of this world, and indeed her very appearance was a striking lesson of dignity and misfortune. Proceeding to the schoolroom, the party received a little address, which was read in French by one of the pupils; the Queen afterwards sent a handsome brooch to the young lady who had read the address, and to the Community a magnificent set of the works of Bossuet, with a little inscription in the first volume written by her own hand.

The conversion of the Dowager-Marchioness of Lothian, which took place in 1851, was a subject of great thanksgiving to the Bishop. A very remarkable movement was going on at this period, and many converts were brought into the Church. Their names are in benediction for the good work they accomplished in their own sphere.

Lady Lothian soon turned her thoughts to

Scotland and its many necessities, and erected a church at Dalkeith, under the invocation of St. David. This formed the nucleus of smaller missions, and after being in the hands of the secular clergy for some years, was intrusted to the Jesuit Fathers, who continued to give their care to the outlying stations of Loanhead, Penicuick, &c., till these places had attained sufficient importance to be established as independent missions, each with its own parish priest. Lady Lothian also purchased a chapel and priest's house at Jedburgh.

The Bishop's health now gave cause for anxiety, and put a limit to his exertions. In consequence of successive severe attacks of illness he put himself under the care of Dr. Gully of Malvern, and underwent a course of hydropathic treatment. Dr. Gully declared that he was threatened with congestion of the brain, which, if not checked, would end in paralysis. After some weeks of medical treatment, considerable improvement was observed, and the Bishop returned to Edinburgh in January 1852. On the 25th of March he laid the foundation-stone of a church at Leith. He was invited to preach the "Month of Mary" of this year in the French Chapel, London. These discourses, delivered in French, were much admired, and the chapel was filled to overflowing. Before the termination of the course the fatal illness of Bishop

Carruthers obliged his coadjutor to return to Edinburgh. On the homeward journey, owing to a collision on the railway near Newcastle, he sustained that injury to the spine from which he never recovered. Bishop Carruthers was dying of typhus fever. During his last days Mother Margaret Teresa visited him, and obtained his blessing for the Community at St. Margaret's. Dr. Gillis ordered prayers throughout the diocese, and the Blessed Sacrament was exposed in the convent chapel. During the last three years the Bishop had resided at Dundee, but notwithstanding his advanced age, he made frequent visits to Edinburgh and other parts of the district.

Fortified by the rites of the Church, and surrounded by his sorrowing clergy, this venerable and beloved prelate expired at St. Mary's, Edinburgh, on the 24th of May, in the eighty-third year of his age, the fifty-eighth of his priesthood, and the twentieth of his episcopacy. The funeral service took place at St. Mary's Church. Dr. Gillis officiated. Bishop Murdoch and Bishop Smith of Glasgow were present, and a large number of priests. His remains were interred in the vault beneath the sanctuary of the church. The increased responsibility, and the many additional occupations which devolved upon Dr. Gillis at this time, left him no possibility of taking the care his health required, after the accident he had met with. He worked on with indefatigable energy, till in 1853 he was once more obliged to return to Malvern. His stay was short, and on his return to Scotland he provided for the spiritual wants of many of the smaller missions. Though unable to devote himself as heretofore to the Community at St. Margaret's, he usually said Mass in the convent chapel on Sunday mornings, and delivered a short discourse; and on all great feast days officiated at Benediction, and preached on the festival that was being celebrated.

The bill for the inspection of convents having been brought into Parliament by Mr. Chambers, Dr. Gillis went to London to unite in the efforts that were made to prevent its passing the House of Commons. It were needless to say with what anxiety this threatened piece of Protestant legislation was watched by the whole Catholic population of Great Britain, nor how the best energies of both clergy and laity were directed against it. In all religious Communities constant prayers were offered that so great an evil might be averted. All these means had the desired effect. Though the bill was brought in for several successive sessions by Mr. Newdegate, it was at last treated with the derision and contempt it merited.

The Definition of the Dogma of the Immaculate

Conception, 8th December 1854, gave occasion to the Bishop to issue a Pastoral, explanatory of the Dogma. He had been in France during the summer of that year to try the waters of Ax, reputed to be efficacious for spinal affection ; deriving but little benefit he returned to Edinburgh, and was much disappointed at learning that the Holy Father had expected him to assist with the other prelates, assembled in Rome, at the grand function of the Definition. The Bishop availed himself of this occasion to instil an increased devotion to the Blessed Virgin in the hearts of his people. A solemn service of thanksgiving was held at St. Mary's.

At St. Margaret's the Thanksgiving Service took place on the 2d Feburary 1855. The holy sacrifice was celebrated by the Bishop, who also delivered a magnificent discourse. In the evening the convent was illuminated, and the Community and the pupils testified their joy by a solemn procession in honour of Mary, ever Immaculate.

CHAPTER XV.

DEPARTURE OF THE FRENCH RELIGIOUS—MOTHER MARY ANGELA LANGDALE NAMED SUPERIORESS—VISIT OF THE DUKE OF MONTPENSIER—PANEGYRIC ON JOAN OF ARC—ARRIVAL OF SISTERS OF MERCY IN EDINBURGH—FATHERS OF THE SOCIETY OF JESUS. 1855-1860.

OUR readers may remember that the first Superioress of St. Margaret's was the reverend Mother St. Hilaire, and that this lady had been obliged in conseqence of failing health to return to France in 1837. She was succeeded by the reverend Mother Mary Emily, another French religious, who, with the exception of a short interval when Sister St. Damian was nominated Superioress, governed the Community till 1855. Mother Mary Emily was a model of every religious virtue, and was much beloved by the Community and pupils. To the sorrow of her Sisters it was observed that her health, never robust, was giving way completely. The Bishop sent her to Malvern to try the hydropathic treatment, along with Sister Jane Frances Macnab, and for a time a marked improvement was the result. A severe winter, however, brought back the alarming symptoms, and this being made known to the superiors in France, an order was sent from Chavagnes enjoining Mother Mary Emily to return to the Mother House with the least possible delay.

The blow was as unexpected as it was painful, not only to the Community of St. Margaret's, but to the reverend Mother herself, who was far from wishing to leave Scotland. The sacrifice, however great, had to be made. The reverend Mother, accompanied by two other French Sisters, bade a long farewell to St. Margaret's, leaving there only one of the original French colony. At the time of their departure Dr. Gillis was in Dublin. Two of the religious were also in that city, whither the Bishop had sent them some weeks previously, to become acquainted with the methods of education followed in the best schools there. These two Sisters resided at the Mother House of the Sisters of Mercy in Upper Baggot Street, where they were welcomed with the greatest hospitality. Letters of introduction from Dr. Gillis were passports to some of the principal convents in and about Dublin, and thus they became acquainted with Mrs. Ball, foundress of the Loretto Convent; Mrs. Aikenhead, foundress of the Irish Sisters of Charity, and several distinguished religious of other Orders.

Archbishop Cullen received the Sisters from St. Margaret's with fatherly kindness, and they were also affectionately received at the Sacred Heart Convent (then at Glasnevin); the Presentation Convent, George's Hill; the Dominican Convent, Cabra, where the deaf and dumb school was a subject of great interest to them, and several other establishments. Indeed, nothing could exceed the warmth of the welcome the two travellers received in all the convents in Dublin, and of which they still retain a grateful remembrance.

The news from home was, however, very distressing to them; and they hastened to complete their work and return to Edinburgh. On reaching Greenock they found Father O'Donnell, and Father Gordon (of Greenock) awaiting them. They were conducted to the Chapel House, and after partaking of refreshment, proceeded to Glasgow, and thence to Edinburgh. The diminished Community at St. Margaret's were overjoyed to see them, and much had to be told on both sides. It was sad to see the vacant places, and many prayers were offered that the arrangements of the Community might be directed for the glory of God and the greater good of all concerned.

The Bishop returned at the end of September, and shortly afterwards Mother Mary Angela Langdale was named Superioress, and Mother Margaret Teresa Clapperton, Assistant

Several postulants joined the Community, and thus again their numbers were filled up. The work of the boarding-school and that for girls of the middle class at Lochrin House, went on prosperously, and the new reverend Mother was fully occupied in training the young members of the noviceship.

On the 23d April 1856 a solemn Requiem Service was held at St. Mary's, for the repose of the souls of the soldiers who had fallen in the Crimean War. The church was prepared with decorations suitable to the occasion. On shields were displayed the names of the battles fought and won, the flags of the allied armies waved over them. The Russian flag below the others, claiming a prayer for her poor fallen soldiers—friends and enemies slept together in death on the battlefield, and were remembered together in the prayers of the Church.

The Bishop issued a Pastoral Letter on the occasion.

An interesting visit was paid to the convent in 1856 by the Duke and Duchess of Montpensier with their suite. The party assisted at Benediction, and then visited the house and grounds. On taking leave, the Duke promised Dr. Gillis that on his return to Spain he would himself search the Escurial, to find, if possible, the relics of St. Margaret, which were believed to have long lain there.

In 1857 the property of the convent was extended by the purchase of the field which lies between the convent garden and the Grange Cemetery. Unfortunately a strip of ground adjoining the garden had already been purchased by Mr. David Murray, who built his dwelling-house on it, and laid out the rest as a garden, thus cutting off all access from the convent to the field beyond. However, it was a great matter to secure that field, as it preserved an open space, free from buildings on that side. The large portion of Warrender Park was purchased by the religious at a later period.

In the same year, 1857, Father O'Donnell was requested by the Bishop to reside permanently with him at Greenhill. This was an arrangement most suitable to all parties. For many years Father O'Donnell had been a zealous co-operator with the Bishop in all that regarded the spiritual and temporal welfare of the convent; and no event of any importance occurred within its walls in which Father O'Donnell did not take a lively interest.

Having been recommended to try the waters of Vichy, Dr. Gillis went to that salubrious resort in the spring of this year, and while there he was requested by his old friend and college companion, Monseigneur Dupanloup, Bishop of Orleans, to visit his episcopal city, and to pronounce the panegyric on Joan of Arc, on the anniversary of the day on which this heroine achieved the deliverance of Orleans from the armies of England.

It was not an easy task; and the Bishop only consented to undertake it on condition that his flock in Edinburgh should benefit by his oration.

In preparation for his discourse he visited Domremy, Chinon, Rouen, and other places immortalised by "La Pucelle," and thus possessed himself of every point of interest in her wonderful life.

The cathedral was crowded on the occasion, and the appreciation of the audience was manifested by their rapt attention to the orator, and their scarcely suppressed applause. The panegyric was magnificent in its power and eloquence. At its close the Bishop of Orleans himself received the offerings of the congregation, for the purpose, so dear to the heart of Dr. Gillis, of enlarging and beautifying the recently acquired Church of St. Patrick in Edinburgh.

In appreciation of the honour rendered to Joan of Arc and the city of Orleans, the mayor and municipality presented Dr. Gillis with the heart of King Henry II. of England, who died at the Castle of Chinon, on the Loire, in the year 1189.

On the return of the Bishop to Edinburgh he turned his attention to the improvement of the poor schools. The chapel in Lothian Street was converted into two schools for girls. These were confided to the Sisters of Mercy established in Edinburgh in 1858. The Bishop had long desired the aid of these religious for the visitation of the sick and the charge of the poor schools, and he invited a colony from the house of the Order at Limerick (then governed by Mother Elizabeth Moore) to make a foundation in Edinburgh. A house had been engaged as a temporary residence for them in Wharton Lane; and to provide for their comfortable reception, Dr. Gillis enlisted the services of the religious of St. Margaret's. These were given all the more willingly, as one of the foundresses—Miss Helen Grant—had been the first pupil of St. Margaret's. She will long be remembered and revered by all who knew and loved her as Mother Mary Juliana.

The Sisters found their abode neatly arranged, and an oratory fitted up with furniture lent by St.

Margaret's. Mother Margaret Teresa was there to welcome them to Scotland, and we may be sure that Mother Mary Juliana's affectionate heart rejoiced at seeing one of her old friends again. The most cordial intercourse existed between the two Communities, whose superioresses had been friends from girlhood.

The Sisters of Mercy continued to reside in their temporary abode in Wharton Lane till 1861. They then removed to the convent under the invocation of St. Catherine of Siena, in Lauriston Gardens, which was erected by the munificence of the late Mrs. Colonel Hutchison, so well and widely known by her holy life and extensive charities.

The Bishop took a lively interest in the progress of the new establishment, and it was a great pleasure to him to see the two Communities of St. Margaret's and St. Catherine's, each in its own sphere, aiding the important work of education.

In 1859 he was able to carry out another long cherished design — the introduction into Scotland of the Fathers of the Society of Jesus, under whose care he placed the south-western portion of Edinburgh.

After occupying a temporary chapel in the

Grassmarket, the Jesuit Fathers erected a spacious church in Lauriston Street. The church was solemnly opened in July 1860, when High Mass was sung by the Very Rev. Thomas Seed (Provincial), and the sermon was preached by the Bishop.

ST. MARGARET'S CONVENT, EDINBURGH, IN 1863

CHAPTER XVI.

ADDITION TO THE CONVENT BUILDINGS—VISIT OF THE BISHOP OF KINGSTON—MOTHER MARGARET TERESA VISITS CHAVAGNES—BISHOP GILLIS GOES TO ROME AND SPAIN—BLESSING OF THE NEW HOUSE. 1861-1863.

THE original building of St. Margaret's Convent having now become too small for the number of its inmates, a large addition was begun according to designs furnished by the late Mr. Edward Welby Pugin. The smallest detail in this building was a matter of importance in the Bishop's estimation. The new wing of the convent was destined for the accommodation of the young ladies' boarding-school, and Dr. Gillis considered it essential that everything in their abode should be in perfect proportion and good taste, though without any approach to luxury or extravagance. The foundation-stone was solemnly laid, November 1861, and the building progressed rapidly. The plans comprised all that could be needed in a great monastery having a large number of inmates both religious and secular. The design formed a quadrangle that would cover a great part of the present garden. If these plans be ever carried out, the building will be magnificent, with a spacious cloister running round the whole. But the finances of the Community would not admit of so costly an undertaking; nor was it required as long as the old Whitehouse was suffered to remain. Consequently only one side of the square has been built; and it contains the dormitories, wardrobe, lavatories, refectory, and class-rooms in convenient proximity to one another.

The time which passed during the erection of this building was a very busy one, and attended by much unavoidable inconvenience to the Sisterhood, which was, however, turned into matter for merriment by the younger members, and into merit by the elders. The Sisters of Mercy were extremely kind in giving hospitality to those who were unable to find rooms at home, owing to the old house being in the hands of the builders who were connecting the two dwellings. The winter, too, was exceptionally severe, and for weeks during which the frost lasted all work had to be supended, and the sunk story of the new building was covered with a sheet of ice.

It was in the spring of 1861 that the reverend Mother received a letter from Dr. Horan, Bishop of Kingston, Canada, announcing a visit to Edinburgh, and of his intention of removing from our vaults the remains of his venerable predecessor, Bishop Macdonell.

Dr. Gillis was then at Malvern, and wrote his orders that every possible attention should be paid to Dr. Horan, that he should take up his abode at Greenhill, and that all the necessary arrangements should be made about the removal of the coffin. A solemn dirge was to be celebrated for the repose of the saintly bishop—to which all the clergy, secular and regular, as well as the lay friends of the Community, were to be invited.

Nothing could exceed the cordiality of Dr. Horan. He was delighted with the reception that was given him. He passed some hours with the Sisters, and spent an evening with the pupils, who exhibited "tableaux vivants" for his Lordship's amusement.

The Requiem Service took place on the 4th June. Dr. Horan sang the Mass, assisted by the Very Rev. Dr. Macpherson, V.G., the Rev. J. Darcy, and the Rev. Father Gascoigne, Father O'Donnell being Master of Ceremonies.

Among the friends present on this occasion was Colonel Macdonell, a relative of the late Bishop.

All regretted the unavoidable absence of Dr. Gillis, but nothing was left undone to fulfil his kind and hospitable wishes towards the Bishop of Kingston, who expressed his sense of obligation in a charming letter to the reverend Mother, and offered a stained-glass window in memory of his predecessor from his diocesans.

It was not often that any of the Sisters left home, but the health of Mother Margaret Teresa requiring change of air, it was arranged that she should visit Chavagnes and remain in France for some weeks. Sister Mary Sales was appointed to be her travelling companion, and they set off on the 29th of July to London, thence to Paris, proceeding to Angers and Nantes (where they were warmly welcomed in the Houses of the Congregation), and at length reached Chavagnes, where the first familiar face that greeted them was that of Mother Mary Emily, in improved health, and now the Assistant-General at the Mother House.

Only those who know how closely the bonds of religion knit hearts together can understand the joy that was experienced at this meeting. How much had to be told on both sides; how many questions were asked and answered, and how interesting were all the details given of old friends and familiar haunts. The two religious from St. Margaret's had a valuable opportunity of observing all the customs of the Mother House, and of obtaining full information on points requiring elucidation. They assisted at the Community retreat, on which occasion the inmates of the house numbered 500.

At the close of the exercises the newly-appointed Bishop of Luçon, Monseigneur Collet, paid his first visit to Chavagnes, and gave the habit and received the vows of a large number of aspirants. After a stay of six weeks the travellers proceeded southwards to Saintes, where they found other old friends, to La Rochelle, and again to Nantes, Ancenis, Angers, and Paris, on their way home. On arriving in London they went once more, and for the last time, to visit their old friends the Benedictine nuns at Hammersmith. That excellent Community shortly after removed to their present abode at Teignmouth, Devon. They returned home *viâ* Birmingham, where they were met by Dr. Gillis, who came from Malvern to see them. Among the memorable events of this visit was an interview with the Very Rev. Dr. Newman, who was kind enough to take them through his school at Edgbaston.

Another visit was paid to the nuns at St. Mary's, York, with whom St. Margaret's had long been on affectionate terms by correspondence. The travellers arrived at home at the end of November, and were welcomed with delight by all at St. Margaret's. Many a recreative hour was agreeably spent in relating all they had seen and heard.

Dr. Gillis began a visitation of his diocese in March 1862, but before he had ended it he was invited to proceed to Rome, to assist at the canonisation of the Japanese martyrs on Pentecost Sunday. He accomplished the journey, and was received in Rome with marked distinction. He explained to the authorities at Propaganda the state of his district, the progress religion had made, the difficulties under which he laboured, and the enfeebled state of his health, and again earnestly begged to be released from the burden which pressed so heavily upon him. This request was not granted. He was told to take the rest he required, and was promised the aid of a coadjutor, but the appointment was postponed.

The Community took advantage of the opportunity afforded by the Bishop's journey to Rome to send an illuminated address to the Holy Father, expressive of their veneration for his person, and their devotedness to the Holy See, and begging the blessing of his Holiness for the Sisterhood and their pupils. The address was accompanied by a miniature copy of the Ecce Homo by Guercino (painted by Sister Agnes Xavier) in a costly frame. Dr. Gillis presented the address and picture at his first audience with the Pope. The reverend Mother soon received a gracious and paternal answer from Pius IX., with the desired blessing, and kind expressions of encouragement to the work of the Community.

Having made a stay of some weeks in the Eternal City, he proceeded to Spain, to prosecute a search for the relics of St. Margaret, Queen of Scotland. It had been a long cherished wish of the Bishop to secure this treasure for St. Margaret's Convent, and he obtained a brief from the Holy Father authorising him to remove the relics, if the Queen of Spain gave her consent. This project had been conceived so far back as the year 1847, when the Bishop had applied to Rome for the brief alluded to. Many difficulties presented themselves. The royal family were at La Granjà, and thither Dr. Gillis followed them to obtain an audience, and the decree requisite for instituting a search in the Escurial, where the relics were believed to be enshrined. He was graciously received by the Queen Isabella II. and King Ferdinand, explained the purport of his journey to Spain, obtained the necessary document, and returned to the Escurial. Unfortunately the Vice-President was laid up, in fever, and was unable even to look at the letter written by the Queen's order by Monseigneur Claret, her Majesty's confessor. Many delays and disappointments ensued.

The Bishop ascertained that the relics in the Escurial had been much scattered during the Peninsular War, and considerable difficulty was experienced in prosecuting the search. Two old paintings (evidently doors of a triptych) representing St. Margaret and Malcolm III. of Scotland were treasures the Bishop was most anxious to secure, but the authorities would not allow of their removal. He obtained, however, a large relic of the saint, together with the necessary authentications. During his stay on the Continent he likewise visited Sens, where he was presented with valuable relics of St. Edmund, and of St. Thomas of Canterbury. In the cathedral at Sens there still exists an altar at which the saint said Mass, and Dr. Gillis obtained leave to have a part of the stone sawed off, to be incorporated in the altar of a reliquary chapel at St. Margaret's, where he intended depositing the relics he had collected.

It cannot be expected that the regular routine of a convent school should afford much matter for history. The days succeeded each other and multiplied into weeks and months, all bringing their appointed round of duties, varied occasionally by a holiday or some extra amusement. The Bishop interested himself in the recreations of the children no less than in their studies, and looked upon the management of the *former* as little inferior in importance to the direction of the *latter*. How delighted he was to reward diligence by some unexpected pleasure! and how anxious to procure for his little friends some joyful surprise! One year when an unusual amount of distress was prevalent about Christmas, the children volunteered to make the sacrifice of their Christmas-tree for the benefit of the poor. Their pocket-money was accordingly expended in charity. The reverend Mother mentioned this trait to the Bishop, who thoroughly appreciated it. Some days elapsed without any notice being taken, when the children were invited to an entertainment at which a splendid Christmas-tree was the event of the evening! If a dramatic performance or *tableaux vivants* were exhibited at the convent school, the kind Bishop was always present if possible, and knew how to encourage the young performers, and at the same time to elevate their taste, and draw useful lessons from the simplest source. These lines may meet the eye of those who will doubtless remember the happy evenings which enlivened their school-days — the wonderful performances of a celebrated conjuror engaged to exhibit his feats of legerdemain; the harmonious strains of the Béarnais Singers; and, still more delightful, when an invitation was given for the children to spend a summer afternoon at Greenhill, on which occasions they were allowed the perfect freedom of the garden ; tea being enjoyed in the conservatory. The festivities concluded with singing some of the Bishop's favourite old Scotch airs, and then *that* "Praise the Lord," which is familiar to every child of St. Margaret's, and in which his own fine voice was always heard. If he loved to share in the innocent joys of the little ones of his flock, he no less sympathised in their sorrows, and in case of the sickness or death of any of their friends, he felt like a true father for the grief of his children, and omitted nothing that could be done to console them.

Who can wonder at the love and veneration with which those who knew him best, regarded him during his life; and still cherish his memory through the long years that have rolled by since he went to that home where we trust to meet him again!

During the summer of 1862 the convent chapel was much improved by the addition of stained glass windows, the gifts of kind friends; two deserve special remembrance—one of these was presented by the Earl of Denbigh in thanksgiving for his reception into the Church; and the other by Mr. Monteith of Carstairs, in thanksgiving for the conversion of Mrs. Monteith. An interesting present was also made to the convent by Mr. Corballis of Dublin, whose nieces had been educated at St. Margaret's. The gift consisted in a set of vestments that had belonged to the late Cardinal York. After his death these vestments came into the possession of the Abbé Taylor, great-uncle of Mr. Corballis, an ecclesiastic of some eminence in Rome, and were by him left to Mr. Corballis, who considered that a Scotch convent was the most fitting place for vestments that had been the property of a Scotch cardinal of the blood-royal.

Many generous benefactors gave pecuniary aid towards the completion of the new buildings, and they have ever since had a share in the special prayers for benefactors, living or deceased, which are daily offered by the Community. The works proceeded, but it was not till the 25th March 1863 that the house was solemnly blessed by the Bishop.

The Feast of the Annunciation being the chief festival of the Ursulines of Jesus, it was most fitting that the new convent should be opened on that day. The morning was happily occupied by three Masses, said by Father O'Donnell, the Rev.

William Grady, and the Bishop. His Lordship's Mass was celebrated at 8·30, at which, according to the usual ceremonial of the day, the religious renewed their vows, and a choir postulant was admitted to take the habit. The Bishop preached on the occasion. In the afternoon his Lordship gave confirmation to a large number of pupils in the two schools, and to several converts. When the service was over the Bishop proceeded to bless the new house. A procession was formed headed by a cross-bearer, the pupils followed, then the religious, the clergy, and the Bishop. Several ladies and gentlemen were invited to follow, and among them were noticed Mrs. Colonel Hutchison, Colonel Macdonell, Mr. Angus Fletcher of Dunans.

Leaving the chapel by the great door, the procession crossed the garden to the new entrance and hall, thence along the cloister to the dormitory and Community room. Here the prayers were recited; returning, the Bishop blessed the lavatory, wardrobe, cells of the nuns, and finally the schoolroom, class-rooms, and refectory. All then returned to the chapel and thanked God for the happy completion of this great work. The Bishop declared this to have been one of the happiest days of his life.

During the following Holy Week, the Bishop

was sufficiently well to officiate at the ceremonies of the Church, even washing the feet of twelve poor men at St. Patrick's on Maundy Thursday. On Easter Sunday he sang High Mass and preached at St. Mary's, and in the evening preached and gave Benediction at the convent.

CHAPTER XVII.

LAST ILLNESS AND DEATH OF BISHOP GILLIS—HIS FUNERAL—LETTER OF HIS EMINENCE CARDINAL WISEMAN. 1864.

In the middle of April 1863 the Bishop went to London to preach at the opening of the Italian Church in Hatton Garden, at the request of his old friend, Cardinal Wiseman. The Bishop urged many excuses, but the Cardinal would accept none, and Dr. Gillis made the exertion. He was so unwell that even at the last moment it was feared he would be unable to speak; and it was but too evident that the effort was beyond his strength. Immediately afterwards he was laid up with a severe attack of jaundice, and it was several weeks before he could return home. He then gave confirmation in several places, where it was due, but during the summer was able for very little exertion of any kind. Even the convent chapel found his place filled by another on the great festivals, which he had delighted to celebrate with his beloved children. When his suffering state permitted him to leave the house he came to St. Margaret's and interested himself in the progress of the children, the arrangements of the new buildings, or the placing of stained glass windows, presented by friends, in the chapel. He seldom came empty handed—often bringing objects of interest for the museum, books or engravings for the school or drawing-class.

He was rarely able to say Mass, and his state was the cause of great anxiety to all around him. His increased sufferings now often prostrated him completely, and feeling it impossible to fulfil the duties of his office he petitioned the Holy See for the aid of a coadjutor.

On the 15th October the Bishop met at St. Margaret's his old friend Colonel Macdonell, who was about to leave Edinburgh for Wardour Castle, there to end his days, but who wished to pay a farewell visit to St. Margaret's. Dr. Gillis took him over the new house, and when the old man of eighty-four knelt to receive the Bishop's blessing, both felt that they should never meet again in this world.

Two days later the Bishop went for a few weeks to Dumfriesshire, to stay with his old friend, Miss Lidderdale, and thence went to Morpeth, where he made a retreat under the direction of Father Lowe, O.S.B. He was very ill while at Morpeth, and was therefore detained much longer than he expected, only returning home on the 11th December.

On the 13th, the third Sunday of Advent, he said his last Mass at St. Margaret's. He breakfasted and spent the forenoon there, visiting two of the Sisters who were sick, and arranging matters of business with the reverend Mother. Next day he was very unwell and consented to send for Dr. Warburton Begbie, who attended him with the utmost devotedness during the few weeks which elapsed till his death. The Christmas festivals were saddened by his absence and the knowledge of his suffering state. Many friends called and sent to inquire after him, and prayers were offered for his recovery. He was most carefully nursed and watched by the religious of St. Margaret's, Father O'Donnell, and his faithful servants. Now and then a change for the better gave a gleam of hope, but this soon vanished.

He sent to the convent many of his valuables, and gave directions as to their destination. On the evening of the 22d of February 1864, the Bishop was taken with a violent attack of illness. Dr. Begbie was sent for, and came immediately, and his prescription took effect for a moment. A bad night, however, brought back the unfavourable symptoms, and he was pronounced to be in danger. In the afternoon of that day, 23d February, he was seized with vomiting of blood. On learning the doctor's opinion, he said, "Send for Father Lowe."

A telegram was instantly despatched, and also one to the Very Rev. Archibald Macdonald, the Vicar-General. In the presence of Father O'Donnell, and some of his devoted children, the religious of St. Margaret's, he received the last solemn rites of the Church at the hands of Father Lowe, with full consciousness. He had a very suffering night, and at five in the morning had another fit of vomiting blood, after which he fell into a comatose state and did not speak again. His last words were the echo of his whole life, "Lord, I have loved the beauty of Thy house, and the place where Thy glory dwelleth."

Who could describe that last day of his life? He was speechless and motionless, while those whom he had loved best were kneeling and praying round his deathbed. Father O'Donnell exposed the Blessed Sacrament at St. Margaret's, and ceaseless prayers were offered for him there. Messengers had been sent to the churches in town to inform the clergy that their Bishop was passing away, and they came to Greenhill to unite in prayer for him. No sound save the voice of prayer and the laboured breathing of the dying man was heard throughout the day, till at a quarter to 3 P.M. the precious soul departed to hear the words so longed for, "Well done, good and faithful servant."

The sacred remains were arranged in full pontificals; all trace of suffering passed away, and the expression of perfect peace stamped on the features of the Bishop seemed to assure those who knelt beside his bier that he had indeed entered into the joy of the Lord. The clergy, the religious from St. Margaret's, Sisters of Mercy, Little Sisters of the Poor, and many old friends, watched by the body till the coffin was closed, and the beloved face hidden from sight.

On the morning of the 27th (Saturday), the coffin was brought to the convent chapel and placed on a catafalque in the choir. After the early Masses, said by Father O'Donnell and Father Lowe, the Very Rev. A. Macdonald officiated at a solemn dirge. The clergy recited the Office for the Dead, and Mass was then sung for the departed.

During the two following days the convent chapel was crowded by persons from the town, who came to pray beside the coffin. On the evening of the 29th it was conveyed to St. Mary's, Broughton Street, and on the following day the solemn obsequies took place. The Right Rev. Dr. Murdoch, Bishop of the Western District, officiated pontifically, assisted by the Rev. Dr. Macpherson as deacon, and the Rev. A. Gordon as sub-deacon, the Very Rev. A. Macdonald acting as assistant priest. The Right Rev. Dr. Gray, coadjutor of the Western District, was also present. Nearly all the clergy of the

Eastern District were assembled round the bier of their departed Bishop, and the church was crowded by a devout and sorrowing congregation.

The church was beautifully arranged, and the whole service conducted with the most imposing solemnity. At the conclusion of the Mass, the funeral oration was delivered by the Rev. Ignatius Grant, S.J., from the words, "Though he is dead, he yet speaketh."

The crowd which filled the space in front of the church, and all along the route of the procession, was immense, and the behaviour of the vast multitude testified to the respect in which Bishop Gillis was held by men of all creeds. His last resting-place was to be his well-beloved convent of St. Margaret's, and thither the long funeral procession now wended its way, passing for the last time his own door. The religious of St. Margaret's and the Sisters of Mercy, with the pupils of both houses, awaited the arrival of the cortege within the convent gates, and accompanied the body to the vaults beneath the chapel, where the last prayers of the funeral service were chanted by the Very Rev. A. Macdonald.

His remains rest beneath the altar which he raised to the glory of God, the altar at which he said his last Mass, and on which the Holy Sacrifice is so frequently offered for the repose of his soul.

Of Dr. Gillis we may well say, in the words of England's greatest poet, "He was a man, take him for all in all, we shall not look upon his like again."

It has not been within the scope of these pages to give more than the merest sketch of his life and works, still less could we attempt to fill in the outline by details of his character and virtues. To the outside world he was known as a man of brilliant talents, matchless eloquence, and great zeal for the glory of God and the advancement of the Holy Church. To those who were privileged to be admitted to his more intimate friendship, he was known and loved as a man of deep and tender piety, charitable to the poor, humble and patient in suffering, merciful to the erring, a lover of little children, who were instinctively attracted towards him, and one ever ready to aid by word or deed where his assistance could avail.

That he was highly appreciated by his contemporaries was abundantly proved by the letters addressed to the Community of St. Margaret's by many who had been personal friends of the late Bishop.

The following letter from Cardinal Wiseman to Sister Agnes Xavier cannot fail to interest our readers :—

"DEAR SISTER IN CHRIST,—I have been prevented from writing more than was absolutely necessary by inflamed eyes, not even yet recovered. On the third day after your good and holy Bishop's death I was able to say the special Mass appointed by the Church for that day, and I have ever since continued my memento, when able to celebrate.

"God, I trust, has heard our prayers for him, and received him to His sweet embrace; for he must have had much of his purgatory here. You must naturally feel like orphans, and endure all the desolation of a fatherless household. But God will be your Father, and your late kind parent and founder will not resign his post to any on earth now that he is near the Fountain of Grace and the Source of Paternity.

"I will not forget to pray for you; for I loved him more than any one else in the same condition and relation with me in the Church. We felt much in common, and thought, I believe, always the same, on all that concerns the Church.

"In return, therefore, I beg your prayers for myself, while I send your Community my affectionate blessing.—Yours very sincerely in Christ,

"N. CARD. WISEMAN.

"LONDON, *March* 15, 1864."

CHAPTER XVIII.

MOTHER MARGARET TERESA ELECTED SUPERIORESS—THE RIGHT REV. DR. STRAIN—ST. JOSEPH'S CONVENT, PERTH—SACRILEGIOUS ROBBERY IN THE CONVENT CHAPEL—VATICAN COUNCIL. 1864-1871.

THE period which followed the Bishop's death was naturally a very sorrowful time at St. Margaret's.

According to the testamentary disposition of Dr. Gillis, Greenhill Cottage was sold and the chief part of the furniture taken to the convent, where it was placed chiefly in the new part of the house occupied by the pupils.

The district was administered by the Very Rev. Archibald Macdonald while awaiting the nomination of a bishop. Father O'Donnell was appointed by the administrator Ecclesiastical Superior of St. Margaret's Convent.

During the summer Mother Margaret Teresa was elected Superioress in place of Mother Mary Angela, whose term of office had expired.

Many fervent prayers were offered by the religious for a blessing on the successor of Dr. Gillis.

Immediately after the Bishop's funeral the Rev. Mr. Strain went to Rome, and several months of suspense were passed. At length, on the 9th of September 1865, Father O'Donnell announced to the Community that Dr. Strain had been nominated Bishop of Abila and Vicar-Apostolic of the Eastern District of Scotland. The Holy Father, Pius IX., himself consecrated the new bishop on the 25th September, and on the 7th of November he arrived in Edinburgh. He paid his first episcopal visit to St. Margaret's on the 10th, accompanied by the Very Rev. A. Macdonald, the Rev. George Rigg (now Bishop of Dunkeld), and the Rev. Robert Clapperton. The Community were assembled in the Community room to welcome the Bishop and receive his blessing. He then visited the new dormitory and cells, and proceeded to the schoolroom, where he spent a short time with the children. On leaving them he went to the chapel, and finally to the crypt, where he prayed beside the remains of his venerable predecessor.

On the 15th his Lordship celebrated Mass in the convent chapel. At the conclusion of the holy sacrifice he addressed a few words to the Community, and imparted to them the Papal Benediction. In the evening of the same day Dr. Strain administered Confirmation to some of the pupils.

The Community were desirous of showing every mark of respect and regard to their new bishop. They did not forget that it was he who had said the first Mass for the little colony in their temporary abode at Argyle Park; and on many subsequent occasions he had manifested his kindly feelings towards St. Margaret's. Besides, they knew him to be the one appointed by God to be their Bishop and Superior; the one to whom henceforth, under God, they were to look for guidance in doubt, for support in difficulties, and for consolation in sorrow. Well might they pray that all graces might be given to him in his episcopal career.

It was with great pleasure that the Sisters offered Dr. Strain a case of church plate and a beautiful alb and rochet, on the occasion of his arrival in Edinburgh, and as a slight testimony of their dutiful sentiments towards himself.

The year 1865 was somewhat memorable.

Towards the close of 1864 the sanction of the Secretary of State was obtained for the admission of religious into the General Prison for Scotland at Perth, with a view to improving the moral condition of the Catholic female convicts confined in that institution, and of instructing them in their faith.

On the 2d of January 1865 the Bishop, accompanied by the Rev. George Rigg called at St. Margaret's, and proposed to the Reverend Mother that the Community should undertake this work at the prison of Perth. No one knew better than Mr. Rigg how greatly the poor convicts were in need of instruction, for he had been in charge of the Perth Mission for several years, and it was owing to his intervention that the aforesaid permission of Government had been obtained. Though no longer at Perth he was still greatly interested in the mission, and the Rev. Dr. Macpherson, who had succeeded him, was equally anxious to secure the services of nuns, not only for the prison, but also for the Catholic schools.

Visiting prisons was a new kind of work to the Sisters; but they considered that it fell within the scope of their institute, as being devoted to *teaching women of all classes*; they therefore gladly acceded to the proposal, and before the end of January the Reverend Mother and Mother Mary Angela went to Perth to look at the house which was offered to them as a residence.

Ultimately, however, Dr. Macpherson determined to purchase Stormont House, which is in every respect suitable for a convent, containing ample accommodation for a small Community, and being situated in a large garden which is surrounded by a high wall. Entry could not be obtained before May, but the interval was busily employed in the necessary preparations for the new establishment. As yet the Sisters had no experience in teaching schools under Government; it was therefore essential that they should be duly qualified and certificated to act as mistresses of the Perth schools, which had hitherto been in charge of secular teachers.

The Sisters who were destined to this occupation prepared to pass the necessary examination, for which purpose they went to Liverpool. On the 16th of May, Mother Mary Angela and her little colony (six in all) took up their abode in their new home, which was placed under the patronage of St. Joseph.

The arrangement of an oratory was their first care, and it was with great joy that they welcomed the hidden God to their dwelling. The rest of the apartments were soon ready; and the Sisters entered on their duties at the Penitentiary on the 1st of June. From that day to the present time they have spent daily several hours instructing the poor prisoners. On Sunday afternoons they likewise attend to conduct devotions for the "associated convicts." In general they have had the happiness of seeing a great blessing follow their labours; and it is only justice to testify to the respect and consideration with which the Sisters have invariably been treated by the authorities of the prison.

One thing is felt to be an imperative necessity for the discharged prisoners. It is, that a safe home should be provided for them, where at the end of their term of punishment they may remain till such time as they are suited with some occupation. All who interest themselves in prisoners must be aware how frequently it happens that, on leaving the gaol, the poor uncaged birds fall into the snares laid for them by evil companions, and probably within a few weeks, or less, find themselves again within the prison walls for a longer period than the first time.

If any charitably disposed person would assist in the establishment of such a refuge as is suggested, it would indeed be a boon to the many poor Catholic girls and women who leave the prison at Perth only to return to the evil surroundings of their former homes.

The little Community at St. Joseph's soon found themselves with as much work as they could accomplish. The schools have prospered under their care. The visitation of the poor and sick is always one of their consoling duties; and Mother Mary Angela was indefatigable in her exertions for the good of all who came under her influence.

The Sodality of the Children of Mary was

established for the young women of the congregation, the Living Rosary, the Guild of the Sacred Heart and Holy Family were likewise set on foot.

The Sisters have invariably met with the greatest kindness from the priest in charge of the mission, and it has been their constant endeavour to assist him as far as they could do so, and under his direction.

Since the re-establishment of the hierarchy the Right Rev. Dr. George Rigg, Bishop of Dunkeld, has made Perth his residence, and in him the religious have found a father and friend, to whom they owe a lasting debt of respectful affection and gratitude.

Since the sale of Greenhill Cottage, Father O'Donnell had resided in temporary apartments at St. Margaret's; but he had taken steps towards the erection of a suitable residence for a chaplain in the convent grounds. This was completed in August 1865, and on the 31st of that month Father O'Donnell took possession of his new house, known as "the Hermitage."

On the 29th of June, Mrs. Hutchison (who has been so often mentioned as a signal benefactress) breathed her last, and went to receive the recompense of her long life of fervour and charity. She was interred within the grounds of St. Catherine's Convent.

The Exaltation of the Cross (14th September) was a distressing and memorable day at St. Margaret's. On entering the chapel in the morning a sad sight presented itself to the Sisters. It was evident that a sacrilegious robbery had been committed during the night. The tabernacle was on the ground behind the altar, the door wrenched off, and the Blessed Sacrament lying within, having been thrown out of the ciborium, which was gone; as also the lunette containing the Sacred Host. Two relics of the True Cross were also missing, one of which was exposed for veneration in honour of the Feast, and the other had been at the foot of the crucifix on the Sacred Heart altar, the small tabernacle on which had also been broken open but was fortunately empty.

Father O'Donnell was instantly summoned, and collected the scattered Hosts into a ciborium, which he deposited in a safe in the sacristy. Mass was said at the Lady Altar, and many acts of reparation were offered by the sorrowing Sisters. No time was lost in communicating with the police authorities. Detective officers attended immediately, took a list and description of the missing articles, and examined the traces left by the thieves. They had entered the chapel by a window, the lower part of which was broken. There were footprints on the floor, and matches were found exactly under the sanctuary lamp. It was matter of wonder that *it* had not been carried off.

The Community and pupils kept up perpetual adoration all day and night, to make what reparation they could for the outrage to the most Blessed Sacrament. The Bishop and several of the clergy called to offer sympathy, and his Lordship ordered three days of exposition as a reparation of honour.

The Bishop celebrated Mass on Sunday the 16th and inaugurated the devotions. During the three days the chapel was visited by many persons from town, who came to unite their loving homage to the Adorable Sacrament with the prayers of the Community. The Triduum ended with a solemn Procession and Benediction of the Blessed Sacrament.

None of the stolen articles were ever restored, nor was any trace found of the thieves. But years afterwards, Father Holder, then parish priest at Perth, told the Sisters at St. Joseph's Convent, that he had been charged with a message to them from a prisoner then undergoing a sentence of punishment for a robbery. The unhappy man requested Father Holder to express to the nuns his regret that he had been one of the party who broke into the convent chapel so long ago. He had often wished to ask their forgiveness, but could not summon courage to call at St. Margaret's, but now he begged the priest to do so for him. It was consoling to know that the poor fellow repented of his misdeeds, and that he had put himself into the hands of the priest to be reconciled with God. Many prayers had been offered for the conversion of those who had perpetrated the crime, and now all rejoiced over the sinner who had obtained the grace of contrition.

The sisterly feeling which exists between the religious Communities of St. Margaret's and St. Catherine's has always been specially manifested on remarkable occasions either of joy or sorrow. The deepest sympathy, therefore, was felt for the Sisters of Mercy, at the death of the Reverend Mother Mary Juliana, which took place on the 5th of June 1867. She had been a "Child of St. Margaret's," and was closely linked to her first convent home by many fond associations, and her memory is still cherished there, no less than in her own Community.

In the following month of August the Sisters of St. Margaret's also mourned the death of Sr. Jane Frances Macnab, who had been for many years in a very delicate state of health. She had been a most active and efficient member of the little Community at Milton House; and had been long in charge of the school at Pentland House and George Square. She was much regretted; but her suffering state had been most distressing for a long time past, and her sorrowing Sisters trusted that her crown in heaven would be proportioned to the heavy cross she had borne so patiently on earth.

The whole Catholic world was united in prayer for the Church towards the end of the year 1869. On the Feast of the Immaculate Conception, the Vatican Council was opened at Rome, and this great event called together nearly all the bishops in the world. So large an assembly of ecclesiastical dignitaries had never met before, and while the deliberations of the Council proceeded, ceaseless supplications were offered for the Holy Father, Pius IX., and for the Fathers of the Council.

Dr. Strain, and Dr. Macdonald of Aberdeen, left Edinburgh on the evening of the 18th November, having paid a farewell visit to St. Margaret's in the forenoon of that day.

When the Definition of the Papal Infallibility was announced, great rejoicings took place, in which all the faithful children of the Church took their part.

Many bishops then hastened to leave Rome, owing to the political disturbances, long threatened, and now close at hand; and also to escape from the intense heat of the season.

On the 30th July 1870, Dr. Strain arrived in Edinburgh, and kindly came to St. Margaret's in the afternoon of that day. He said Mass at the convent next morning, and breakfasted with the Community, spending the forenoon with the Sisters and children, giving interesting details of his stay in Rome, and of the magnificent service in St. Peter's after the Definition of the Council.

Among all the important duties of the last few months, the Bishop had not forgotten his flock at the convent. He brought a souvenir for every one; and to the children at St. Margaret's, rosaries blessed by the Holy Father.

It had long been a subject of regret to the Community that there was no likeness of Dr. Gillis, excepting two miniatures, painted many years ago by Sister Agnes Xavier, and, latterly, some photographs. It was determined to have a life-sized portrait, painted by a first-rate artist, from these small likenesses. Inquiries were made to find a painter who would undertake the work; and the celebrated Sam Bough was introduced to the reverend Mother as the one most likely to succeed in this not very easy task. Mr. Bough was a great admirer of Dr. Gillis, and had frequently attended his sermons at St. Mary's. He had, therefore, the aid of memory to further his work. The portrait was brought to St. Margaret's as soon as it was finished, and was placed in the Refectory. Though not absolutely perfect, it is still a wonderfully good likeness, considering the difficulties under which the artist laboured, and the Community rejoice in possessing it. The following year it was exhibited in Dublin at the exhibition of paintings in that city, the reverend Mother acceding to Mr. Bough's request on that subject.

The addition to the convent was carried out during the year 1870. A new laundry was erected adjoining the Hermitage, and this permitted the arrangement of the old laundry buildings (close to the entrance gate) as apartments for a few lady boarders. These rooms have been constantly in use ever since they were opened in January 1871.

CHAPTER XIX.

REMOVAL OF FATHER O'DONNELL TO FALKIRK—VISIT OF THE EMPEROR AND EMPRESS OF BRAZIL—THE FATHERS OF THE SOCIETY OF JESUS—FUNERAL OF MR. HOPE SCOTT—NEW BELL—BANNERS FOR PARAY LE MONIAL—POOR SCHOOLS AT YORK LANE AND MARYFIELD. 1871-1875.

NOTHING is stable in this world. This is a truth which we all know in theory; nevertheless, when some great change comes over our life, it would seem as if we had never realised that we live in a world of change, and that we must all the more cast the anchor of our hope on that shore which is eternal.

A great trial was about to fall on St. Margaret's—the greatest, after the death of Bishop Gillis, that could have befallen the Community. It was all the more keenly felt because it was wholly unexpected.

On the 21st April 1871 Dr. Strain called on Father O'Donnell at the Hermitage. His Lordship then went to the school-room to show the children the medal of the Vatican Council, and after visiting the lady boarders, he left. How little did the Community suspect the purport of his visit! In the afternoon Father O'Donnell sent word to the Reverend Mother that he wished to see her and the senior Sisters at five o'clock, and would then give Benediction. The worst was soon told. Father O'Donnell was to leave St. Margaret's, having been appointed by the Bishop to take charge of the mission of Falkirk, in place of the Rev. John Gillon, lately deceased.

After Benediction the Community were apprised of the Bishop's decree. Father O'Donnell announced his removal, and then added, "and I leave you to-morrow." He went on to exhort the Community to accept the will of God with perfect resignation.

The following day was indeed a sad one. For five and twenty years Father O'Donnell had been intimately connected with the convent. In joy and in sorrow he was always at hand to console and sympathise, to assist and encourage. He had worked hand in hand with Dr. Gillis for the welfare of the establishment, and there was no one in the house, from the superioress to the youngest child in the school, who had not experienced his interest and solicitude.

Father Walmesley, S.J., called that forenoon, little thinking what had happened. When he was told that Father O'Donnell was going to Falkirk, he exclaimed, "I should as soon have expected to see the large ash-tree in the court removed from its place."

The sad farewells were said at last. As the devoted Father and friend of St. Margaret's crossed the threshold he said, "God's will be done! God bless you all!" The Sisters all retired to the chapel to pray for the grace to make their sacrifice generously, and that every blessing might attend Father O'Donnell in his new career.

For many weeks nothing was settled as to a successor to Father O'Donnell, and the Sisters would have had many spiritual privations had it not been for the immense kindness of the clergy attached to St. Patrick's, and to the Jesuit Fathers at Lauriston.

Father O'Donnell, though chaplain to the convent, did a great deal in town, and always had a confessional at St. Patrick's, which he regularly attended. Regret at his removal from Edinburgh was not therefore confined within the convent walls. The congregation of St. Patrick's resolved on presenting him with a handsome testimonial as a tribute of regard and esteem.

The clergy all called at the convent, offering to do what lay in their power to give the Sisters Mass and Benediction regularly till some permanent arrangement should be made by Dr.

Strain. It is a pleasing duty to give expression to the gratitude which will ever be felt at St. Margaret's to the reverend Fathers who so kindly came forward to supply the spiritual necessities of the Community at this time of sorrow and suspense. The names of Father Hannan, Father William Turner, Father Byrne, and Father Healy, of St. Patrick's; and of Fathers Walmesley, Clifford, and Pearson, S.J., of Lauriston, will ever be remembered in the prayers of the Sisters.

Father O'Donnell was obliged to come over from Falkirk to attend to the removal of his books and other effects, but his visits were always short. At length it was arranged that Colonel and Mrs. Gordon (old friends) should reside with him at Falkirk, and this being carried out, proved to be most suitable for all parties.

Towards the end of May the Bishop announced that he had appointed a chaplain to the convent, who would arrive the following day. The chaplain's rooms at the Hermitage were accordingly prepared, and the Bishop came out on the 26th May with a Dutch priest, whom he introduced as the Rev. Mr. Berentzen. At the same time the Bishop requested Father Walmesley to act as confessor to the Sisters, which he kindly consented to do.

On the 3d of August, Sister Mary Gertrude

Burn, who had long been ill of lingering consumption, breathed her last. As Father O'Donnell was one of her trustees, he was summoned by telegraph, and came over in the afternoon.

Shortly after his arrival, a carriage drove up to the door, and a gentleman inquired if visitors were permitted to see the convent. The portress asked their names, and was told "the Emperor and Empress of Brazil," with two ladies and a gentleman-in-waiting. Of course so illustrious a party could not be refused admission, and they were taken to the parlour, where the Reverend Mother, the Mother-Assistant, and Father O'Donnell went to pay their respects. It was explained that the Imperial party had been driving in the neighbourhood, and had noticed the convent and asked what building it was. On being told it was a convent, the Emperor exclaimed, "I cannot pass a Catholic convent in this Protestant country." Their Majesties visited the chapel and house, and were most affable in their manner to the Sisters and children. They were particularly interested to learn that Father O'Donnell was a native of the island of St. Helena, and that he distinctly remembered the funeral of the Emperor Napoleon.

Their Majesties appeared much pleased with their visit, which was duly noticed in the papers next day.

The Congregation of the Ursulines of Jesus at the Mother-House had now the joy of receiving documents from Rome, announcing that the holy founder of the Congregation, the Abbé Louis Marie Baudouin had been declared "Venerable." The Community at St. Margaret's were informed of this event, and united their rejoicings with those of their Sisters in France.

On the 2d July 1872 the Community were again without a chaplain. The Rev. Mr. Berentzen, being in bad health, gave up his appointment, and left for Rotterdam.

Once more the kindness of the clergy in town was manifested by the regularity with which the services in the convent chapel were performed. At a time when *all* were kind it is hard to particularise one more than another. It may, however, be permitted to name one who has lately gone to his reward, the Rev. Walter Lomax, S.J., who was always ready to officiate at the convent, and to take the place of any other priest in this work of charity. May his eternal reward be great!

The departure of Father Walmesley from Edinburgh was a great loss to St. Margaret's, where he had acted as confessor since the removal of Father O'Donnell.

Much difficulty being experienced in finding a suitable chaplain for the convent, application was made to the Very Rev. the Father Provincial of the Society of Jesus, and permission was obtained for the services at St. Margaret's to be performed by the Fathers residing at Lauriston. This has been maintained ever since, to the great benefit of the Community, who can never be sufficiently grateful for all the graces they have received by means of the Society.

The close of the year again found the Sisters in sorrow. On the 3d of December they lost Sister Agnes Xavier Trail, whose name has so frequently occurred in these pages, and who had been so distinguished a member of the Community. After a long period of failing health she expired on the feast of her patron saint, fortified by all the blessings which the Holy Church lavishes on her faithful children at that supreme moment when they are about to enter on eternal life.

In the following May the remains of Mr. Hope Scott of Abbotsford were laid in the vaults beneath the chapel. In the life of this eminent man it has been mentioned that he had a special affection for St. Margaret's Convent. He was a most kind and generous benefactor to St. Margaret's, and also to St. Joseph's, Perth; and was, moreover, ever ready to assist the superiors by his advice and influence. On the death of Mrs. Hope Scott, which occurred in an hotel in Edinburgh in 1858, Dr. Gillis offered

Mr. Hope Scott a burial-place in the crypt at the convent; and there (as Mr. Ornsby has told the world) the grandchild of Sir Walter Scott reposes, along with her two children, Walter and Margaret. Mr. Hope Scott expressed a wish to be also buried at St. Margaret's. After a solemn service had been performed in the Church of the Jesuit Fathers, Farm Street, London, on which occasion the Very Rev. Dr. Newman delivered a touching discourse, the remains were conveyed to Edinburgh.

The funeral took place on the 7th of May, and was attended by a large number of the friends and relatives of the deceased, and a numerous body of the clergy. All were anxious to testifiy their respect for one who had been so great a benefactor to the Church in Scotland, and whose private life had been a model to every Catholic gentleman.

The Sisters now undertook the duty of visiting Craiglockhart Poorhouse regularly, for the instruction of the Catholic inmates of that institution. Permission for this good work was given by the Board, and after a short time further facilities were granted, by which the religious were allowed to furnish a room as a chapel, where they assembled the Catholics on Sundays for devotions and instruction, and where Mass is occasionally celebrated.

A lady interested in the work presented a beautiful set of pictures for the Way of the Cross.

Archbishop Strain authorised the solemn erection of the Stations, and this devotion has been greatly appreciated by the poor people.

The Sisters have met with every kindness from the governor and matron of the Poorhouse, and their labour of love has done much to soften the unavoidable trials which attend the lot of its inmates.

A most interesting function took place in July, one which is another proof of the decay of bigotry in Scotland. It is well known that the churches belonging to the established religion are alone legally entitled to have bells, and it had happened on several occasions that the attempt to contravene this statute of the realm had been followed by disagreeable interference on the part of the magistrates and others.

"The Convent Bell," so necessary in fact as well as familiar in fiction, had hitherto been rung at a bell-turret in the house, but now the Community received the present of a large church bell, cast by a firm in Dublin.

The bell was solemnly blessed by Dr. Strain, assisted by Father Hannan, Father Pope, S.J., and Father W. Turner, who acted as master of ceremonies.

The Bishop gave a short address explanatory of the ceremony, and proceeded with the blessing according to the ritual. The bell was named "Margaret," and was first tolled by the Bishop, and then by the donor and godmother.

Within a few days the bell was hung in the belfry of the chapel, and from thence its voice has been heard many times a day by all the surrounding neighbourhood. In one instance, at least, it was the means of leading to a conversion. The Angelus bell was remarked as being rung in a different manner from the other bells, and a gentleman living near the convent inquired of a friend the reason of this peculiar way of ringing three times daily. The Catholic thus interrogated gladly availed himself of the opportunity afforded, and explained various points of Christian doctrine regarding the Incarnation, devotion to the Blessed Virgin, &c. Some years later an eminent ecclesiastic requested permission to say Mass in the convent chapel, and then, for the first time, the Community heard of the good work that had been begun by the bell, and which had resulted in the conversion of this gentleman, who became a priest. and who came to give glory to God for these graces, in the chapel where the bell rang to call the Community to assist at his Mass.

The English pilgrimage to Paray le Monial took place in August 1873. Many will remember the enthusiastic devotion to the Sacred Heart which was manifested by all classes of Catholics on this occasion. Clergy and laity alike were eager to join the pilgrimage, and those who could not go in person subscribed the means to send a substitute to present their homage and petitions in the favoured spot where our Divine Lord manifested Himself to His faithful servant, the blessed Margaret Mary Alacoque. A deputation from Scotland joined the pilgrimage, headed by Lord Henry Kerr, and many fervent Catholics, both priests and laymen, ladies and gentlemen. As each deputation was to have its own banner, it was requisite that one should be made for Scotland. This delightful task was proposed to the nuns at St. Margaret's, and was undertaken by them at the request of Lord and Lady Henry Kerr. At the pilgrimage the banner was carried by Lord Walter Kerr, and it was considered a beautiful specimen of work, both in design and execution. It was placed in the chapel at Paray le Monial, and there, as we trust, it represents Scotland before the altar of the Sacred Heart; and its motto, "Cor Jesu, miserere Scotiæ," is a constant prayer for our beloved country.

The crowded neighbourhood of Greenside had long been in want of a school for the numerous Catholic children who roamed about its closes and alleys. The Bishop and the Rev. George Rigg offered the charge of a school in York Lane to the nuns; a second school in Maryfield was also opened, and both were fully attended. At a later period the school at Maryfield was put into the hands of the Marist Brothers, who reside there and conduct a boys' school, and the labours of the Sisters were confined to the girls' school at York Lane. The purchase of a house in Albany Street enabled the Sisters charged with the children to reside in that locality till July 1880, when the death of several members of the Community obliged them to relinquish this interesting branch of usefulness, and the schools were transferred to the care of Franciscan nuns from Glasgow, who have since retained the charge.

CHAPTER XX.

VISITS FROM THE MOTHER-GENERAL OF THE FRENCH CONGREGATION AND FROM THE RIGHT REV. DR. ULLATHORNE — PURCHASE OF PART OF WARRENDER PARK—SUNDAY SCHOOL AT DAVIDSON'S MAINS—NEW LADY ALTAR. 1875-1878.

EARLY in July 1875 the Sisters at St. Margaret's had the pleasure of a long-expected visit from the Reverend Mother Marie Néophyte, Superioress-General of the Congregation in France. She was accompanied by Mother St. Clémence, one of her assistants. The reverend Mother had spent many years at St. Margaret's, and had been one of those religious who had accompanied Mother Mary Emily to France in 1855.

After an absence of nearly twenty years she returned to spend a short time in her old home, which she had never ceased to love, and where she was welcomed with the most affectionate cordiality. Mother St. Clémence had never been in Scotland, so that everything was new to her; and it was with some surprise that she found in this Protestant country so large a convent and so numerous a Community.

Many changes had taken place since 1855, and many dear old friends had passed away; so that joy and sorrow were mingled in Mother Mary Néophyte's feelings. Still she found many who knew and loved her already, and those who had not known her till now were won by her sweet gentle manner, and the air of unostentatious sanctity which distinguished her.

It was a great happiness to possess her, though the time flew only too quickly, and the visit was far too short.

This opportunity was taken to obtain information as to the usages of the French Congregation in various points of rule and religious discipline. It was suggested by the Mother-General that it might be advisable for St. Margaret's to be united to the French Congregation under certain conditions; but so serious a step, and one so completely at variance with the original intentions of Bishop Gillis and the foundresses, required to be maturely considered, and nothing could be said on the subject beyond the promise of considering it in all its bearings, and taking advice from those most competent to give it.

The reverend Mother Mary Néophyte and Mother St. Clémence took their leave with many regrets at the end of July. The visit had been a real pleasure to all parties, and had drawn still closer the union between the two branches of the Congregation. The delicate health of the Mother-General made it very unlikely that she would ever again be able to come to Scotland, and when the Sisters said farewell all felt that they would never meet again in this world. She died on the 13th August 1879.

The proposal made for the union of St. Margaret's to the French Congregation was duly considered, and it was thought advisable to obtain the opinion and advice of the Right Rev. Dr. Ullathorne, Bishop of Birmingham, on the subject, his Lordship being one of the highest authorities on all matters of religious rules. With the sanction of Dr. Strain the reverend Mother applied to Dr. Ullathorne, who kindly came to Edinburgh with his nephew, the Rev. John Ullathorne, and remained at the Hermitage from the 15th to the 23d of October. During these delightful days the Bishop's kindness to the Community was truly paternal. His Lordship devoted every forenoon to a meeting with the Sisters, in which all their business matters were thoroughly discussed. In the evening he joined the Community at recreation, and charmed every one by his affability and his interesting and instructive conversation.

Towards the end of the visit Dr. Strain was present at the morning conference, when Dr. Ullathorne summed up his advice by recommending the Community of St. Margaret's to remain independent of the French Congregation as to government, while continuing that sisterly union of hearts that has always existed between the separate establishments. Dr. Strain thanked the Bishop of Birmingham, in his own name and that of the Sisters of St. Margaret's, for all the interest he had taken in their affairs, and for the time he had devoted to them.

During this year the Sodality of the Children of Mary made considerable advances. For several years it had been affiliated to the Prima Primaria in Rome, but few persons beyond the pupils had become members of it. Now, however, it became better known. Dr. Strain gave permission for Benediction to be given once a month to the Sodalists. On these occasions an Instruction was likewise given by the Rev. T. Williams, S.J.; and during the month the ladies undertook a certain amount of work for poor churches. These pious and useful practices have been perseveringly followed ever since; and at various times handsome presents of church linen and vestments have been given to destitute missions.

The first public Retreat to ladies in the world was given at St. Margaret's by the Rev. Edmund Vaughan, C.SS.R., in the month of August. This, too, was the beginning of an excellent work which brings good results.

Those who remember St. Margaret's in its early days will recall the situation as being quite removed from any other dwellings. Greenhill Cottage and Bruntsfield House were the only houses within sight, and it was hoped that this seclusion might long continue. Years had brought many changes, and amongst others that of a great increase in the buildings in Grange Loan and all the streets leading towards Morningside.

The Greenhill Parks (purchased by Dr. Gillis) were feued for buildings, and rows of villas, in every style of architecture, were erected opposite the convent. The old trees were cut down, and the "shady lane," which had been such a pleasant approach to the convent, no longer existed. Still, there were the Warrender Parks, and surely *they* would never be touched! Alas for the uncertainty of human things! The reverend Mother received intelligence that these beautiful fields were also to be feued for building purposes, and that if the Community wished to escape a row of houses close to their boundary wall on the north side, their only means of protection was by purchasing a portion of the land in question.

The matter was too important to admit of delay or even hesitation. A large piece of land was purchased at a considerable sacrifice; but it was thought only justice to the Community, in all time coming, to obviate so great an annoyance as would have been the threatened houses in such close proximity to the convent grounds.

As soon as the purchase of the field was concluded, it was solemnly blessed by the Bishop. The ceremony was very striking. The pupils were dressed in white and wore long veils. They carried a banner of the Blessed Virgin; the Community followed, with the banners of St. Joseph and of the Sacred Heart. The Bishop was vested in cope and mitre. The procession went all round the field singing the Hymn of the Sacred Heart, the Litany of the Blessed Virgin, and the Hymn of St. Joseph, the Bishop blessing the field with holy water and the usual prayers. On the return of the procession to the chapel, his Lordship gave Benediction.

A high wall was afterwards erected round the newly-acquired property, but the houses soon overlooked it, and increased the gratitude of the Community that they were not in closer proximity.

The field has proved a most agreeable addition to the convent grounds, and, by means of a gate, communication was also opened with the southern parks, thus affording extensive recreation-ground to the nuns and pupils.

The Bishop requested the aid of some of the Sisters during the year 1875 in giving Christian instruction to the Catholics living at Davidson's Mains, a village about three miles to the north-west of Edinburgh. It was arranged that the catechism should be given in the village school-house, which was lent for the purpose on Sunday afternoons. A considerable number of children and adults attended these classes with admirable regularity. The children were prepared for the sacraments, and their elders were renewed in their first fervour. This good work continued till 1882, when, by the exertions and generosity of Mrs. Craigie Halkett of Cramond House, a temporary chapel was arranged, and the Rev. Michael Turner went to Davidson's Mains as resident priest. After his removal to the more important town of South Queensferry in 1885, he requested the Sisters to resume their attendance at Davidson's Mains, which they gladly consented to do.

Early in May 1877 the Bishop went to Rome, accompanied by the Rev. Dr. Smith, for the celebration of the jubilee of his Holiness Pius IX. On this occasion the Sisters of St. Margaret's sent an offering to the Holy Father, with an illuminated address, which was presented by the Bishop, and to which a gracious reply was sent with the Papal blessing.

The solemn Triduo for the Pope was observed at the convent by every possible demonstration of joy. The Blessed Sacrament was exposed, and ceaseless prayers were offered for the Holy Father. The devotions concluded with a "Te Deum."

On the return of the Bishop from Italy he paid a visit to St. Margaret's, and gave a most interesting account of his stay in Rome, and of the manner in which the festivals had been celebrated there.

For many years it had been the desire of the Community to embellish their chapel by suitable altars to the Sacred Heart and the Blessed Virgin. Many former pupils had already subscribed towards this object, and the development of the Sodality made it highly desirable that the Lady Altar should be placed without further delay. Mr. George Goldie of London, was asked to furnish a design, and the work was executed under his direction by Mr. Earp.

The statue was presented by Mr. Clapperton of Fochabers, and an elegant lamp by Lord Ralph Kerr.

To assist in defraying the expenses connected with the altar, a little bazaar was held in the classrooms of the convent in January 1878.

Many friends sent contributions towards the

stalls, and a Christmas tree was a great point of attraction to youthful visitors.

At the close of the bazaar it was found that the necessary funds had been obtained, and that all expenses had been cleared. The altar was much admired, and has been conducive to increased devotion to the Immaculate Virgin. The monthly meetings of the Sodalists always take place in the Lady Chapel, as well as the exercises of Retreats for secular ladies.

CHAPTER XXI.

RE-ESTABLISHMENT OF THE HIERARCHY—RETURN HOME OF ARCHBISHOP STRAIN—MARCIA, LADY HERRIES—SACRED HEART ALTAR—GROTTO OF LOURDES—LAST ILLNESS AND DEATH OF FATHER O'DONNELL—DEATH OF ARCHBISHOP STRAIN. 1878–1883.

AT the end of the year 1877 Dr. Strain again went to Rome. An important work was about to be accomplished. The ancient Hierarchy was about to be restored to Scotland, and great was the anxiety felt on all sides while many rumours of the deliberations reached home. All was decided at length; but when the news arrived the joy was mingled with sorrow. The re-establishment of the Scotch Hierarchy was the last act of the Holy Father, Pius IX., who died on the 7th of February 1878. The whole Church mourned for his death. During his long Pontificate he had become endeared to every Catholic heart, and his children felt truly orphans.

A magnificent requiem service was celebrated at St. Mary's, attended by almost all the clergy of the district; an eloquent panegyric was delivered by the Rev. George Rigg.

THE MOST REV. JOHN STRAIN, D.D.,
Archbishop of St. Andrews and Edinburgh.

A solemn service was also celebrated in the convent chapel for the Holy Father.

Many were the prayers now offered for the blessing of God on the election of the successor of Pius IX. This took place on the 20th January 1878, and was the occasion of great thanksgiving and rejoicing in the whole Catholic world. By order of the Bishop a solemn "Te Deum" was sung after Mass on Sexagesima Sunday.

His Lordship lost another dear friend while in Rome, the Very Rev. Dr. Grant, who had been Rector of the Scots College for many years, and who was universally esteemed by his numerous friends. He died on the 27th March.

The death of Pius IX. naturally retarded the arrangements of Scotch ecclesiastical matters, and it was not till the 28th March that the official announcement was made of the re-establishment of the Hierarchy, the division of the dioceses, and nomination of bishops.

On the 10th of April Dr. Strain returned to Edinburgh as Archbishop and Metropolitan; and on the 12th he paid a visit to St. Margaret's. As soon as he entered the court, the bells were rung, and the Community and pupils assembled to receive his blessing. His Grace spent some time in the convent, and gave most interesting details of his stay in Rome, of the death of Pius IX., and the election of Leo XIII.

The functions of Holy Week prevented any special festivities in honour of the Archbishop; but on the 25th April the Community had the happiness of presenting his Grace with their congratulations on his appointment to the Archiepiscopal See of St. Andrews and Edinburgh. His Grace was conducted to the Community room, where he was presented with a beautiful alb. He dined in the Refectory with the Sisters, and afterwards went to the schoolroom, where the children were prepared to receive his visit. An appropriate address was read by Miss Kate Barry, and a lace rochet presented along with an illuminated copy of the address from the school. His Grace expressed how much he was touched and gratified by the congratulations he had received, and gave an affectionate blessing to all present. He officiated at Benediction in the evening, when a "Te Deum" was sung.

The appointment of the Right Rev. George Rigg as Bishop of Dunkeld brought about several changes in Edinburgh. The Very Rev. William Smith was appointed Vicar-General, and from that time has always taken a lively interest in the welfare of St. Margaret's.

One whose life was devoted to good works, and whose name is in benediction, was at this time a frequent inmate of the apartments allotted to lady boarders—the late Dowager Lady Herries. If the life of this saintly woman is ever made known to the world, it will be seen that her virtue was closely allied to that of the most eminent servants of God, and that in all things, and at the cost of any sacrifice of personal feeling, she strove after perfection. The first object she had in wishing to spend some weeks at St. Margaret's was to live in retirement, where she could be near a chapel; her second wish was to economise her means, the better to further the foundation of a Convent of Nuns of Perpetual Adoration.

From the time of her first visit Lady Herries retained great regard for St. Margaret's, and it was a pleasure to the Sisters as well as herself that she came again and again to stay for Lent, the Month of Mary, or other seasons of special devotion, during the remaining years of her life. She was a constant subject of edification by her fervent piety, her charity, and her mortification. Had her life been prolonged, she would have spent her last years in a religious Order. In the eloquent sermon delivered at her funeral, it was mentioned that her last journey to Rome, was undertaken to make necessary arrangements for carrying out this holy vocation. An indisposition, which at first caused no uneasiness, developed dangerous symptoms; and in a few days Marcia, Lady Herries, breathed her last. The convent, for which she had worked and prayed, was opened in the following autumn, and is only one of many monuments to this holy woman.

The erection of the Lady Altar in the convent chapel made it desirable that the altar to the Sacred Heart should be in the same style. Mr. Goldie was again requested to furnish designs, and in the course of the summer of 1880 the temporary altar was superseded by the stone and marble one, now in the west aisle. The statue of the Sacred Heart was presented by John Mellon, Esq., a constant friend to all good works, and a generous benefactor to St. Margaret's.

Another addition to the devotional attractions at the convent is the Grotto of Our Lady of Lourdes, in the garden. A model of the Grotto was sent from Lourdes, for the purpose of ensuring the resemblance of the one at St. Margaret's to the favoured Sanctuary of the Immaculate Virgin in the Pyrenees. A statue of Our Lady was presented by Mrs. Miles Fletcher, and after remaining for two days in the Grotto at Lourdes, came without accident to Edinburgh. The Grotto in the convent garden was finished early in June, and was solemnly blessed on the Feast of St. Aloysius.

The Rev. Father Whyte, S.J., gave Benediction, and in the evening of that day he delivered an interesting instruction explanatory of pilgrimages to holy places, and especially to Lourdes. A procession was then formed; the pupils carried a banner of the Blessed Virgin; they were followed by the Community, acolytes, and Father Whyte.

The favourite hymn "Immaculate" was sung while the procession advanced to the Grotto, which was adorned with lights and flowers. Father Whyte blest the Grotto and Statue, and then the procession returned to the chapel.

A petition was presented to the Holy Father, for an indulgence for those visiting Our Lady of Lourdes, and this was graciously accorded.

An Ex Voto Tablet has recently been placed in the Grotto by the grateful parents of a little girl, whose cure, when dangerously ill, was obtained by the use of water from Lourdes.

It was with deep sorrow and anxiety that the friends of Father O'Donnell learnt that he was in a precarious state of health. On the Festival of Corpus Christi he officiated for the last time in his church at Falkirk, and then was obliged to acknowledge himself unable to do more.

The Archbishop went to Falkirk several times to see Father O'Donnell, and requested Mother Margaret Teresa to go and nurse him, which she gladly consented to do, and with the assistance of another Sister did all in her power to relieve his sufferings till he expired.

The Archbishop had hoped the invalid might have recovered sufficiently to be removed to his old home at the Hermitage; but it was evidently impossible. The daily bulletins sent by Mother Margaret Teresa gave no hope. On the 24th of August the Archbishop went to Falkirk, in the forenoon, and brought word that Father O'Donnell was dying; the telegram announcing that all was over arrived in the afternoon. The Community sorrowed deeply and long for the loss of one who, after the death of Dr. Gillis, had been to them as a second father.

As he had himself requested, his remains were brought to Edinburgh for interment in the Grange Cemetery. The leading gentlemen of Falkirk, both Catholics and Protestants, accompanied the coffin to the station; wishing thus to testify their respect and esteem for one who had endeared himself to all classes during his residence of eleven years in that town. Several members of the Catholic body,

THE VERY REV. ALEXANDER O'DONNELL.

and of the Young Men's Association, came to Edinburgh, and claimed the privilege of lifting the coffin when occasion required. Several of the clergy were waiting with a hearse at the Waverley Station when the train arrived, and the body was taken to St. Mary's, where the Vespers of the Dead were chanted. The church was crowded, and numbers of Father O'Donnell's old friends remained there in prayer, till late at night.

The funeral took place on the 29th August.

The coffin was placed on a handsome catafalque before the altar, and in the sanctuary was a large number of priests. Monsignor Smith officiated, assisted by Father Hannan as deacon, and Father Woods as subdeacon. The Archbishop occupied the throne. Bishop Rigg was also present. At the conclusion of the Mass, the Archbishop made a touching panegyric of Father O'Donnell. The absolutions were given by the Rev. Alexander Gordon, Bishop Rigg, and the Archbishop. When the clergy had entered their carriages, they were followed by hundreds of people, all lamenting the death of one so beloved and revered. On reaching the cemetery the "Young Men" of Falkirk carried the remains to the grave, situated in the ground belonging to St. Margaret's, where the last prayers were said by the Archbishop.

A marble cross was erected over the grave of Father O'Donnell by the nuns of St. Margaret's.

The Rev. Father Burke, O.P., having come to Edinburgh to deliver one of his lectures at the Church of the Sacred Heart, Lauriston Street, was kind enough to call at the convent. His visit, though short, was a great pleasure to all who saw him. He was then in very suffering health, but no one who heard his cheerful conversation and merry jokes with the children could have guessed how much pain he was enduring.

The year 1883 was to be again one of mourning to the Church in Edinburgh. The Archbishop left home in May, being called by business to Rome. The circumstances of his illness, his sad homeward journey, and his death, are still too recent to require a detailed account. It was inexpressibly sad to all his flock to see the venerable Archbishop so enfeebled and ill, and he himself fully realised his position. Still, he was present at Mass in the Pro-Cathedral on the Sunday after his return home, being wheeled into the sanctuary in an invalid chair. Before leaving the church he addressed the congregation, and imparted to them the Papal blessing. Every one present was deeply touched, and many earnest prayers were offered for his restoration to health.

For a time it was hoped that he might recover; some improvement was observable, and he was able to take carriage exercise in the fine summer evenings. On one of these occasions he called at St. Margaret's. He was accompanied by Monsignor Smith, Father Donlevy, and Father Woods. The large gates were thrown open and the carriage driven into the court. The bell soon brought the Community and the pupils together. His Grace was assisted to alight, and he sat down in the hall, talking of his visit to Rome and the kindness of the Holy Father. He gave an affectionate blessing before leaving, promising to return soon again.

The reverend Mother went to St. Mary's to see his Grace on Sunday, the 1st of July, and he was able to walk across the room and show her the altar where Mass was said every morning; he also spoke of the preparations that were being made for the celebration of his jubilee, and expressed a wish to see the Sisters after the fatigues of the festivities had passed off.

The following day, as is well known, the Archbishop went down to the church to inspect the arrangements. Shortly after returning to his room his attendant was attracted by a change in his breathing; Monsignor Smith and Father Donlevy were summoned, and in a few moments the Archbishop expired.

The preparations for the jubilee were changed for the sad mourning of the Dirge and Requiem Mass, the funeral service taking place on the 6th July.

The Pro-Cathedral was crowded by a sorrowing congregation, the impression being deepened by the sudden revulsion of feeling from joy to grief. The remains of the Archbishop were deposited in the vaults beneath the sanctuary of the church.

The Archdiocese of St. Andrews and Edinburgh now entered on a long period of widowhood, more than two years elapsing before the nomination of the Most Rev. William Smith to the Metropolitan dignity.

CHAPTER XXII.

CELEBRATION OF MOTHER MARGARET TERESA'S GOLDEN JUBILEE—FOUNDATION STONE LAID OF ST. ANN'S SCHOOL—A FAMILY FEAST. 1883-1885.

ON the 6th of October 1833, Sister Agnes Xavier and Sister Margaret Teresa consecrated themselves to God in holy religion, and received the habit at Chavagnes. Since that time many changes have taken place, and many who shared in the joy of that Rosary Sunday, have gone to sing their Alleluias with the angelic choir. Bishop Gillis and Sister Agnes Xavier have both been taken to their reward; but Mother Margaret Teresa is yet with us, and the celebration of her fiftieth year of religious life was naturally a matter of importance to her Community.

It was sadly against her own wishes to be brought thus prominently forward, but, as the first nun in Scotland since the Reformation, it was desired that all honour should be paid to her on this occasion.

The old friends and pupils of the house most

affectionately and generously wished to unite with the Community in celebrating the feast, and many letters were received, inquiring, "What would Mother Margaret Teresa like? What would give her most pleasure?" There could be but one answer from those who knew Mother Margaret Teresa. "Something for the altar, or something for the poor."

When the time drew near gifts arrived from all quarters. Magnificent candelabra from the old pupils; a splendid ciborium from her brothers; vestments from other Communities and friends; clothes, tea, sugar, and tobacco for the dear poor. How many times was heard the exclamation, "How pleased she will be!"

The blessing of the Holy Father had been asked for, and it arrived with a beautiful photograph of himself, forwarded by Monsignor Campbell of the Scots College, Rome.

On the morning of the 6th October, early Masses were celebrated in the convent chapel.

At ten o'clock High Mass was sung by the Right Rev. Monsignor Smith, Administrator of the Archdiocese, assisted by Father Selby, S.J., as Deacon, and the Rev. Robert Clapperton as Subdeacon.

The music was Haydn's Second Mass.

At the conclusion of the holy sacrifice, Monsignor Smith addressed a few suitable words to the jubilarian, congratulating her on the occasion of the fiftieth anniversary of her religious life, and in conclusion, saying, that it was his privilege to impart, and hers to receive, the Papal Benediction. After pronouncing the blessing, he intoned the "Te Deum," which was enthusiastically sung by the choir and congregation.

The pupils, religious, clergy, and guests then proceeded to the Community room, which wore a truly festive appearance—the walls were festooned with wreaths, and the panels in the ceiling filled alternately with shields bearing appropriate mottoes and devices, and wreaths of flowers. At the end of the room was displayed a scroll with the words, "Be thou faithful unto death, and I will give thee the crown of life."

The beautiful gifts were arranged on a table at the side of the room.

Among the honoured guests on this happy occasion were members of several other religious Orders—Sisters of Mercy, Sisters of the Good Shepherd, Oblates of Mary, Franciscans, and Little Sisters of the Poor.

When all were assembled, Mother Margaret Teresa was conducted to her place by Mother Mary Angela and Sister Mary Stanislaus. Monsignor Smith then spoke, in the name of all present, renewing their congratulations and offering the gifts that had been presented.

Father Gordon, the senior priest present, himself a jubilarian, was requested to return thanks, after which the clergy and company sat down to a *déjeûner*.

Benediction of the Blessed Sacrament was given in the afternoon, and a merry evening was spent with the children, who shared in all the festivities of the day.

The locality occupied by the day-school in Castle Terrace had long been found inconveniently small, and otherwise ill-adapted for educational purposes. Many an afternoon was spent in looking out for a house which might be purchased for St. Ann's, but without any satisfactory result. It was therefore decided that a house should be built at the extremity of the Strathearn Parks, on the convent property, and that it should be arranged as commodiously as possible for this long-established school.

The foundation-stone was laid on the 21st September, and was solemnly blessed by Monsignor Smith, who also read the inscription, which was placed in a bottle embedded in the stone. Besides the inscription, which was engrossed on parchment, the bottle contained a copy of the Catholic Directory for the year 1884, a florin of Queen Victoria, a medal of Leo XIII., &c.

The trowel, level, and mallet used on this occasion were the same used by Bishop Gillis when he laid the foundation-stone of the new buildings at the convent in 1860.

While on a visit to Edinburgh in October 1884, Monsignor Dillon (of Sydney) kindly called at St. Margaret's and spent some time in the schoolroom. He gave a most interesting account of his visit to the shrine and miraculous picture of Our Lady of Good Counsel, at Genazzano, near Rome, strongly urging devotion to the Blessed Virgin under this title. He left some oleographs which had touched the original picture as memorials of his visit.

The jubilee of the convent, according to date, ought to have been kept on the 26th December 1884, but the celebration was deferred till an Archbishop of St. Andrews and Edinburgh should be present. The Community, however, observed the day as a family feast. The statue of St. Margaret (presented by Mrs. Campbell of Lochnell) was placed on an altar beautifully ornamented. A catalogue of the names of all the Sisters who had formed the Community of St. Margaret's was enclosed in a silver gilt heart and suspended round the neck of the statue by Mother Margaret Teresa, the Sisters singing the Psalm "Ecce quam homum" the while.

The 28th was a day specially devoted to thanksgiving, it being the fiftieth anniversary of the first Mass celebrated in the convent. Father Selby sang Mass at 10 o'clock. The Blessed Sacrament was exposed till Benediction, at which the "Te Deum" was sung. All present were deeply moved with love and gratitude to God for all His goodness during these past fifty years, and all renewed the consecration of their lives to the service of the Word Incarnate, and thus entered on the second epoch of the life of the first convent in Scotland since the so-called Reformation.

CHAPTER XXIII.

DEATH OF MOTHER MARY ANGELA—ST. ANN'S SEMINARY —CONVENT EDUCATION. 1885.

THE name of Mother Mary Angela is familiar to our readers, and dear to the memory of the many children who owe to her much of the happiness of their early years; to the poor, who called down blessings on her head, and above all, to the Sisters, over whom she presided for a long period of time, both at St. Margaret's and at St. Joseph's.

It was with inexpressible sorrow that the Community watched over the close of her life, wasted by a terrible malady, which she bore with heroic patience. Everything that medical skill could do was tried to alleviate her sufferings, but without avail. Every spiritual succour was lavished upon the beautiful soul, whose whole life had been spent for God. As long as she could leave her room, the dear invalid was present at Mass, Benediction, and the exercises of the Community. One by one, these were relinquished, and as she was missed from her accustomed place, it was felt that another step had been taken towards the end of her way of the cross.

Within a few days of her death she was consoled by the blessing sent her by the Holy Father. In Holy Week it became evident that her strength was fast failing, but she lived till the 10th of April, Friday in Easter Week, when she passed from her cross to her crown.

Mother Mary Angela had been so widely known, and so deeply respected and beloved, that her funeral was attended by a large number of the clergy. Bishop Rigg came from Perth, and several priests from distant missions, all desirous to pay their last tribute of esteem to the departed religious.

Monsignor Smith had been obliged to go to Rome a few days previous to her death: from him, and from others, unavoidably absent, the reverend Mother received letters of condolence, all testifying to the general feeling of regard entertained for Mother Mary Angela by all who knew her.

The new house in Strathearn Road was now finished, and the pupils attending the school in Castle Terrace, were to be transferred to this locality at the beginning of May. To make the school villa known to the Catholics of Edinburgh, it had been resolved to inaugurate the establishment by holding a Drawing-room Bazaar in the new house, the time being fixed for the three last days of April.

Mr. Smith Sligo of Inzievar, one of the oldest friends of the Community, kindly consented to open the bazaar, which was generously supported by many friends, whose kindness furnished the stalls, or purchased the useful and ornamental articles displayed in the various departments.

In the afternoons and evenings, concerts and recitations were given by the pupils of St. Margaret's and St. Ann's, and by ladies and gentlemen who volunteered to assist, thus adding to the attractions of the bazaar.

An opportunity was thus afforded for every one to inspect the house, and all expressed their satisfaction with the arrangements for the pupils.

The classes were opened on the 4th of May, and they have been well attended during the past year, even through an exceptionally severe winter.

So much has been said and written on the inexhaustible subject of education, that it is evidently one of the most prominent thoughts in the minds of men of every civilised country. How many and what contradictory theories are advanced! what an endless variety of methods invented, followed for a time, and then superseded by new plans, which in their turn will, after an ephemeral existence, be allowed to sink into oblivion!

There is no accusation against the Catholic Church more general, or more false, than that she is the enemy of intellectual progress. Where would be the intellect of Europe at the present day, if the Catholic Church had not fostered its germs in the monastic institutions of the Middle Ages, stigmatised as "dark" by self-conceited scientists of later times?

It is in religious houses that the question of education, its end and its scope, have been most practically studied; and it is from monastic schools that have come forth, not only the great luminaries of mediæval times, but, in our own days, those men and women who are always in the front of every battle for the cause of truth and virtue, and whose daily lives are the surest test of the excellent training they received in their early years.

The common outcry against the enforced ignorance of Catholics is generally supplemented by abuse, especially levelled at what is known as "Convent Education." This comes naturally enough from Protestants, but that it should be echoed by Catholics is more than surprising. Yet, every now and then, some newspaper article is brought under the notice of religious bodies devoted to teaching, and the vulgar accusations are again and again adduced, that monks and nuns are "behind the age," and therefore unfit to develop the intelligence of the rising generation; and these things are said by liberal Catholics!

Fortunately for the teaching orders, they have brave champions who are ready to take up the gauntlet that ignorance or prejudice has thrown down, and the most eloquent words have been uttered by their defenders. Their best defence, however, is the fact, that in the tests of public examinations the pupils of Catholic colleges and schools take places equal to those gained by pupils of Protestant institutions. In the matter of education all that Catholics ask is a "fair field and no favour," and it will be seen that they can hold their own.

The ever-increasing pressure on the education question of course necessitates a corresponding amount of exertion on the part of both teachers and pupils, and in a city so devoted to learning as Edinburgh, there is naturally much competition among the numerous establishments that exist, attached to sects of every shade of belief. Hence it became incumbent on Catholics to hold their rank high in the lists, and St. Margaret's came to the front by sending pupils to the Local Examinations held at the University. The young candidates have invariably attained most satisfactory results, and prizes have been frequently awarded. The pupils from St. Ann's Seminary who have been presented at the University Examinations have likewise always passed successfully.

While doing their utmost to promote the intellectual advancement of their pupils, the religious of St. Margaret's strive still more earnestly to instil the principles and practice of sound religious doctrine into the minds and hearts of the dear children confided to their care; and it is their greatest happiness to watch the development of their young charges in knowledge and virtue. The children become much attached to their mistresses, and it is a mutual pleasure when they can, in after life, revisit the happy convent home where their early years were spent. The practice of retreats for ladies in the world enables the old pupils of the house to reassemble occasionally at St. Margaret's, and then the old days are recalled, old memories are refreshed, and the old affection becomes even stronger than before.

It is a great joy when the noviciate is augmented by a former pupil; the children declare they are "quite proud" when they see one whom they remember at school become a member of the Community. Indeed, besides the Community at St. Margaret's, there are many other nuns in England and Scotland whose first love and esteem for religious life was imbibed in the little chapel at St. Margaret's, and among the Sisters who guided their early years.

CHAPTER XXIV.

CONSECRATION OF ARCHBISHOP SMITH—HIS RECEPTION AT ST. MARGARET'S CONVENT AND AT ST. ANN'S SEMINARY. 1886.

THE time which elapsed during the absence of Monsignor Smith in Rome was one of considerable anxiety and suspense. The Very Rev. William Grady was named Administrator of the Archdiocese, and he ordered prayers in all the churches, that the nomination of an Archbishop to the See of St. Andrew's and Edinburgh might speedily be made, and all other ecclesiastical matters be satisfactorily settled.

At length Monsignor Smith announced his return home. He was joyfully welcomed on the 9th of September; and on the 21st the news was made public, that he had accepted the mitre, and that the flock, so long without a shepherd, would henceforth be ruled and guided by his firm yet gentle hand.

The rejoicings were general; shared alike by the clergy and the laity. Nowhere were they more heartfelt than at St. Margaret's.

XXIV.

HIS RECEPT... AND AT ST. A...

...ng the absence ... was one of consi... The Very R... administrator of ... prayers in all ... of an Archbish... and Edinburgh might ... other ecclesiastic...

... announced ... welcomed on the ... the news was ... the mitre, and ... shepherd, were ... his firm ...

... where were ... more heartfelt ... Margaret's.

THE MOST REV. WILLIAM SMITH, D.D.,

Archbishop of St. Andrews and Edinburgh.

The Archbishop-elect soon favoured the Sisters and children with a visit, and arranged to make his retreat, previous to consecration, at the Hermitage. How honoured and happy the Community felt when he expressed his wish to this effect; and with what pleasure the little necessary preparations were made for his reception and comfort!

On the departure of his Grace, the Hermitage was again honoured by episcopal presence. The Bishop of Hexham and Newcastle, accompanied by the Rev. D. L. Ramsay, stayed there for a week, that they might be present at the consecration and the subsequent festivities.

The 28th October, Feast of SS. Simon and Jude, was a truly memorable day.

The convent chapel was occupied during the morning hours by several masses; and after these early devotions were concluded, the delightful excitement of the children, and the equally joyous, but more quietly expressed, happiness of their elders, found relief in the preparations for attending the consecration of the Archbishop, at the Pro-Cathedral.

The late Archbishop having been consecrated in Rome, no such ceremony had taken place in Edinburgh since Bishop Gillis was consecrated in 1838. The ceremonial was therefore unknown to the greater part of the vast congregation who assembled to witness it. Long before the hour of eleven, the church was crowded. The sanctuary had been enlarged, for the better accommodation of the numerous body of clergy who were expected to attend, and it was not a foot too large. When the bell announced that all preparations were complete, Gounod's "Marche Romaine" was performed by the organ and orchestra. As the procession advanced up the church, it was watched with great interest, as, after the altar boys and St. Joseph's guild, the clergy followed in cassock and surplice, many well-known faces being recognised. Then followed the bishops and their chaplains, deacons and subdeacons, the Archbishop-elect, and finally Archbishop Eyre of Glasgow, the consecrating prelate.

The magnificent ceremonial began, amid the rapt attention of the congregation, who watched every movement in the sanctuary with intense interest. Needless to describe what is still so fresh in the memory of all who were present, and has been so fully chronicled elsewhere. Let us rather address to Archbishop Smith the words with which the consecration service concludes, "Ad multos annos," praying that he may long be spared to fulfil his high and sacred functions, and that the blessing which he pronounced over his flock may be likewise bestowed by Almighty God upon himself, and that all his undertakings for the glory of God and the advancement of religion in the Archdiocese may be crowned with success.

On the evening of this eventful day Archbishop Eyre and Bishop M'Lachlan of Galloway visited St. Margaret's, and again the following day Dr. Eyre called, bringing one of the consecration loaves to the children. A visit from his Grace is always an immense pleasure to the children, for every one of whom he has a kind word and a blessing.

The first care of the Community, after the consecration of Archbishop Smith, was to beg his Grace to spend a few hours at the convent, to receive the congratulations of the Sisters and pupils. He fixed the 25th of November to come to St. Margaret's, and the 26th to go to St. Ann's —both afternoons at five o'clock.

The 25th of November 1886 will ever be memorable in the annals of the convent. It was a day of universal joy to all the inmates of St. Margaret's,—hailed with gratitude and delight. From early morn the excitement of pleasure in the children was manifest, and during the day their joy was hardly controllable, and found its best safety-valve in their eagerness to share in the preparations for the evening.

The school apartments were adorned and decorated by all that respect and affection could suggest. Evergreens, flowers and flags, were displayed in every available space. The two arches of the beautiful cloister leading to the schoolroom were outlined with wreaths of evergreens, fastened in graceful festoons by a scroll, bearing the words, "Welcome to our loved Archbishop," which attracted much admiration. On each side of the arch were two large flags, so artistically placed as considerably to enhance the beauty of the effect.

The reception-room was particularly elegant; white lace curtains draped the windows, crowns of roses, ferns, and flowers were suspended from the gasaliers. The walls displayed the insignia of the Archiepiscopal dignity; the mitre, crozier, and pallium were emblazoned on shields, encircled with wreaths of holly, while a variety of choice hot-house plants and bright geraniums produced a charming harmony of colouring. The Archbishop's armorial bearings were placed above the folding doors at the end of the schoolroom. Below the shield was a scroll, with the inscription, "Ad multos annos." At the upper end of the room a raised seat was prepared for his Grace. When all was ready, the most anxious and critical scrutiny could not but admire the good taste which had presided over the arrangements, as well as the skill with which these had been carried out.

At five o'clock, the religious, the children in spotless white, and a numerous assembly of clergy and friends (a larger gathering than has been seen at St. Margaret's for many years), were awaiting his Grace's arrival.

Vested in purple, with rochet, mozetta, pectoral cross and ring, he entered the room, looking every inch an Archbishop!

The brilliant overture to Tancredi (arranged for two pianos, and four performers) was played; and as the music ceased, Miss Ethel Thornton advanced with two of her companions, and having read an address from the pupils of St. Margaret's to the Archbishop, begged his acceptance of a handsome copy of the canon of the Mass (the gift presented by the school), and an illuminated copy of the address.

All the young ladies then came forward to kiss the Archbishop's ring and receive his blessing, after which his Grace expressed the pleasure he felt at their affectionate welcome, and assured them of his constant interest in their welfare and happiness.

Father Whyte, S.J., in the name of the reverend Mother and the Community, thanked his Grace for the favour of his visit; and after some very enjoyable music had been performed by Madame Woycke and her pupils on the violin, the company adjourned to the refectory, where refreshments were prepared.

On the following evening the Archbishop honoured St. Ann's Seminary with his presence. A large number of the parents of the pupils assembled, to be present on the occasion, besides the clergy from every parish.

One of the guests must be named with special regard—the late Sir George Harrison, M.P. It was only on the preceding evening that he had been elected, in the Liberal interest, to represent the Southern Division of Edinburgh in Parliament. At a moment when his time and thoughts must necessarily have been engrossed with many important matters, the Community of St. Margaret's will never forget his kindness in coming to St. Ann's, nor his genial cordiality in all his dealings with the Sisters during the years of his provostship.

To return to the Seminary. On this auspicious occasion the schoolroom was decorated with flags, plants, and scrolls, bearing appropriate mottoes of welcome to the Archbishop.

As his Grace entered the room, a pianoforte

quartette was played by four of the pupils, and this was followed by a chorus, "Many hearty greetings to-day," composed expressly for the occasion, and sung by all the children, who were arranged in tiers on either side of the alcove, where a beautiful statue of St. Ann was embowered amid flowers and lights.

In compliment to the Archbishop, whose mother was a M'Donnell of Glengarry, badges of white heather, and scarfs of M'Donnell tartan, fastened with brooches on the shoulder, were worn by the pupils.

The address to his Grace was read by Miss Mary Bolan, who was supported by two of her companions, one of whom carried a travelling writing-case, and the other an illuminated copy of the address mounted on gilt rollers.

In reply, the Archbishop thanked the children for their congratulations and the good wishes expressed in the address, and also for the writing-case, which he promised to preserve. He gracefully alluded to the compliment they had paid his family by wearing the M'Donnell tartan, and expressed his pleasure at seeing the class of little boys in full Highland costume.

The Archbishop's speech, and the announcement of a holiday with which it concluded, were received with much hearty applause.

Father Hannan, of St. Patrick's, thanked the Archbishop, in the name of the children, for his presence among them that evening, and also expressed his own kind feelings and good wishes for the prosperity of the old school, in the new house.

Mr. M'Nally then favoured the company with a solo on the violoncello. Miss M'Hardy also contributed some beautiful Scotch songs; — the pupils were not behindhand; they performed duets and quartettes, and sang various character songs, which were much appreciated by the audience. Even the little boys did their part with great spirit.

The company afterwards adjourned to the spacious class-rooms, opening into one another by large folding doors, where refreshments were laid out. After some time, pleasantly spent in conversation, the visitors dispersed.

The Sisters and their pupils felt very happy at having received the blessing of their pastor, and the reiterated assurance of his paternal feelings towards them. They feel sure that the two bright evenings which have been described (at St. Margaret's and St. Ann's), will never fade from the memory of those present; and that the kind and winning words of the Archbishop will be enthroned in the hearts of the little ones whom he addressed as the "Lambs of his Flock."

At the close of the festivities in his Grace's honour, all united with one heart and voice in those oft-repeated words—

"AD MULTOS ANNOS."

BIOGRAPHICAL SKETCH

OF

SISTER AGNES XAVIER

(ANN AGNES TRAIL).

SISTER AGNES XAVIER TRAIL.

CHAPTER I.

PRELIMINARY—JOURNEY THROUGH ITALY TO ROME

In a retrospect of fifty years how many memories crowd our hearts and minds! How many well-known faces rise before our eyes, how many well-known voices, long silent, seem again to sound in our ears! And thus, while celebrating the Jubilee of St. Margaret's Convent, recalling those who were most intimately connected with its rise and progress, we would fain dedicate to each dear Sister a few lines of loving remembrance.

Time and space alike forbid so considerable an addition to this little work; besides which, the lives of those who lived and laboured at St. Margaret's and who have gone to their reward were for the most part too uneventful to be of interest to the general reader. Their names are very dear to the Community, where each one filled her appointed place and accomplished her allotted work, whether in the schools, among the poor, or in the lowly and hidden occupations of domestic care. Their remains rest beneath the chapel where they spent so many hours in prayer, and where now others pray for them; they are not forgotten by their Sisters, whose only desire is, to carry on the work of the Institute as perfectly as it was begun by those who entered on it in 1834.

There is one, however, who cannot be thus enshrined in memory alone. She was too widely known in her day to be yet forgotten even by the outer world; and we feel sure that a short sketch of her life cannot fail to be acceptable to many who may still remember her.

Sister Agnes Xavier, Ann Agnes Trail, was born at Panbride, Forfarshire, on the 16th of February 1798, and was baptized on the 25th of the same month. Her father was the Presbyterian clergyman of Panbride, and was much beloved and respected by his flock. Of him and of her mother she always retained the most affectionate remembrance; indeed she was deeply attached to all her family. Though for a time, after her conversion to Catholicity, her parents and relatives manifested much displeasure at the step she had taken, and some coolness ensued, Mr. Trail was himself too conscientious to retain enmity against his daughter, who soon convinced her friends that she had acted from the purest motives, and only after mature reflection and deep study had rendered her convictions unchangeable.

At the suggestion of the Rev. Thomas Glover, S.J., her spiritual director, she has herself given us the history of her early years and religious experiences. These give us an insight into the effect of Calvinistic teachings on a mind that is brought up under the influence of these gloomy doctrines. It is pleasing to be able to contrast these early mental terrors with the perfect peace and joy which Miss Trail experienced after her submission to the Catholic Church, and which only increased and deepened in her religious life. Her letters to Father Glover were written very soon after her abjuration in 1828. In those days a convert from Protestantism was rare. Mr. Ambrose Lisle Philipps, the Honourable and Rev. George Spenser, and a few others, had indeed been brought into the Church; but it was not till many years later that the transition "from Oxford to Rome" became so frequent as to be no longer matter for surprise. Many converts have published their reasons for abjuring Protestantism, and it is always interesting to trace the different action of the grace of God on different souls. It is, however, still rare to find a convert from Presbyterianism, and therefore Sister Agnes Xavier's letters will be perhaps useful to some who belong to that body, and who may be seeking to serve God rather from love than fear.

In her letters she gives a sketch of her youthful days, which we supplement by some further details and by the account of her journey to Italy. She here depicts herself as a pious and uncompromising Protestant, constantly acting up to her conception of what was right and true; and thus, unconsciously to herself, preparing for that gift of faith which was to be bestowed upon her, and which was to change the whole tenor of her life.

Her wonderful talent for painting attracted attention while she was still a child, and her parents and other relatives did all in their power to further her progress, by affording her the best instruction at their command. She soon, however, surpassed her teachers, and it was felt to be desirable that a higher standard should be placed before her. It was, therefore, most willingly that Mr. and Mrs. Trail consented to their daughter's making some stay in London in 1824, under the care of relatives, whose kindness she constantly remembered and referred to, when speaking of her early life. It was to herself a real sorrow to part from her home and family; and during her absence she was a most punctual correspondent, never omitting to give every detail of her life, and her progress in the art of miniature painting, to which she now entirely turned her attention.

Her master was Mr. Andrew Robertson, one

of the most celebrated artists of his day. She was an indefatigable student, and during the ensuing five years the number of portraits she executed is well-nigh incredible. Her acuteness of sight was very remarkable. We have heard her describe the lid of a snuff-box which she painted for the late Lord Panmure; it bore three miniatures, the Emperor Napoleon, the Empress Maria Louisa, and the young King of Rome. Round the neck of the Empress was a gold chain with a locket, on the locket was a replica of the portrait of the Emperor. As another proof of her wonderful sight she told us, that having painted a miniature portrait of a young lady, holding an open book in her hand, she inscribed a favourite verse of a hymn on the page of the book.

It was delightful when she related anecdotes of her youth. She had seen so many changes, and gave such good descriptions of men and things. Among other stories which amused us, was one illustrative of the ways and doings of London beggars.

Her cousin, the Hon. Mrs. Erskine, with whom she resided, had a lady's maid who one day came to her mistress to announce her approaching marriage, and consequently to resign her situation. Mrs. Erskine had a great regard for the young woman, and made some inquiries about the future husband; all of which were satisfactorily answered. When the wedding day approached, the maid told Mrs. Erskine that her fiancé had taken a house in —— Street, and that if ever her lady happened to be in that neighbourhood, she would be very proud to see her.

It happened some months afterwards that Mrs. Erskine, walking with a friend, was overtaken by a heavy storm of thunder and rain near the street named. The two ladies thought themselves fortunate in being near a friendly shelter, and went to the house of the *ci-devant* lady's maid, who was delighted to see her old mistress. Everything was in perfect order; the house nicely furnished, the young woman neatly dressed. She offered her visitors tea, which was served with perfect attention to all the requirements of a refined tea-table. Mrs. Erskine was much pleased to see her old servant so comfortable, and said, "I suppose your husband is still engaged in his business; what trade does he follow?" The poor wife blushed and looked confused, but at last said, "Well, madam, my husband is an asker." "An *asker*," said Mrs. Erskine, "what sort of business is that?" It turned out, on explanation being given, that the man was a regular street beggar, who took his station on one of the bridges. He had held this post for years, as a supposed cripple, and received daily alms from the passers-by. Thus he made a good livelihood, and kept his wife in a comfortable home.

After profiting much by the lessons she took in London, it was considered advisable for Miss Trail to go to Italy, still further to perfect herself in her art. In the spring of 1826 she returned home for a short visit, and then started for Italy. How little she thought of the momentous importance of that journey! In her letters to Father Glover she had spoken of her feelings respecting it. She has, besides, left some fragments of letters to a friend, descriptive of her journey, which give a still further insight into her mind and heart.

The first of these letters is dated from—

"CHAMBERY, *13th June* 1826.

"MY DEAR AGNES,—When I left London I intended, in a series of letters to a few dear friends, to communicate whatever I thought worthy of notice; but day after day has passed, and I am arrived thus far on my journey towards Italy without having commenced. But to-day I have enjoyed too much, not to wish to share it with those I love, especially with you.

"Oh, how your imagination and every feeling would have been enchanted in ascending the majestic Alps, the lower range of which I have passed to-day! My heart is full; but my pen can give but an inadequate idea of the scenery. At first rich swelling hills present themselves; then an immense valley surrounded by precipitate rocks, by the edge of which the road winds; next, you are shut up amid rocks, and enter the passage of the Echelle, a long gallery of 900 feet, after passing which your road lies through rocks heaped on rocks, wild in the extreme, as if Nature had just tossed them from her hand. Every moment the prospect varies; here a perpendicular tabular rock, there a peak; now immense blocks of stone huddled together, covered with the loveliest wild flowers, interspersed with box-pine, walnut, mulberry, and other trees. This abundance of verdure amidst the bare rocks is beautiful in the extreme.

"Now you begin to descend again for about two hours towards Chambery, a lovely town, embosomed in the Alps; we reached it a little before seven o'clock. I got a little maid from the hotel, and proceeded at once to the Cathedral, which is an old Gothic building, and rather fine. They were, I suppose, at vespers, so I knelt down. There is something almost irresistible in such numbers assembled to worship, and amidst the emblems of superstition, I still felt it was the house of prayer; and from thence I sallied forth to the Boulevards, a fine walk shaded by trees, and thence towards the country, where I took a small sketch and returned to dinner at eight. It is now about half-past nine, so I must say good-night and go to bed. I travelled all last night, and am to be off again at three in the morning. Farewell,—our heavenly Father is present everywhere, on Alpine steep as in our native land.—I, too, am ever your affectionate A. A. T."

"*26th June* 1826.

"DEAR AGNES,—I took it into my wise head to be romantic, and, like most romantic people, must suffer for it; having selected a lovely spot on the top of a crumbling terrace on the side of a hill commanding a fine view of the Gulf of Genoa, I sat down to write to you, when, alas! my ink bottle fell, and with it all my hopes of using pen and ink till I get another; however, I do not like to be baffled, so I have taken my pencil, which had scarce been laid aside from taking a sketch of one of the most beautiful views on which my eye ever rested. Our *vetturino* has laid by for three hours during the heat of the day, and all other travellers have hid themselves within walls from the mid-day sun, now intensely hot; but seated under a fig-tree, I enjoy the air, the prospect, and a refreshing shade at the same time.

"What a lovely world has our heavenly Father

given us to dwell in, were it not marred by sin; but peace with God again enables us to contemplate it with delight. When I cast my eye now over the rich intervening screen of vines, figs, &c., and rest it on the soft blue of the Mediterranean, and on Genoa, and the mountains receding in the distance, my heart exclaims, 'And was this fair scene all made for ungrateful man?' Ah! the infinite goodness of Jehovah,—it was not enough to satisfy all our wants, but every sense must be gratified: the eye with beauty, the ear with music, now faintly poured from the branches around; the grasshopper's chirp, too, is sweet—all is harmony, and I enjoy it the more for being alone. There is society where none intrude.

" *Wednesday.*—I had scarcely finished the above when I was summoned to the *vetturino,* where I had to join a motley group of Italians—only one of whom could speak a few words of French, our conductor, too, could not understand me, so that I felt myself indeed *alone,* a stranger in a strange land; but there was so much to attract the eye, that a silent day was an enjoyment. Every turn winding along the shore between Genoa and Sestri presents a new prospect, each disputing the palm of beauty, so that had Paris been called on to decide, I know not to which he would have thrown the apple. Perhaps, on the whole, the spot from whence the commencement of this is dated is the finest ; it is the most extensive and varied ; I also attach to it some pleasing recollections which will endear it to my memory.

Rambling about in search of the best spot for taking a sketch, on the acclivity of the beautiful terraced hill which overhangs the inn where we rested at midday, I found a cottage. Its singularity struck me, I entered, and in the lower part found a cow, which seemed much startled by my appearance ; on the side next the door were a few open wooden steps with a rope—I ascended, and found a family consisting of a mother with I think five young children. She welcomed me with a smile which denoted she was pleased to see me. I had fallen on my way up the hill and had hurt my arm, I showed it to her, and she immediately applied some wet paper, and seemed most anxious to relieve the pain. I tried to enter into conversation, and with a few words of Italian and signs made myself tolerably understood. I showed her some of my tracts, which I always carry in my little sack. I found she could not read ; but she told me her children were at school, and she was quite delighted with two I gave her, and immediately locked them in a trunk. May the Lord send their contents home to the hearts of these poor simple peasants, thus may they become wiser than their teachers, of whose ignorance and vice I had lamentable proof in one of my *compagnons de voyage*, while taking my sketch near the cottage. One of the children came and sat by me; there was something in the confidence placed in me which went to my heart, but I could only pat its head and give it a little piece of money, which seems always acceptable. After the accident of the ink bottle I again visited the cottage, to get my hands washed, and I found the master of the mansion had arrived for dinner, I suppose, which consisted of salad and bread, baked something like an Irish potato cake on a girdle, but mixed with onions. They invited me to partake, and I did so, delighted with their hospitality, and pleased to see something of the manners of the peasantry of the country, always the most interesting, because the most original and also the most numerous class in every country. The physiognomy of these people was quite distinct from that of the peasantry of our country. The man especially had a dark quick eye, rather short face and projecting chin, with a black beard of perhaps ten days' growth. He seemed rather amused at my attempts to express my ideas, but very respectful, for, if I may judge by his gestures, he refused to sit down to dinner while I was present. But I pointed to his seat at the table, where his wife and children were already placed, and then he sat down; and I went away, never I believe to see them again on earth; but if the words of eternal life, sown in hope, should spring up, and bear fruit, we may yet meet, when this fleeting pilgrimage is over, in the land of everlasting rest—and there shall be no stranger there, but one heart and one tongue shall unite all the happy multitude that surround the throne of the Lamb, and they shall praise Him for ever and ever. That we may unite in this song is the prayer of—

Your affectionate, ANN A. TRAIL."

The above letter clearly indicates that the writer was a sincerely pious Protestant. She lost no opportunity of instilling the doctrines of the sect she believed to be the true Church of God, and thought she did a good work in trying to shake the faith of the peasants she encountered.

Fortunately, we possess a note to the preceding letter, in which Miss Trail says:—

"The same month, three years after, in 1829, I passed by the same route on my return home; we rested at mid-day at the same albergo. Blessed then with the light of the true faith, I bethought myself of my poor friends in the cottage, with whom I had left my tracts with a good intention; but, as I now knew them to be a useless or pernicious present, I set out, and with some difficulty found the cottage. I entered and saluted my old friend, the mother, who instantly recognised me. The children were grown, and just returned from school. I asked if she remembered the little books I had given her. 'Si, signora;' and opening her chest, where, no doubt, they had been carefully locked up ever since, she presented them to me. I took them, saying, 'They are bad books; I was a heretic when I gave them to you.' I warned her as to receiving such gifts for the future; after which I sat down and heard the children their catechism.

"How wonderful are the ways of God! how true it is that He leads the blind by a way that they know not!"

Sister Agnes Xavier often said how relieved her mind was to know that these tracts had done no harm—the thought of her ill-advised attempt at proselytism had been a great source of uneasiness to her at the time of her conversion, and this was only allayed by the result of her second visit to the good woman. The account of her journey reads like a bit of ancient history in these days of railway travelling. Our present speed gives no time for sketching or minute description of lovely views and fine buildings such as our dear artist delighted to record.

Her third letter is as follows, but without date:—

"DEAR AGNES,—I find the old proverb true, 'Nothing teaches like experience.' I had been warned of the effects of the sun in these warm climates, but foolishly thought I could brave it, so followed my own vagaries the other day, as you know by my former letter. But the following day I had such a bad headache, I was hardly able to look up, except now and then to see the country, which now lay a little inland amidst hills beautifully and richly clothed with vines and fruit and other trees. At mid-day we rested again, but I was neither able to go out nor to write; and after waiting till past twelve for a cup of coffee, which, when ready, was so bad I could not drink it, I took some cake and milk, and went to rest for an hour. About two we again set out, and soon got a glimpse of the sea, and for some miles our road lay along the shore. I got out and washed my hands in the Mediterranean. Here I saw hedges of aloes.

"Next morning we started at five. Our route was beautiful in most parts, but not so picturesque as the two preceding days. I reached Pisa about ten, and to-day have been engaged in seeing the Duomo, Baptistery, and wonderful leaning tower, of which you must have seen so many descrip tions, it is useless for me to give you one. I ascended to the top, and was much gratified by the view, which is very extensive; the sea and Gulf of Genoa on one side, the Apennines on the other. The port of Leghorn is visible in the distance; and also, in clear weather, Florence, but to-day it was too heavy. The Duomo, or Cathedral, is a fine old building—the high altar most magnificent, composed of the most precious marbles. There is in the Baptistery a beautiful font of white marble, carved in the most exquisite manner; and the pulpit is of alabaster, with fine bas-reliefs—the birth, presentation in the Temple, death, and ascension of our Saviour; and the fifth is the last judgment. The Campanile is a very elegant building, the arches are of the most beautiful construction I ever saw." . . .

Miss Trail resumes the chronicle of her stay in Italy in November 1826:—

"After passing between four and five months at Florence, I set off for Rome in company with the Hon. Miss F. Mackenzie of Seaforth, and our celebrated painter, Wilkie. We chose the route by Perugia, as being on the whole the most interesting, and also as possessing the best roads—no trifling consideration at this season of the year after very heavy rains.

"On the 22d, about half-past seven in the morning, Miss Mackenzie and I got packed into our vehicle, and went to take up our friend, Mr. Wilkie, who, we found, had been awaiting us nearly two hours. However this was a small evil; but at the city gate it was found that his passport was not in order. We were now in a sad dilemma. It was impossible to remain without the gate till mid-day, till which time we were told the passport could not be signed, and it was equally out of the question to return within it, and have all the same work to go over again. So after a short consultation it was resolved that Miss Mackenzie and I should proceed with the luggage, and that Mr. Wilkie should follow us in a light cabriolet as soon as possible. The day was fine, and though so late in the season, the country still looked beautiful, the grey olive, the green ilex, and the various shades of yellow, red, and brown on the still unscattered foliage of the other trees, gave a charming effect. We immediately began to ascend, and at a few miles from the town looked back upon Florence, embosomed in wooded hills. It seemed from thence well to merit the title of "Fair," which has been so often bestowed upon it. We began now to descend, however, and of course lost sight of it, I cannot say with a sad heart, but yet many pleasing recollections and some tender regrets lingered round it. I could not say farewell without a wish to revisit it, and offering up a prayer for the few kind friends who had rendered my stay there agreeable.

. . . . . .

"After we lost sight of Florence there was little of interest that presented itself on our first day's journey, excepting here and there a convent picturesquely situated on a rising ground; for, to do the inmates of these mansions justice, they have generally had the sagacity and taste to select the most beautiful spots for their habitation, and have sometimes charming views from some apartments of the convent; but from sharing which, the eye of woman is of course excluded. I often feel inclined to be a little angry; but after all, it is but fair that if the monks are shut out from many of the pleasures of society, they should enjoy as much as possible those which nature and solitude afford. Peace be with them; I envy them not!

"Between one and two o'clock we stopped for a few minutes at a wretched café in a town which, from its size, must, I think, have afforded better. There we got some indifferent coffee without milk, sour bread, stale eggs, &c., but hunger made us put up with bad fare; and we proceeded onwards towards Montevarchi, where we passed the night in an albergo outside the walls, and situated beautifully on a river bank and in sight of a seemingly old and most picturesque convent.

"As we arrived early I was tempted by the beauty of the scenery to take a ramble, and after doing so, and making a little sketch, I returned to the albergo, where I found Mr. Wilkie had rejoined us, and both he and Miss Mackenzie were seated beside a fine blazing wood fire, when we enjoyed ourselves, after a very comfortable dinner, by reading a few chapters of Walter Scott's last novel.

"We then went to bed, out of which we were called at a very early hour next morning, and proceeded on our journey.

"As the grey dawn began to disappear before the beams of the rising sun, our eyes were saluted by a view of the Apennines, with their tops covered with snow, which formed a contrast we in more northern climes seldom behold, with the varied tints of the trees. Midway up the mountain, the clouds were rolling in large volumes, while the snowy tops were basking in the full rays of the orb of day, and reminded me of the beautiful lines of Goldsmith—

"'Though round its breast the rolling clouds are spread,
Eternal sunshine settles on its head.'

"At mid-day we stopped for two hours at Arezzo,

the birthplace of Petrarch. After getting breakfast, we rambled a little through the town, and went to the Cathedral, which stands on a fine site overlooking the town. It is a handsome building, and inside it contains some curious monuments; amongst the rest, I observed one to Gregory IX., and a high altar wrought in the manner of a monument. There are several pictures by modern artists of merit; among others, one which is much admired, by Benvenuti, of the martyrdom of a saint.

"We walked about a little and saw the outside of the court of justice, a curious-looking old building. We then returned to the albergo, where we found our *vetturino* ready to depart, so we set off. The weather was very disagreeable, and we amused ourselves the best way we could, with reading and chat, till we arrived at Camuscia, where we slept at a poor inn. Camuscia lies just below Cortona, one of the most ancient cities of Etruria, and of which we got a sight next morning, at a little distance, situated on a hill.

"We were now drawing near the scene so celebrated by the operations of Hannibal, and it was a disappointment that it rained heavily all the time we were passing by the Lake Thrasymenus, which prevented us from enjoying its beauties. We reached Perugia late, but there we had a comfortable dinner and good beds. We got up next morning as soon as it was light, and went out to see the pictures of Pietro Perugino, justly celebrated both for his own works and as being the master of the inimitable Raphael. His works appear to me full of beautiful simplicity, nature, and expression; indeed it seems difficult to distinguish between his and the earlier productions of his scholar; and the finest parts of the works of Perugino are often, though most probably unjustly, attributed to Raphael. The heads, especially, have a great deal of the same style about them. When we returned to the albergo, we got breakfast and then proceeded to a church a little out of town, to see some other beautiful things by the same master; from whence also there was a magnificent view, which we enjoyed much, as the weather had again cleared up, and the sun was shedding all his glory over the beautiful landscape. Having admired everything, both inside and outside this convent church, we returned to the city gate, where we met our *vetturino*. After a pleasant journey, we reached Foligno for the night, but too late to see anything of the town. The albergo was indifferent enough, or, at least, our accommodation in it; but we found out that they were expecting no less a personage than Jerome Bonaparte, so we were obliged to content ourselves with second-rate fare.

"We were ushered into an immense hall without a fire; however, when we insisted on having that comfort, we were led down stairs to another which seemed common property, being shared with children, dogs, and servants of both sexes. We got it cleared a little, and had dinner at one end of a large wooden table that might, I believe, have served thirty persons at least; the fireside was ornamented with our sheets, which Miss Mackenzie took particular care should both be clean and well dried, neither of which seemed very common, and sometimes when they were told they had been used, they did not even attempt to deny the fact. During the night it blew a sirocco, and early next morning, our window being blown open, I was astonished, on approaching to shut it, to find the air quite hot—the temperature was entirely changed from the intense cold we had experienced before we left Florence and during the former part of our journey.

"Sabbath morning, we set off before light; early in the morning passed the temple of Clitumnus; we alighted a few minutes to see this small piece of ancient architecture, though not of the best line of the art; it is situated on a rock almost overhanging a stream. After resting in the forenoon outside the walls of a considerable town, I believe Spoleto, we entered some beautiful scenery like our Scotch glens, but richer perhaps in wood, whose varied tints glowed in all the luxuriance of autumn, though now winter. Such is the felicity of this climate. Lovely Italia! thy Maker's hand hath formed thee fair, but sunk as thou art now by moral degradation, darkened by superstition, and depressed by tyranny, I would not give the most barren spot in my native land for all thy enchanting beauties, which while they ravish the eye, make (by sad contrast) the heart recoil the more from thy mental horizon. About sunset we entered Terni two or three miles distant from the celebrated falls. I wished much to see them; but the weather being so wet, and both my companions having seen them, we resolved to pass on; and next morning accordingly proceeded towards Narni, a small town most picturesquely situated on the side of a hill; there we were obliged to have two bovi or oxen attached in front of our horses, to aid in pulling our vehicle up the steep. Having gone through the town, we continued to travel over very high ground, which commanded extensive views of the surrounding country, which was wild and mountainous; at midday we stopped about two hours at Civita Castellana; a wretched breakfast we got; but it was amply compensated by a view of the magnificent scenery around. Mr. Wilkie conducted me to a bridge just at the entrance, from whence, with his assistance, I took a sketch.

"On our return to the albergo we found Miss Mackenzie and our vehicle had both deserted us. Miss Mackenzie had gone out to sketch, and our *vetturino*, from a blunder, followed her; however, we found both waiting us at a bridge at the other side of the town. From thence till we reached Nepi the country was not particularly interesting. At Nepi we passed the night—our accommodation very indifferent. How strange that they appear worse as they approach the capital; but such is the fact—our bed-chamber was a great desolate room opening from the common hall, where were assembled travellers of all descriptions and different countries. I found our door did not fasten properly, and to prevent any unwelcome intrusion I set a heavy chair behind it, and we kept a light burning; but the night passed quietly, no banditti, no adventure, and early on the morning of the 28th we proceeded towards Rome.

"We soon entered the Campania or great plain which surrounds this far-famed city; but it seems a desert: scarce a habitation is to be seen for many miles. Man has fled its noxious precincts, for many months infected by malaria. At mid-day, we rested at a solitary mansion, the squalid countenances of whose inhabitants told but too plainly the unhealthiness of its situation, and on enquiry we found that the master has suffered from malaria three of the summer months.

"A few miles from this spot, from the stupidity of our driver, our carozza was completely overturned; but most providentially we escaped with a few bruises and scratches, though the glass was broken to pieces, and I was undermost. I believe I suffered least, from the circumstance of my being at the moment on my knees in the bottom of the carriage enjoying my first glimpse of the dome of St. Peter's; such things appear to us too often accidental, but I would acknowledge it as an additional proof of the kind care of my Heavenly Father, whose gracious hand hath conducted me safely through all my wanderings. In a few hours more we entered Rome" (28th November 1826).

Arrived in Rome, Miss Trail devoted herself to the immediate object of her journey thither. Having established herself in a quiet apartment in the vicinity of the Vatican, it was in that treasury of art that she spent many hours daily, studying the works of the great masters, whose *chefs-d'œuvre* are the admiration and wonder of all who behold them.

In May 1827, she left Rome, in company with the Rev. Mr. Middleton and his wife, and travelled with them to Venice, and round by the north of Italy to Parma, where she spent four months; after which she returned to Rome and there spent the greater part of the year 1828.

During this time she copied Raphael's representation of the miracle of Bolsena; and in her letters she alludes to the impression made upon her by this picture, while her own religious belief was wavering.

We here leave her to tell her own tale in her letters to Father Glover, S.J. Her conversion now took place, and was the great turning-point of her life, changing its whole aspect and aim.

It naturally brought much suffering upon her, not only by reason of her own mental anxieties, but on account of the sorrow her change of religion could not fail to inflict on those most dear to her. But we have been told that "Sorrow endureth for a night, but joy cometh in the morning;" and so it proved in the case of Miss Trail. Her whole life, from the day of her reception into the Church, was one ceaseless act of praise and thanksgiving to God for the wonderful gift of faith.

CHAPTER II.

AUTOBIOGRAPHY OF SISTER AGNES XAVIER (ANN AGNES TRAIL), WRITTEN AT THE REQUEST OF THE REV. THOMAS GLOVER, S.J.

LETTER I.

"REV. AND DEAR FATHER,—I take up my pen at your suggestion to give a short sketch of my religious life from childhood, and thus as it were to trace step by step (as far as memory will serve me) all the way by which a gracious Providence led me, till that happy day when He brought me into the Ark of His own true Church, where I have at length found that rest which, like Noah's dove, I had sought elsewhere in vain.

"And while I recall to remembrance the goodness and longsuffering of my God, and my own wanderings and perverseness, may my heart swell with gratitude, while it sinks low in humiliation and exclaims with one of old, 'Lord, I am not worthy of one of the least of all Thy mercies;' and may this short account of the bounty of my Heavenly Father, and my own misery, be to the praise and glory of *His grace*, who hath 'called me out of darkness into His marvellous light.'

"To no one can I so properly address this; as to yourself, honoured Father, to whom the secrets of my conscience were first made known, and who, therefore, can estimate more justly than any one else the amazing wisdom and loving-kindness of Jehovah, in adapting the dispensations of His Providence to my peculiar character and turn of mind.

"You are aware that my father is a clergyman of the Presbyterian sect; and few, I believe, have been more justly esteemed, both for his ministerial and private virtue;—pious without enthusiasm; just without severity; sincere without rudeness; mild and patient, yet firm; a kind master, and indulgent parent, he seldom, I may say never, found fault, excepting when moral delinquency called forth his just reproof. Liberal in his sentiments, charitable to the poor, the peacemaker among his friends, faithful himself in the discharge of his parochial duties, I never heard him blame or criticise others who were more remiss; indeed, detraction of all sorts (even though couched under a witty sarcasm) he was sure to disapprove of, and though fond of an innocent jest, nothing approaching to impurity was ever heard from his lips or countenanced in his presence. Of my dear mother I need only say, she is worthy of being the partner of my honoured father; beloved by him, her children, her dependants and friends, almost, I may say, the idol of every guest who visits at her house.

"You will forgive me for paying this tribute to my beloved parents, for whom, while I weep over the errors of their faith, I can never cease to feel the strongest affection and highest respect. To them I owe that I was brought up in the fear of the Lord, and that as soon as my infant lips could lisp the name of father, I was taught to raise their accents to Him who is in heaven. I well remember that my dear mother used frequently, especially on Sunday evenings, to call my sisters and me together and speak to us on the love of the Saviour till both our hearts and eyes would overflow. As we advanced a little in years, my father himself took the charge of instructing us in our moral and religious duties, and continued to do so regularly till we were about fourteen. Thus we were taught both by precept and example to regard religion as the one thing needful. Though a very lively child, and when with others the gayest of the gay, I was always fond of solitude; and when very young often did I retire into some quiet nook or unseen corner, where, gazing on the starry heavens or the lovely moon, I would muse on the angelic inhabitants of those bright regions, or think on the goodness of God who had hung out all these lights, as I then thought, solely for our benefit.

"My great delight was musing and reading the scripture histories of the Old and New Testaments, the Psalms, some parts of the prophecies and the last discourse of our Saviour to His disciples. The words, 'In My Father's house are many mansions: I go to prepare a place for you,' were the frequent subject of my meditations and prayers, in which two exercises I early experienced great pleasure. Prayer was, I think, my refuge in all my troubles, the first instance of which that I distinctly remember was when, I suppose, I must have been between eight and nine years old. My eldest brother, who was then an infant, had pushed a small pebble up his nose, to extract which we had to send for a surgeon; meanwhile my mother, &c., were in great distress; on seeing which I retired into a place apart, and with great earnestness entreated God for my little brother; and I think it was before I was much older, that I used to beseech God to pour out upon me the spirit of grace and supplication, to give me a very tender conscience.

"I think it was soon after this period too, that on reading some religious books, particularly 'Todd on Death,' I became deeply impressed with the necessity of leading a religious life if I would be happy hereafter. I immediately set about many practices of devotion, such as frequent set hours for prayer, reading the Scriptures, &c., but my devotion was by fits and starts, and sometimes, I fear, altogether forgotten; which then caused me much unhappiness.

"One day that I was alone, offering up prayer, but I believe, much in the spirit of the Pharisee, an internal voïce (for I never imagined I heard it with my outward ears), exclaimed, 'Thou shalt not be always thus.' The impression was so strong that I instantly started from my knees, and the meaning conveyed to me was, 'Thou shalt be no longer happy in thy self-conceited sanctity.' I entered the room a proud Pharisee, I left it a conscience-smitten sinner; I think I must then have been little more than twelve years old. From that day, for upwards of two years, I was one of the most miserable of human beings; I saw myself an undone sinner, I knew there was an Almighty Saviour; but 'would He be merciful to such a wretch as I?' was the heartrending question, to which I dared not reply in the affirmative. I was a Calvinist, and I thought myself already numbered with the damned, but I felt I deserved it, and as far as I can remember, I never in the midst of my misery charged God with injustice. I even recollect that in reading 'Clopstock's Messiah,' wherein he describes the different characters of the lost spirits, he represents one as having been the last to quit the ranks of the blessed, and as spending his time in hell, not like the others in blaspheming God and maliciously devising the ruin of man, but in mourning his loss of heaven. I fell down on my knees and implored that if, as I dreaded, I must inevitably be lost, I might never at least speak against God, but only blame myself, and mourn my having shut myself out from His blessed presence. I began with intense anxiety to study religious works, and some of them on the most profound subjects, others calculated to awaken the careless sinner, neither of them adapted to my then state of mind; but I had no one to direct me, and I swallowed alike milk and strong meat which I was not able to digest: thus I derived little benefit and received little comfort. Is my heart renewed? Have I true faith? Am I one of the elect? Have I not perhaps committed the sin against the Holy Ghost? were questions upon which my mind perpetually dwelt, and drove me almost to despair. The agony of my mind was often such, that I withdrew where I was sure no human eye could discover me, and there, prostrate on the earth, I have groaned and wept for hours; I should have welcomed death, had I not dreaded hell, and I only feared lest in some awful moment of temptation I might destroy myself: but God, infinite in mercy, though He permitted me to have many a fearful struggle, yet would not suffer me to be tempted above what I was able to bear; a ray of light now and then shot across the gloom, darted from some of the sweet promises of the Gospel; hope, though darkened, was not altogether extinct: it sometimes whispered, 'Though now in misery, God will yet deliver you.' One text of Isaiah often brought me consolation: 'Thus saith the Lord to the man that feareth the Lord, and hearkeneth unto the voice of his servant, who sitteth in darkness and hath no light, let him hope in the Lord and stay himself on his God.' This I endeavoured to do, and as it were to hope against hope.

. . . . . .

"The merciful arrangements of Providence, about this time, placed in my way duties which in a great measure forced my mind from almost constant meditation on itself and turned its energies into a totally different channel: but as this brings me to the close of one period of my history—that of my childhood—it reminds me also, that it is time to conclude this long epistle, with which I almost fear to have exhausted your patience, notwithstanding the kind interest you are pleased to take in one who considers it her honour and her happiness to subscribe herself,—Your obedient and affectionate daughter in Jesus Christ.

"ANNE AGNES TRAIL.

"*February* 1829."

LETTER II.

"REV. AND DEAR FATHER.—In my letter I gave you an account of the first fourteen years of my life; and I now enter upon that period when the mind, full of ardour and of hope, usually regards the world as an earthly paradise, and deceived by these false ideas, pursues the vain dream of worldly bliss, and often awakes but too late to the sad reality that 'All is vanity and vexation of spirit.' I no doubt shared to a certain degree in the general delusion; but God had early impressed deeply upon my mind,' 'Arise, and depart, for this is not your rest, because it is polluted;' and had made me experimentally to feel that nothing but the favour of God could make me happy; it was indeed my want of certainty as to possessing this favour, which caused all my misery, the depth of which I can hardly now recall without sensations of horror. What might have been the consequence had my mind been left much longer to prey entirely on itself, I know not, but a gracious Providence, without affording me any direct spiritual comfort, yet provided effectually for my relief.

"For upwards of seven years, my dear mother, finding her other household cares too great to allow her to attend as she wished to our education, had employed an accomplished female to instruct us in the various branches of knowledge with which it is thought necessary for women to be acquainted. A few months after I was fourteen she thought it proper to part with this lady, (my elder sister being at the time in England), to consign to me the instruction of my younger brothers and sisters. This occupied me at least eight hours a day; and as I was most anxious for their improvement, my mind was as it were forced from itself, and by degrees I became more calm, and at least less miserable.

"In the course of the same summer we had a visit from a cousin who had lately become very religious, full of enthusiastic piety, and adorned with all the gentle and more amiable virtues. His only pleasure seemed to be either to converse with God in prayer, or of God to others. I was, perhaps, his most deeply interested, as well as his most frequent listener, and I began to long for the same assurance that he seemed to enjoy, of being one of the elect of God. To attain this desirable end I naturally thought the best means was to imitate him as well as I could, and I adopted most of his opinions both as to doctrine and practice. With respect to the former, his sentiments were what are generally termed evangelical; and as to the latter, his ideas were very strict, particularly with regard to an entire renunciation of worldly pleasures and amusements, a thing not very difficult for one who was removed from almost every temptation of entering into them, as I then was. However, though I thought he was right on the whole, I tried to persuade myself that there could be no harm in my seeing a little of such things, that I might judge for myself, which I was always most anxious to do. I confined my reading almost entirely to works on religion, having entirely excluded novels, romances, plays, &c., as either pernicious or useless; I even for a considerable time gave up reading poetry, of which I was passionately fond, that I might bring my imagination into proper subjection.

"Thus passed away three or four years, till, when I was seventeen or eighteen, I went to pay a visit to my mother's relatives in the north of England. I remained with them a year and a half, during which time, though little favourable, I fear, to my growth in internal piety, I still adhered conscientiously to what I considered my religious duty. The first hour of every day I spent in prayer and reading the Scriptures; again, a short time before going to bed, and the whole Sunday after attending church, I devoted to the study of books on religion. On week days I employed my time, of which I was then entire mistress, in cultivating my taste for music and drawing, especially the latter; and in improving my mind by the study of scientific works on botany, astronomy, chemistry, and geology. I also acquired a little general knowledge of the rudiments of natural philosophy, which afforded abundant food for my natural disposition towards ratiocination, a disposition which, if under the guidance of the Spirit of God it has at length been a great instrument in bringing me to the knowledge of the truth, has likewise, when left to its own proud exercise, led me several times to the verge of infidelity. The last few months of my stay in England being passed in a city, and with relatives who seemed to live for little else than amusement, I was immersed in a vortex of gaiety, which produced a deadening influence upon my mind that it did not recover for some time after it was placed in a more healthy atmosphere. For one thing, however, I cannot cease to bless God, that though I was then a good deal in the society of gay and fashionable young men, and of course had my share of attention and adulation, my aversion to the thought of marriage was rather increased by the account I received of the general character and conduct of men of the world; of the corruption of which I had till then little idea. On my return home, I resumed, in conjunction with my eldest sister, the office of instructing the younger ones. I was entirely removed from all the follies of the world, but I had tasted of the Circean cup, and my heart felt a little hankering after it for a few months, till I got hold of a sermon on 'Lovers of pleasure more than lovers of God,' which so completely convinced me of the evil tendency of what are generally termed *amusements*, that I made a determined resolution to renounce them all; and from that day never set my foot in an English theatre or public ball-room, gave up playing at cards or any other games of chance, and almost considered it as a sin for any one to do so.

"These sentiments were soon after strengthened by the arrival of a cousin (sister to the one I before mentioned), endowed with the same piety as her brother; and having passed through affliction, which had entirely weaned her affections from the world, she endeavoured to inspire us all with the same contempt for it, and the same ardent devotion to Christ crucified. She was, I believe, useful to us all, but more particularly to me, in again arousing in me a lively interest for my eternal salvation, and an ardent desire after Christian perfection, which from that time I think I never lost, but which only served again to plunge me into frequent distress. I had most firmly embraced the principle, that faith alone is necessary to salvation; but I believed, likewise, that my faith, if sincere, must inevitably be productive of a holy life, and finding myself still defective in that perfection after which the Christian is urged to aspire, I often fell into doubt whether I believed at all or not, and who was to solve for me this tremendously important question, upon which was to hang my eternal destiny? I could only cast myself trembling into the hands of my Saviour and say, 'Lord, if I have faith, increase it; if I have not yet obtained it, bestow it on me.' 'My God, if I love Thee not as I would, or as Thou deservest to be loved, at least I desire to love Thee above all things, and I desire that I may never be happy in anything short of Thee; that I may never rest satisfied till I have attained the true knowledge of Thee.' Indeed, however much of mental suffering I have had to endure throughout my life, I think I can mark this, that I never so much prayed to be delivered from *it*, as from its *cause;* which I always felt assured must be either sin, ignorance, or unbelief, for it requires but one glance at the Christian religion to perceive that it was intended to proclaim 'Peace even on earth to men of good will.'

"My dear cousin, after a stay with us of about six months, returned to Ireland, carrying me with her, and there I remained for the space of nearly two years; and I look back to it with peculiar pleasure, as having been profitable both for my mental and moral improvement. Animated by the bright example of my cousins, I wished only to imitate them, and heartily united in most of their works of active charity, devoting several hours two or three times a week to instruct the poor children in the ladies' charity school; one or two hours more every Sunday, and frequently on week days, to visit the hospital for the sick, to strive to carry comfort to these children of affliction; to teach those to read who had not previously learnt; to distribute religious tracts to those who had; to exhort the careless or immoral to repentance and amendment; and to give general religious instruction by reading a sermon to the whole assembled together. At other times we visited the poor in their own houses, and there, I acknowledge with gratitude to God, I learned to feel for human misery, and to deny myself almost every superfluity, that I might have wherewithal to relieve at least a small portion of the distressing poverty with which I was surrounded; for who could visit the wretched hovels of the Irish peasantry and not feel that it was indulging a culpable selfishness to throw away even a small sum upon folly or vanity, while numbers around were in want of the bare necessaries of existence! Meanwhile I was no less diligent in cultivating internal devotion; almost all my spare hours were spent in reading and in prayer, in which latter exercise I was often so fervent, that my dear cousin, who was generally in the next room employed in the same way, was at length compelled to entreat me to restrain my vehemence. She observed that my mind was in distress, and I acknowledged it. I remember she replied, '*You* feel in danger of despair, *I* of presumption.' Ah, my dear sir, I believe every thinking Protestant is in danger of being shipwrecked either on the one or the other; for he must either, self-satisfied as to his own discoveries of the truth, believe himself privileged, either by nature or by grace, above every other; or, mistrusting his own conclusions, and equally doubtful of those of others, he is but too likely to fall into despair or infidelity. To God's grace alone I owe that I did not fall into either extreme, but He alone knows how near I have often been.

"I had almost neglected to mention a temptation (for I cannot regard it as anything else) which I had just on my first going to Ireland. We had on board the ship in crossing the Channel, a very clever young gentleman, a Socinian; and as usual we soon began to talk on religion, and we had a long discussion, in which I thought I had controverted his arguments; but they recurred to me afterwards, and excited doubts in my mind with respect to the Holy Spirit; so much so, that for several Sundays, feeling that I could not conscientiously say, 'I believe in the Holy Ghost,' I always missed that part of the creed when read in the Church; but my unbelief, I hope, was not wilful. I was confounded and distressed to find myself in any doubt upon a point which I considered as fundamental and which I had hitherto regarded as certain; though I had not read anything in direct proof. I immediately read Jones on the Trinity, which fully satisfied me, and from that time I never had any further misgiving with respect to the Blessed Trinity. Rest, however, I found none. Being naturally of a very independent mind, strengthened by the circumstances in which I had been placed; and having imbibed as a principle that I ought to search for myself in the Scriptures for the proof of every individual point of faith, you may well imagine I found it no easy matter to satisfy myself. Having many friends of different persuasions, each desirous of drawing me to their own party, I had read and examined the tenets of various sects, comparing them likewise with Scripture; and I came to the conclusion, that all had erred, and that each approximated near to the truth upon some particular point, either of doctrine or practice. These being my sentiments, I thought I might as well remain in the communion of the church in which I was educated, as I could discover none that on the whole appeared better; but as I was still at liberty to adopt what opinions and practices I chose, I did not scruple to select what I thought best out of each, believing this must lead me nearest to primitive and perfect Christianity, and I wished to be called by no other name but that of Christian. One good I gained by this was that I avoided all that prejudice which is the natural result of party spirit; and that I regarded with charity all whom I believed sincerely to love the Lord Jesus. And thus were removed some of the barriers which might have prevented me from seeing the truth, when the Lord's good time was come for placing it before me. How true it is that, 'The Lord leadeth the blind by a way they know not.'

"I cannot but frequently look back with wonder and admiration at my own path, when I mark how nicely every, even the minutest circumstances of my early life were adjusted to forward the Lord's gracious designs with respect to me; how by degrees I was taught, by my own bitter experience, that the principles I had, however conscientiously, acted upon, were unable to conduct me to that certainty of faith, which alone can convey peace to the soul that is anxiously inquiring after truth; again, how my early sentiments on the point of marriage, strengthened, from a diligent perusal of the writings of St. Paul, by the firm persuasion, that in a single life I could devote myself more entirely to the service of God, preserved me from many of those entanglements by which the youthful heart is led but too frequently, if not into sin, at least into folly; whilst the affections are kept from that object which alone can fully satisfy them. Further, how by little and little I was inured to opposition, learned to contemn the opinion of the world when it ran counter to what I believed the will of God; and to sacrifice even my dearest passion, the love of praise, at the shrine of conscience. Whilst in Ireland I gave up, even in private, an exercise of which I was very fond, and in which I thought myself to excel—viz., dancing—that I might the more readily excuse myself from entering into societies whose sole end was that amusement, and to which, much to the mortification of some of my friends, I determinately refused to go.

"On leaving Ireland it was determined that instead of returning home I should go straight to London for the purpose of improving my talent for painting, by affording me the means of studying under some first-rate artist. There I was received by relatives (whose kindness must ever be engraved on my heart) of rank and fortune far superior to me, as if I had been their own child. Their house, carriage, and servants, were all at my command. I found myself in a situation which would have been the envy of most young persons. Placed in the midst of affluence and splendour, having it in my power to be introduced into some of the first society in town, and to enter into all its diversions, God enabled me to stand firm to the resolution I had made, and after a stay of almost six months, I left London without having once entered a place of public amusement, or even having attended a single private *fête*. I cannot say, however, that I effected this without some severe contentions with my own spirit. Too deeply interested in religion to feel the renunciation of worldly pleasure any deprivation, I was yet keenly alive to the love of praise, and I well knew that my principles and practice, on these and some other points, were at utter variance with those of many whose esteem and goodwill it was both my wish and interest to cultivate; and once, especially, I remember, that it cost me some hours of painful internal combat and much earnest prayer, to come to the resolution of refusing an invitation, and giving such a reason as I felt assured would be a tacit condemnation of the person who gave it, and who was one of those who had shown me most kindness and attention. Conscience, however, at last gained the victory, and I had never cause to repent it, even on a worldly account; for I found that by consistency I gained the esteem and confidence of those even who regarded my strictness as blameable, or at least unnecessary; and I had the happiness some years after of receiving the acknowledgment, from some of my friends, 'that my example and conversation then was one of the most powerful causes of turning their attention to the one thing needful.'

"Returned to the bosom of my own family after so long an absence, I need not say I was received with every demonstration of tender affection; but it seemed the will of Providence that I was never again for any length of time to enjoy the sweets of a retired and peaceful home. A friend who was much interested in our welfare, and who knew that my father's circumstances, though comfortable, were not affluent, and who likewise thought it a pity that my talent should be thrown away, proposed to me to take some likenesses for her, for which I was offered a handsome compensation. Having overcome the foolish pride, which first made me feel a repugnance to the idea of doing anything for money, by the reflection that God had not bestowed on me the talent, and afforded me the means of improving it, for nothing; that as I did not wish to marry, the most honourable thing I could do would be to render myself entirely independent of my relatives; and I think that the words of the Apostle, 'Working with your own hands that you may have to give to him that needeth,' had no slight influence on my determination. From that time I continued to exercise my pencil, but more in a private way, for favour, than as a public artist. However, I soon became known, and one of our greatest connoisseurs in the art in our Scotch capital, begged me to do a set of miniatures for him, which occupied me nearly two winters. This naturally led me to reside frequently in town; and there I sought to cultivate chiefly the acquaintance of those who were most noted for their piety and zeal, and sought most earnestly after every means of religious instruction; exhorting at the same time every friend whom I thought to be careless, to seek after his soul's salvation; and defending at all times, and in every society, the cause of religion from the attacks of the worldling or the infidel. But my own breast was not the seat of peace: constantly harassed by doubts for which I could find no solution; sometimes a prey to fears, which however legitimate, I was told was a want of faith; and thus, instead of relief, I was plunged deeper into distress. Thinking myself too unworthy, I had for nearly two years abstained altogether from approaching the communion; but as I had been always changing place, this had passed unobserved, as I could not bring myself to open my mind to any one. At length, however, a friend speaking to me about an approaching solemnity, and taking it for granted I was to go, I acknowledged to her the fact. She was surprised I believe, as I had been for years noted for a more than common devotion to religion. She asked me if I would like to converse on the subject with the Rev. Dr. Gordon, a clergyman of great celebrity both for his talents and piety. I consented, though with some reluctance; he was written to, but ere he could find time to see me, the day arrived. I went to church early, and remained till the evening (at least eight hours), without any refreshment excepting a morsel of biscuit I had carried with me; but the mind was too intensely occupied to think of the body. With a heart almost broken with grief, I saw hundreds receive the Sacrament, which I longed to partake of, but dared not.

"The day at length arrived fixed for my seeing Dr. Gordon, and I approached his gate with nearly as great fear and trembling, as, for the first time, I did your confessional; so naturally averse was my proud heart to acknowledge its wretchedness. I prayed to God, however, several days before and all the way there, to enable me to do so; but when I revealed the state of my mind, I found my pastor little able to help me. How could he? his own heart, I believe, often shared in the same difficulties. Ah, what a heartrending thing for a clergyman to be in any doubt whether he himself knows the truth he is bound by his office to teach to others! His kindness, notwithstanding, encouraged me to return, and I did so several times; yet with little effect; excepting that on the subject of the Eucharist, my apprehensions were entirely removed, by Dr. Gordon succeeding in persuading me most thoroughly, that there was nothing in it, but the simple elements of bread and wine, to give a more lively representation of our blessed Saviour's passion, than could be done by words; and thus to excite our faith more strongly; and that, in short, there was nothing more awful in going to the communion, than in putting ourselves in the immediate presence of God, by prayer or reading the Scriptures. He likewise greatly removed my fears that I might be in, or left to fall into, a state of reprobation, but still I was unsatisfied. Intense search and reflection upon this subject for two months, (during which time I frequently did not sleep more than three or four hours), reduced me so thin, that it was observed by my friends, though they did not know the cause. Alone or in society, by day or by night, I may almost say sleeping or waking, my thoughts revolved but on one subject; all others for me had entirely lost their interest. It would be impossible for me now to state all the doubts and difficulties which suggested themselves to my mind; indeed I must now regard many of them as mere temptations; but unable to distinguish these from my own thoughts, mistaking the fear of unbelief as being itself that deadly sin, advised not to reason with my doubts, whilst at the same time the reasonings of my own feeble intellect, or the meaning of Scripture was to be my only rule of what I ought to believe; I often felt myself like a ship at sea, with a compass indeed, but without a rudder, and without a pilot, or like a drowning person, catching in vain at something to keep his head above the waves.

"Yet, in the midst of this dismal chaos, God gave me sometimes to enjoy a sweet sense of His gracious presence in prayer, and a firm dependence upon that promise, 'Then shall we know if we follow on to know the Lord.' The hope that I should, at some future day, attain, through God's mercy, to the knowledge of the whole truth, afforded me a degree of consolation; but I could not call it peace. It increased, however, with my advancement in practical devotion; in which I hope God enabled me to make some small progress during the three following years; the greater part of which time I passed in Edinburgh where I had every means of grace at my command, that could be afforded in the Protestant faith. My great delight was in hearing sermons, and attending missionary and prayer meetings, where devotion and zeal, however misdirected, are undoubtedly awakened and kept alive. My hours of daylight were generally occupied in the exercise of my pencil, and my evenings, as I had entirely withdrawn from parties, were devoted to reading books on religion, excepting when now and then I went, in a quiet way, to visit some friend, when religion was usually the theme of conversation; indeed, so noted had I become for my lectures and exhortations, that a friend at some distance, seeing an advertisement in the newspaper that a lady was about to preach, concluded instantly that it must be me—a mistake, however, as I never thought of exercising my gift of speech in that way; though had I been a man I should certainly have become a missionary, and the great object of my ambition for my brothers was that they might devote themselves to the service of the Saviour in the work of the ministry, an object for which I offered up many prayers which I hope it will yet please God to answer. For the clerical character I had always a deep reverence; yet from the principles I had imbibed, I could not and I did not yield an implicit credit to any. I cultivated their acquaintance, and listened to them with delight; but if my impression of the meaning of Scripture was different from theirs, I followed my own judgment, and professed openly to do so, knowing them all to be as fallible as myself. This, though the natural result of Protestant principles, led inevitably to a proud dependence on my own opinions, which I perceived to be contrary to the spirit of the Gospel, and much did I pray to be delivered from it: but how are we to attain to the docility of a child, and act in consistency with the right of private judgment?

"Struggling thus between opposing principles, I carried my grief to my pastor. I lamented my want of that childlike disposition, without which Our Saviour had declared 'we could not enter the kingdom of Heaven.' I was told that this very complaint was the result of pride, and a wish to find something in myself to recommend me to God. Faith was declared to be the *all in all;* that is, a firm confidence that I was already saved, and in possession of eternal life. In theory I embraced this, but it sometimes failed me in practice. I was, however, constantly exhorted by my truly pious, though mistaken pastor, to live as became an heir of glory; and this it was my earnest endeavour and prayer to be enabled to do. I hope I truly loved my Saviour, and that it was the chief desire of my heart to please Him, and to induce others to do the same. With this end in view I gave as much money as I could spare to missionary and other religious societies, and prevailed on many of my friends actively to engage in the same. I never missed attending the prayer meetings for their success, and gave an hour every Sunday morning to private prayer for the same object. The diligent employment of my pencil had become in my mind an object of duty; but when I had a spare hour I generally occupied it in some work of charity or devotion, my evenings in study and in prayer. At one thing, I daresay, you will smile, when I tell you, that impressed with the idea that women ought to do all in their power to remedy the evils they were the sad cause of introducing, I took a particular charge of all the young men of my acquaintance. Seeing them, especially in our northern capital, exposed to the seductions of infidelity on the one hand, and profligacy on the other, often from the want of a home and good society, exposed to seek the worst, I used to invite them to come to see me, on purpose to give them good advice, and had the happiness to find it not unfrequently succeed. I became noted for my zeal and intrepidity, and perhaps also, from having made it an object of more deep study than many, and thus generally being ready to render a reason for my opinion, I found my judgment looked up to, not only by my own sex, but the other, and even by clergymen themselves—a sad temptation to a heart like mine, and might have ruined me altogether had not my own frequent doubts and difficulties served to humble me, and keep me always at the foot of the throne of grace; where, I believe, no sincere suppliant was ever rejected. Things were going on thus, and I had reached the age of twenty-eight, when various circumstances made me embrace the resolution of visiting Italy; but as this enters on the most important epoch of my life, I shall reserve it for another letter, and conclude this with subscribing myself—Yours in Jesus Christ.

"ANNE AGNES TRAIL.

"*March* 1829."

LETTER III.

"REV. AND VERY DEAR FATHER,—I cannot resume my pen at this moment without sheddin tears, but they are not those of sorrow but of gratitude. 'Would,' as the prophet expresses it, 'that my head were a fountain of these tears,' that I might pour them out at the foot of the Throne of Grace in thanksgiving to God for His gracious Providence towards me.

"The recollection of the moment of my departure for Italy brings with it a crowd of thoughts and feelings which it would be difficult to express. Eight and twenty years of my life had already passed away, and I think I may safely say that sixteen of these years had been almost uninterruptedly spent in an ardent search after Truth, which seemed constantly to elude my grasp. I had examined, reasoned, and reflected, till at last I had come to the conclusion, that truth without mixture of error was not the possession of any religious body existing on earth. I could not, therefore, be presumptuous enough to think that I alone had found it, or that it was very likely I ever should do so; and I began to strive to rest satisfied with the knowledge of one simple truth of which I felt fully assured, viz., 'That Jesus Christ came into the world to save sinners,' and that 'He that cometh unto Him He will not cast out,' endeavouring at the same time to obey the injunction of the Apostle, 'Be ye followers of God as dear children.' I made it my constant prayer that God would enlighten me more and more, and mould me entirely into His own will, and that He would never suffer me to rest satisfied, or enjoy happiness, till I was truly what He would have me to be. I never entered upon any project of importance, I never changed my abode, nay, I believe, I seldom went to pay a visit of civility or charity, or even to take a walk, without seeking first the direction and blessing of God. Thus, you may well suppose, that when it was proposed to me by some of my friends to visit Italy in order to improve my taste for painting, I did not make up my mind to do so till I had made it a matter of earnest prayer, and felt fully satisfied that it was the path which Providence at that time meant me to follow.

"As to all my worldly plans and prospects, it was certainly the most eligible step I could take. I was urged to it by several friends, and had the full concurrence of every other who had any right to interfere; my parents had given their full and ready consent, and my favourite pastor, whom I also consulted on the occasion, gave it as his opinion that it would be rather for my spiritual good than detriment. Under such circumstances, could I doubt that in going I was following the will of God? Yet I can hardly express the distress I suffered at the idea of abandoning the privileges I then enjoyed, and casting myself, as I thought, into a barren wilderness with respect to spiritual things. Indeed, desirable as it was to me on many accounts, I never could have brought my mind to it, had it not been the firm persuasion that it was the path of duty, and being so, I felt assured God would supply me with the necessary grace; my chief prayer was that it might be for His glory and my spiritual good. I frequently put up the petition of Moses, 'Except Thy presence go with me, carry me not up hence.' Having with a sad heart listened to the last advice of my beloved pastor, and bid him and my other friends farewell, having fixed upon an hour for mutual prayer, in which we were to recommend each other at the Throne of Mercy, and having passed a few days with my own family, I set off on my journey, accompanied only by the prayers of my Christian friends; for I went quite alone, at which some expressing a little anxiety, I replied, that I felt such confidence in the protection of my heavenly Father, that I felt safer in simply committing myself to Him than if I had an army around me. With this sentiment, you may believe, I felt no vain fears, either in the prospect, or during the progress of my journey; my simple prayer all the way was: 'Let Thy presence go with me, and do Thou give me rest.' At London, where I remained about a fortnight, I was chiefly engaged in seeking my own spiritual improvement and that of my dear relatives, and especially in praying for and using every effort for the conversion of *one* who was sceptical as to the Christian religion; but as he had a pious sister, I agreed with her for an hour of prayer for him and another brother who was in the same situation. Another hour every Sunday morning, besides my public and private devotions, I set apart for prayer, in union with many whom I knew to be occupied in the same way and at the same hour, for the success of Christianity throughout the world. I mention these things to show the confidence I felt in the efficacy of united prayer, the beautiful spirit of which in the Catholic Church was one of the things in which my mind first sympathised, and which struck me most forcibly in entering Catholic countries. The churches always open, the people assembled at the evening Benediction or during the day; the scattered, yet united worshippers, at their silent devotions, was a spectacle my heart could not resist, and I generally knelt down that my prayers might ascend with theirs; yet, believing their mode of worship erroneous, I frequently added a petition for them, and entreated the Father of Lights, to deliver His Church from all darkness and error. My God! how can I sufficiently thank Thee, or admire, that the prayers I thought to offer up for others, were for myself, and that Thou didst in mercy return them into my own bosom! My general sentiments with respect to the Catholic religion at the time of my leaving England were, that it was grossly superstitious, and in some instances perhaps even idolatrous, but this only amongst the ignorant; the priests I believed frequently as ignorant as their flocks, and such I regarded as objects of compassion; but I could not exculpate the more talented and learned from the charge of wilfully deceiving the people, by teaching them for doctrines the commandments of men, fancying they taught them to rely more on a multitude of outward observances than on the purity and devotion of the heart. To counteract this evil, I carried with me for distribution a quantity of Scripture and other tracts, not, however, directly attacking any doctrine of the Catholic faith, though, I doubt not, they would do so insidiously, but chiefly, as I thought, to lead from outward to internal religion. Upon the same plan, I endeavoured, according to the advice of my pastor, to regulate my own conduct, by showing in my every action the influence of Christian principles, that others, without the word, might be won by my example.

"To Paris I carried letters of introduction to several of the most eminent and zealous Protestants, clergymen and others, who were most actively engaged in Bible Missionary Societies; and my zeal for such institutions, made me be received by them all with distinguished marks of affection; and I suppose, from the liberality of my sentiments, I gained during my short stay the confidence of all. By this means I likewise discovered their clashing opinions, and suspicions of each other: this grieved me; for I knew that Christians should be united, and not regard each other with bitterness. But though I lamented the effect, I had no suspicion of the cause; yet, I doubt not, it was in the designs of Providence that I should perceive the evils of Protestantism, whilst still its undoubting and zealous advocate, for the right of private judgment was to me the dearest that I possessed, and which I allowed no one to dispute with me, though on the principle of the Apostle I sometimes abstained from what I thought lawful, that I might not offend a weak brother, I defended, nevertheless, my *absolute right* to follow in religious matters the dictates of my own conscience; and this, I frankly acknowledged, did not agree entirely with the principles of any sect, nor could have allowed me to be the minister of any; as I could not have conscientiously sworn to their articles of faith. Yet though I could not entirely coincide with any Protestant profession of faith with which I was acquainted, still further was I removed from what I had always been taught was that of

Catholics; and not doubting but that the representation had been correct, I had no intention whatever of inquiring into their doctrines. The external splendour of their worship had for me no attractions, as I believe my chief reason for preferring the Presbyterian to the Episcopal Church, was the simplicity of its forms and the republican nature of its government, two points in which it is farthest removed from the Catholic. The first impression made upon my mind by the multiplicity of representations of the Crucifix, Dead Christ, &c., too frequently executed with wretched taste, was that of disgust; processions, &c., seemed to me things for the amusement of children, so that I may truly say there was nothing in the outward form of the Catholic religion which tended to conciliate me; on the contrary (as I think must always be the case where the surface alone is regarded), there was much to confirm my preconceived prejudices; but happily God had endowed me with a mind that was never satisfied with barely surveying the surface of anything; and I never lost an opportunity of inquiring into the purpose and meaning of everything of which I was a spectator, and *that*, if possible, always from Catholics themselves, convinced their information must always be the most correct. Thus by degrees my prejudices against many outward observances were removed, and the more I entered into the meaning of the various ceremonies and institutions of the Catholic Church, the more did I perceive how well they were calculated to inspire and increase devotion in the generality of minds. Besides, after remaining some time in Italy, I could not shut my eyes to the fact, that amongst the people there was much more of the primitive spirit of Christianity than even amongst our most enthusiastic religionists. I perceived amongst them that humility and docility of spirit for which you may almost search in vain in our Protestant land. I perceived that respect for, and devotion to, their clergy; that love for the service of the sanctuary, not only on *one* but *every day* of the week, which from the writings of the Apostles we find animated the first followers of the Redeemer. I saw, too, a noble generosity in contributing of their temporal substance to the purposes of religion, which is so lamentably deficient in Britain; for notwithstanding the large sums which are lavished upon missions and Bible societies, and some other things which happen to be the fashion of the day, yet with what difficulty do we contrive to pay an additional clergyman, or raise a new church even where the glaring deficiency is acknowledged by all. Here, too, charity was not blazoned to the public, but the rule followed, 'Let not thy right hand know what thy left hand doeth.'

"Then, religious zeal was evidently so much more universal, and also the real spirit of charity, which mourns over the errors it cannot but condemn. Revolving in my mind these observations, I often said to myself, how is it that a religion so full of error is yet more imbued with the genuine spirit of Christianity than one which is freer from it? Still, early prejudice was so strong, that a suspicion never entered my mind that it might possibly be the true faith; but a natural love of justice made me acknowledge whatever I saw among Catholics that was good, and defended their conduct from many of the unworthy motives imputed to them most uncharitably by Protestants; and while I still lamented over, and prayed against their supposed errors in faith and worship, I often reproved my fellow-countrymen and women for their indecent behaviour while attending the latter. I endeavoured myself, as much as possible, to unite in the general spirit of devotion, though disapproving of the mode in which that devotion was manifested.

"In the public ceremonies in which the Pope made his appearance, my mode of acting was, I believe, somewhat singular; whenever it appeared to me that the homage that was paid him partook more of the temporal than the spiritual sovereign, I bent my knee as I would have done to my own prince; but if it was attempted to be exacted from me as an acknowledgment of his spiritual dominion, I peremptorily refused to do so — on both occasions regardless of what was done or thought by others—for I detested alike the insolent rudeness manifested by some who pretended to despise *popery*, and, in fact, contemned all religion and all authority, and the crouching servility of others, who could bow before *one* whom they inwardly despised and openly abused as an impostor and a hypocrite. Personally, I always esteemed and defended the Pope, Leo XII., because from everything I heard I believed him to be a good man and zealous for the religion which he believed to be true; and I condemned loudly the want of charity, shown even by many of my most pious acquaintances, in imputing to him, and the Catholic hierarchy and clergy in general, the most flagitious conduct, and the worst of motives for the best actions. Ah! where had the gentle spirit of Christianity fled, when Christian could thus accuse his fellow-Christians of crimes that would have caused a heathen land to blush? For I dare say, I need not tell you, dear Father, that the immorality of the clergy is one of the great bugbears held up to frighten Protestants from the Catholic faith. I must confess that the first few individuals of that body whom I met with, were not calculated to make a favourable impression; but I felt always unwilling to believe that the mass of the ministers of *even an adulterated Christianity* could wish to seduce the people committed to their care; and I rejoiced when further observation convinced me that the accusation was groundless; and that if among Catholics there were likewise some who abused their priests, I generally found them to be those who sought in the errors of their teachers an excuse for a conduct at variance with the precepts they taught; but as I found them beloved and respected by the most pious, I could not reasonably doubt they were as a body worthy of that affection and esteem.

"Character, and the causes which contribute to form a certain state of society, had always been favourite objects of my study, and of course claimed their share of attention in a country so interesting as Italy, where from constantly residing in families of the middle class, while I visited a few of the higher, I had opportunities which few possess of forming a correct judgment. It appeared to me that (contrary to what I had been led to expect), if some crimes were more common, the balance on the whole was rather in favour of Italy—at all events not against it; whilst, at the same time, the overbearing pride and self-conceit of my own countrymen, so contrary to the spirit of the Gospel, forced themselves upon me in a very striking manner. Still, however, during the first winter of my stay at Rome, I may say, that my prejudices were removed rather from Catholics, than from Catholicism, which I continued to regard as a most erroneous system; and I well remember that when a young priest, for whom I had a great esteem on account of his virtues and amiable qualities, made some little attempts to bring me over, I told him it was much more probable that the cardinals, clergy, and people of Rome should all turn Protestants, than that *I* should turn *Roman Catholic.* Unaccustomed to reason with heretics, his arguments brought no conviction to my mind, but his affectionate earnestness, his evidently ardent desire for my conversion (for which he assured me he prayed and fasted, and would willingly shed the last drop of his blood), convinced me of the sincerity of his own faith, and manifested a spirit that is rare indeed among Protestants, but which I had often longed to find. Once he said to me, 'I think you believe in and love the Lord Jesus, and therefore I hope we shall meet in Paradise,' —'A very liberal sentiment,' said I, 'for a Catholic priest.' But when he explained himself, I found that his hopes were founded on an assurance of my sincerity, and love of the truth, and that therefore God would not fail to give me more light, and that I should finally become a Catholic—

a thing I thought nearly as impossible as that I should become a Mahometan.

"But God's thoughts are not as our thoughts, and how wonderful are the ways of His divine Providence, and how great His goodness towards them that seek Him, which I continued to do constantly and earnestly in private prayer. On Sundays I was one of the most regular attendants at church and communion, and I had likewise joined myself to a few pious Protestants who met privately once a week for prayer, reading and expounding the Scriptures; and conversation on their eternal interests. I went very little into general society, and usually spent my evenings as formerly in study and prayer;—and these were the sweetest moments I enjoyed. Now and then some friends called, and they often wondered to find me so solitary and yet so cheerful; but they knew not that I never felt less alone than when left in peace to converse with God.

"I esteem it as an especial Providence, that from the time I left home I never enjoyed a more comfortable state of mind; and harassed by no particular doubts or difficulties, I could more calmly turn my attention to the contemplation of religion in general; and it likewise precludes the suspicion that unhappiness in my own faith made me think of embracing the Catholic religion. Quite the contrary:

my spirit was entirely at rest; an entire abandonment into the hands of Providence made me take no thought for the morrow with regard to temporal things; a firm confidence in the paternal care of my Heavenly Father made me, in every difficulty and danger, fly to His protection; and I had met some wonderful deliverances in direct answer to prayer—a humble hope in my Redeemer's merits, whilst my own conscience, which acquitted me of indulging in any wilful offence against God, made me regard futurity rather with joy than dread.

"Such, as far as I can recollect, was the state of my heart and judgment when an apparently accidental occurrence turned my mind to the study of that faith which I had hitherto regarded as so erroneous, but in which I now hope ever to subscribe myself—Your obedient and affectionate daughter in Jesus Christ, ANN AGNES TRAIL.

"ROME, *April.*"

LETTER IV.

"REV. AND DEAR FATHER,—I do not require to tell you, who are so intimately acquainted with my interior, that my besetting sins were the pride of intellect and the love of praise. Aware, however, of these defects, and I trust sincerely desirous that they should be subdued, and every thought brought into the obedience of Christ—though I had been much flattered on my reasoning powers, and felt a great pleasure in their exercise and display—I had, ever since my entering Italy, rather avoided discussions on religion with Catholics, (though I doubted not but that I had truth on my side), lest in doing so for the love of argument, or in the spirit of pride, God might as a punishment allow me to fall into error.

"At length, however, being at a party one evening, I was placed near a lay prelate, Monsignor Zacchia, afterwards Cardinal Priest and Governor of Rome, a clever man, with whom I had previously had several conversations, but always on indifferent subjects. That evening, however, I hardly know how it came about, but the conversation turned on religion, and he began to press me to pay attention to the Catholic faith, offering at the same time his services to answer any objections or clear up any doubts I might have. Doubts indeed I had none, but plenty of objections, and I had little idea of becoming a learner, where I deemed myself rather in condition of being the teacher. I felt no wish to enter into discussion with him, but I feared that my refusal might be taken as an acknowledgment of the weakness of my cause, and thought it would be tantamount to a denial of the *truth*. I therefore accepted his challenge, and an evening was fixed for his paying me a visit.

"I attached a good deal of importance to this meeting, and when the day arrived, on bidding farewell to a dear friend with whom I had dined, and who was, I believe, the only one acquainted with the circumstance, I begged her to pray for me; I made no other preparation. About nine o'clock Monsignor came, and we instantly began a discussion which proved so animated and interesting, that it was an hour past midnight when, looking at his watch, he felt that propriety compelled him to withdraw, though we were still in the midst of our argument. I thought I had sustained my cause very well, by abundance of Scripture quotations, which of course I applied in my own way. At that time I knew nothing of the writings of the Old Fathers, and besides, told my opponent I would give nothing for the whole of them if they spoke against the truth. No suspicion as yet had entered my mind that the *truth* might possibly be in the system I was so strongly opposing. No way daunted, however, by my pertinacity, perhaps perceiving that my warm opposition was more the result of ignorance than determined prejudice, my friend returned to the charge in about ten days, and we had another discussion of about three hours, which, though it did not in the least convince me of the truth, yet showed me Catholic faith, and affected me very deeply with the thought of the difficulty of finding the truth. Here, thought I, are two; each thinks the other in dreadful error, each sincerely anxious for the other's eternal interest; and yet, how are we to know who is right? I believe I am; but it is possible it may be otherwise. Has our merciful Heavenly Father left us no sure means to ascertain this? Oh, the agony of this uncertainty! With a pain at my heart, and I believe tears in my eyes, I bid Monsignor farewell in these words: 'Your arguments only show me more the need we all have to ask the aid of the Holy Spirit to enlighten us;' and he was no sooner gone than I think I knelt down to pray for him and myself.

"I had no further conversation at that time with Monsignor, as a few days after I left Rome with two friends, a clergyman and his wife, to make a tour round the north of Italy; but previously I received from my zealous friend a book, which I had promised him to read attentively and as far as possible without prejudice. It was 'Forest's Method of Instruction for the Protestants, to bring them back to the Church of Rome.' For my note of thanks for this book I wrote:—'If it contains the truth, I pray God to enable me to perceive and embrace it; if error, I pray to be preserved from its contamination.' This prayer, offered in the sincerity of my heart, and repeated, I believe, every time I opened that book, ascended, I doubt not, to the Hearer and Answerer of prayer, as you will find by the sequel.

"The evening before I left Rome, which was I think about the 20th of May, my friends and I went to take a last look at St. Peter's. We entered that noble temple, calculated to inspire devotion into the coldest heart; but at that moment every circumstance conspired to make us feel its power: it was the hour of Complin; my friends sat down to hear the music, and I knelt down to pray, as I thought, for the Catholics; but in reality for myself, as I offered up the petition, that God would deliver His Church from all error, and enlighten all with the light of His truth. On my return to the house, I received a farewell visit from the young priest I formerly mentioned, who sitting down by me, expressed his sorrow at my departure, especially in ignorance of the truth; 'But,' said he, 'I hope God will yet hear my prayers for you; since the first day I knew you, I have always prayed for you, and I will continue to do so every day in the Mass, along with my mother and sisters.' 'I pray for you too,' said I. 'Ah!' exclaimed he, with great energy, 'thank God I was born a Catholic, or I might have been worse than you, for your error is that of birth and education, more than of the heart; *that* is too good.' This might have been considered a compliment; but it was not a time for adulation; and I was too much affected to feel flattered; on the contrary, I was grieved, because I thought his expression savoured of an error, of which I believed Catholics guilty, *that* of counting too much on human merit, and I immediately disclaimed the application of the term 'too good,' either to myself, or any human being. He said, 'I do not mean before God; *there* we are all sinners, but only with respect to man.' I was more satisfied with this reply, and besides was not in a humour to enter into controversy. He bid me 'Adieu,' entreating me to seek my salvation by searching into the truth of the Catholic faith. I did not indeed expect to find my salvation there; but after all that had passed, I should have almost felt myself culpable in not paying some attention to the subject; and I resolved to do so as soon as I was again settled, and prayed God to remove from me all prejudice, that I might view the question fairly.

"We set out on our tour, and at Florence I received from a great friend, a Swiss clergyman, the Communion for the last time in the Protestant Church. I there likewise refused two offers, either of which, had I accepted, would in all probability have defeated the Lord's gracious designs with respect to me; and I can only attribute it to His kind care that I still retained my preference for a single life, or I should probably have yielded my hand to one who was possessed of almost every quality I could have desired in a husband. I love in these incidents to mark an overruling Providence constantly exercised on my behalf.

"We continued our tour to Venice, where we immediately paid a visit to the English Consul, Mr. Monney, a most worthy and pious man, but an ardent Protestant. By him and his lady I was received as an old friend, though we had never before met; and they pressed me to return and spend the winter with them—an invitation which it would have delighted me to accept; but having left a large picture unfinished at Rome, I was obliged to decline. While at Venice we happened to go into a church at the hour when they were teaching the 'Dottrino,' and both I and my clerical friend were much struck and delighted at their mode of giving instruction, and also with two sermons we heard, which appeared to us both admirable doctrine. All these things made an impression which, if not at the time, were useful afterwards when my eyes began to open to the light of truth.

"From Venice we proceeded to Milan and the

Lakes, where I met a countryman, a convert to the Catholic faith, and who knowing something of my family, expressed a wish to see me, and showed me great kindness and attention. I felt great curiosity to see him, and measured his skull with a scrutinising eye to see whether he had got a competent quantum of brain or not; still so strongly was my mind impressed with the absurdity of many Catholic doctrines, that when he took me to see the body of the great St. Carlo Borromeo, I stood unmoved, while he bowed in reverence; on which, and I believe some other things, I remarked on leaving the church. I had now bid farewell to my dear friends, and proceeded alone to Parma, for the purpose of making a copy of the celebrated St. Jerome of Correggio. *Parma* I must ever recall with great interest, as *there* was first awakened in my mind *that doubt* which, by being resolved, ended all those which had harassed me for years; but I must proceed, if I can, with order. I entered an Italian family, to whom I carried a letter of introduction from Rome, and the mistress of which was a perfect example of unaffected piety and virtue, but had neither talents nor learning for controversy; the husband still less inclined to enter upon it, so that religion was only spoken of in a general way. There were no English residents, and I made no acquaintances excepting a few of the professors of the art I had gone to cultivate; so that my time was uninterrupted and my mind left free to ruminate, without any one to bias it, on the important subject to which God was about powerfully to call my attention.

"In the midst of a city my soul almost enjoyed the solitude of a cloister: eight or nine hours daily employed at my painting; the remainder of my time, except perhaps a solitary ramble along the walls or in the palace garden, I passed in my own apartment reading or writing—quiet without and peace within. This state of isolation was a singular Providence, as it removed me entirely from the influence either of Protestant or Catholic friend; and if, on looking around me, I might have said, 'No man careth for my soul,' I believe my gracious Heavenly Father was taking it under His more peculiar care. It was the first time in my life that I had been placed where there was no Protestant place of worship, and to remedy, as far as I could, the want of it, I used regularly at the hour our church met for worship at home, to shut myself up in my room, and strive to unite in spirit with them, by reading or singing a psalm or hymn, then proceeding to prayer and the reading of Scripture, in which way I occupied the usual time of divine service. I generally likewise spent some time, morning or evening, in some Catholic church, that

I might have the pleasure of offering up my devotions in what I still considered the house of prayer, though polluted by superstition. There, too, among the fervent adorers, I could not doubt that many were worshipping God in spirit and in truth. During these visits I remembered the deep devotion of Catholics, especially whilst at communion, and I believed it to be the effect of their peculiar belief. 'The effect is good,' said I, 'but is the cause a truth? I believe not. Yet, if the Catholic religion were not full of error, it is certainly furnished with much more abundant means of salvation than the Protestant.' These observations caused me to reflect deeply, and I could not unravel the mystery, that a faith which I had been always taught was so corrupt, should be productive of such effects. But the time was at hand when the scales were to fall from my eyes, and the pure light of divine faith, without mixture of error, was to burst on my astonished sight.

"I had read the greater part of Forest's work, and my mind was as yet untouched by the force of the arguments, when I came to the subject of the Blessed Eucharist. To part of the reasoning on that too I had replied, but ere I came to the conclusion, I was forced to acknowledge the Catholics had all fair arguments on their side. I instantly laid hold of my Bible, and turned to every text that I thought could in the least bear on the subject; and I saw clearly that Scripture likewise, if taken in its literal sense, was all for them, and I said to myself, 'If, in this doctrine alone, Catholics are right, though in error on other points, it were well to be a Catholic; but how am I to know in what sense my Saviour means me to take these words?—that is all I desire: to accept them as He wishes me.' This doubt excited others with respect to the foundation of the Protestant faith, and threw my mind into great agitation. I prayed, but I knew I had no right to expect a miraculous interposition of Providence, and that it was my duty to make use of every means in my power for discovering the truth; and I instantly resolved on applying to a Catholic divine, a good old Franciscan friar, confessor to my landlady, and who was generally esteemed for his learning and piety. I had made his acquaintance about ten days before, when at my request she had asked him to dinner, and when I was afraid I had hurt his feelings by some remarks I had made. I took up my pen, however, and first made an apology, or rather asked his forgiveness, and frankly stated the doubt that had arisen in my mind, requesting a conversation with him. Next morning I carried the note to the convent, and sent it in. The good Father, surprised, you may believe, but pleased, granted my request, and offered to call on me. I preferred, however, going to him, as I was desirous no one should know.

"I can never forget the scene of our first conference—conducted through the church into the sacristy, where the good old man, beckoning me to follow, led me into a little cell furnished with two chairs, shut the door, and sat down. I immediately put a number of questions to him with respect to how he felt on receiving the Blessed Eucharist, and a number of other things, some of which were curious enough; amongst the rest, whether he had ever repented becoming a friar. In short, I believe I ran over the greater part of the common Protestant objections to the Catholic faith. He heard everything with the greatest patience, and his replies pleased me much, and enlightened my mind on many points, both of doctrine and practice on which I was either entirely ignorant or grossly misinformed. I repeated my visit several times, and every time I came home with a deeper impression that the Catholic faith was *probably* the true one, and the conflict this raised in my mind, I cannot express. On the one hand, anxiety to know the truth made me wish and determine to search further; on the other, the fear of being seduced into error, made me almost afraid to yield my judgment even to arguments which seemed most convincing. This was my chief fear, and made me act with the greatest caution; and oh! with what earnestness, I may say agonising prayer, did I entreat God not to punish my pride by allowing me to be deluded, and this, not only for my own sake, but likewise that I might not be a scandal to others.

"Then the situation in which I should be placed, should I change my religion, arose to my mind in all its horror; slighted and contemned by those who had hitherto honoured and courted me; regarded as an outcast from grace, and pointed out as a beacon to warn others, by those religious persons who had heretofore marked me as an example to be followed, and for whose esteem and regard I had most value; perhaps abandoned by my friends and relatives, many of whom I knew to be most hostile to the Catholic faith. But what wounded me most deeply was the thought of the affliction into which I knew I must inevitably plunge my beloved parents and family—perhaps I may bring my father's grey hairs with sorrow to the grave, perhaps I may break the tender heart of my affectionate mother, of whom I have hitherto been the pride; my own will break soon, too, thought I, but no matter, I must follow the dictates of my conscience; but, if my conscience be mistaken, what then? to lose *all* for *this* world and the *next!* Yet, would my Saviour suffer this, when I am willing to sacrifice everything I value most, even life itself, for His sake? Nay, when, were I even sure of being saved in the Protestant faith, yet should the Catholic faith be more pleasing to Him, I would embrace it at the hazard of all I possess in the world. Surely no!

"Ah, my dear Father, could you but conceive half of what I then suffered, you would weep with me now. Without a friend to whom I could reveal my distress;—in fear whether God was not at that moment forsaking me, I could only cling closer to Him and entreat Him not to abandon me. If stones could speak, those of St. Giovanni would bear witness to my sighs and tears; for there, usually as I returned from my painting, I retired to pray and meditate; and I sometimes withdrew into the most obscure chapel, where, throwing myself down on the pavement, with my forehead on the cold marble steps of the altar, I would truly pour out my heart before God, to beseech Him to preserve, or deliver me from error, and to enlighten me with the light of truth—the whole truth. Then, my God! let me suffer what Thou wilt—nay, I would rather suffer, should it be more for Thy glory and the honour of religion. From two things alone, I think, I prayed God to spare me; that, should the Catholic religion be the true one, and God enabled me to perceive and embrace it, I might not be doomed to break the hearts of my parents, nor be myself reduced to the necessity of accepting a partner. I know I prayed likewise that I might have no worldly inducement, that I might feel more sure of my own sincerity, and that the world might not be able to impute an interested motive. How graciously my Heavenly Father heard and answered all these prayers. Ah, pray for me, that I may correspond to so much mercy by an entire devotion of myself, body, soul, and spirit, to God.

"Thus passed the last six weeks of my stay in Parma; for I find, by the date of various letters, that the first serious doubt entered my mind about the 20th of September. I left Parma on All Souls' Day; on the preceding evening I went to bid farewell to the dear old Father who had with such patience done all he could to instruct me, by conversations, letters, and books. He wept as I kissed his hand (the first time in my life I had ever condescended to do so to any one), and said he felt assured God would show me the truth; assured me he would never forget to pray for me, and conjured me to let him know as soon as I should feel convinced, and embrace the Catholic Faith,—which I promised to do.

"I resolved to return to Rome by way of Loretto, that I might see that celebrated sanctuary. Doubtful with respect to its miraculous history, I yet felt it was an object of deep interest, as the reputed place of the incarnation of the blessed Redeemer, and I entered it with a feeling inexpressible, and a wish or half expectation that God might there show me some miracle, which should make me know the truth. I knelt down in it to pray, while my companions went through the usual ceremony of kissing the Scudello, &c. I think I kissed it too, but I am not sure. After remaining about an hour to see all the treasures, &c., we passed on towards Rome, my mind still immersed in doubt and distress. But the further progress of my convictions I shall reserve for another letter; and meanwhile subscribe myself, with grateful devotion towards you, dear Father in Jesus Christ—Your obedient and affectionate daughter,

"ANNE AGNES TRAIL."

LETTER V.

"REV. AND VERY DEAR FATHER,—From the circumstances I recounted to you in my last letter, you would naturally conclude that I returned to Rome with a firm determination to inform myself fully, and to satisfy myself thoroughly whether or not the Catholic was indeed that Faith once delivered to the saints; and for this purpose I brought with me letters to two ecclesiastics who should be competent to give me every information.

"Had I allowed myself in the least degree to be guided by my feelings, I should certainly have delivered these letters immediately; but when the first serious doubt entered my mind, I had written to my much esteemed pastor, Dr. Gordon, and likewise to a learned and pious female friend; and I felt that it was acting both most prudently and most conscientiously, to wait at least some time for an answer to the former, before I proceeded further in my inquiries.

"According to my calculation, there had already been ample time for a reply, and the urgent nature of the letter led me to expect it would be answered without delay; three weeks, however, passed away, and still not a line; till at length I judged it my duty to wait no longer, and kneeling down in prayer to my Heavenly Father to direct me, I went straight to the post, taking with me my letters of introduction, resolved that should I find nothing, I would deliver them without loss of time. My inquiries were all in vain, so that it appeared to me that without a direct resistance to the manifest will of Providence, I could not do otherwise than proceed in my search with respect to the Catholic Faith.

"I returned not to the house, but turned my steps towards St. Calisto, in order to find a Benedictine, Abbot Beni, to whom one of my letters was addressed. He was at home, and after having read the letter, he offered his services to give me any instruction I should wish, and asked me the points on which I was most anxious to be satisfied. I mentioned several, especially that of the Blessed Eucharist; he promised to procure me books and to call on me. On leading me through the church he bowed before the altar, and perceiving my unaltered attitude, he took me by the arm, saying, 'I bowed to the Holy Sacrament, and I hope it will not be long ere you do the same.' I replied, 'When I am convinced: never till then,' and walked away. I believe he thought he had got a most stubborn animal to deal with, for I would not be satisfied with hearing or even seeing in modern books quotations from the ancient Fathers, but insisted on seeing them in the original ponderous folio Latin volumes which I could not read, but I had them translated for me by a learned Protestant, that I might not be cheated by a false or partial construction of the text. My Protestant friend, however, was obliged to allow, that the testimony of these great luminaries of the Christian Church was quite in favour of the Catholic belief, and the more I read, the more I became convinced of this fact. A glance, too, at Bossuet's 'Variations of the Protestant Churches,' &c., showed me how false were the principles, and how unchristian the motives, which led to, as well as the mode in which was conducted, the pretended Reformation.

"The mist of prejudice began to disperse before the rising light of the Sun of Faith, but it was by slow degrees, as my habits of reasoning led me to fight every inch of ground; and though I began to perceive something of the folly of the so much boasted right of private judgment in matters of faith, yet in practice I knew not how to give it up.

"Meanwhile I may say, I spent day and night in earnest prayer; for my sleep was broken by the agitation of my mind, and I often arose in the midst of it to throw myself on my knees; and during the day, though I regularly employed my pencil, it did not hinder the aspirations of my heart towards Him who is in every place. Besides, my painting itself afforded me food for meditation, as the subject was the Mass of Bolsena, the history of which, you know, regards the Real Presence in the Blessed Sacrament. My employment thus leading me to the Vatican, was fraught with another advantage, that of having it in my power to visit St. Peter's almost daily, and there every morning, before I began my work, I used to go to the altar of the Blessed Sacrament and pray to my divine Redeemer, that if He were really present in the Sacred Host, He would make me know it, and ere long to receive Him in the Communion. I believe I owed much, very much, to these prayers, and oh, how much more to that grace that caused me to offer them, and then answered them so abundantly! It is singular that from the time the first doubt arose in my mind, I was never again permitted to receive the Lord's Supper in the Protestant communion, though I had the wish and intention of doing so more than once; for I still considered it my duty to attend public worship, and I did so for several months after my return to Rome. The first time, however, that I went with the intention of receiving the communion I was taken ill, and obliged to leave the church just before the commencement of the service. The second time that I had the intention of going, it came on such a heavy rain that I could not possibly go, as I was at a considerable distance; and instead, I ran across to a Catholic church which was opposite, where I prayed, during Mass, for the service I think I did not then thoroughly understand. A third occasion occurred, but by that time my mind, though not completely satisfied, was so far convinced of the truth of the Catholic faith—at least upon that head—that my conscience would not allow me to partake.

"The Carnival season then came on, and instead of going to any of the public diversions, I went with some Italian friends to the Pauline Chapel to pray. Soon after, at my particular request, the same friends introduced me to the Rev. A. Magee, one of the friars of the SS. Apostoli, to whom I acknowledge myself much indebted for his unwearied attention and perseverance in giving me instruction, and procuring me able English works, which have been of great service to me. You may imagine how glad I was to be able to converse on the subject in my native tongue and with one of my own countrymen; for hitherto all my discussions had been with foreigners, who could not altogether enter into my sentiments, nor make the necessary allowance for my prejudices. A few days after I made the acquaintance of Mr. Magee, I requested the Italian Prelate who first spoke to me, to introduce me to the English Bishop—Right Rev. Dr. Baines, and they had the kindness to call upon me both together. God had thus afforded me ample means of instruction, of which I was not slow to avail myself; but it was like Nicodemus when he came to our Lord by night—I did not wish it to be known. As my convictions strengthened, however, my boldness increased; and my friends, beginning to suspect my change of sentiments, wrote to the Protestant clergyman, and begged his interference. He offered me a visit, which I most readily accepted; for I had no desire but that of knowing the truth. Yet fully aware of the feelings with which he would naturally regard me, I felt a considerable degree of agitation at the prospect of the announced visit. To assist me, I had previously written out several of the questions I meant to put; but in the morning of the appointed day, as soon as I got up, I went, as was my frequent practice, to look into my Bible for a text, and I opened upon, 'Think not beforehand, neither do ye premeditate, for it shall be given you in that self-same hour what ye shall speak.' Whether erroneously or not, I immediately applied these words to myself, and considering my written preparation as a want of faith, I tore the paper in pieces—confiding, that if the truth were on my side, 'the Lord would be to me a mouth and wisdom which none should be able to gainsay or resist,' and if not, that He would make use of Mr. Burgess as an instrument to show it me.

"I believe I spent nearly two hours before his arrival in earnest prayer; that his visit might be for the elucidation of truth, that we might meet in the spirit of mutual Christian charity, and that God would sustain me in the novel circumstance in which I was then placed, of meeting as an opponent the minister of a party I had hitherto warmly supported, and acknowledging myself seeking for wholesome food for my soul, in a field which he thought only covered with poisonous weeds. My soul was deeply agitated, but as I arose from my knees God brought most seasonably and strongly to my remembrance the words of the inspired Prophet, '*Fear not*, for *I* am with thee; be not dismayed, for I am thy God, I will strengthen thee, yea, I will help thee, yea, I will uphold thee with the right hand of My righteousness.'

"Soon after Mr. Burgess made his appearance, and on my thanking him for his visit, he apologised for not having called on me earlier; mentioning several mutual friends, &c. As I wished to let him know I was quite aware of the motive of his coming, I said, 'I believe, Mr. Burgess, I am indebted for this visit to ——,' naming the friend who had written to him. 'Yes,' he replied, 'but had I known, I should have called earlier as your clergyman; for,' said he, rather pointedly, 'you are one of *my flock*, are you not?' I felt it was better to be quite open, and answered with emphasis, 'I *was* one.' With apparent surprise he said, 'And surely you can have no thought of leaving us?' 'Very serious thoughts,' said I. He then expressed his astonishment that one who had known the truth and been distinguished for my religion as I had, should think of abandoning the faith, &c. We then began to discuss several points of doctrine; and seeing—what I suppose he did not expect—that I had a reason ready on every point, he began to try to confound me with some sophistical quibbles. As soon as I perceived this, I said, 'Mr. Burgess, I thought you came with the intention of elucidating truth, and in that spirit I met you.' He seemed ashamed of himself, and gave up; but at the end of our discussion I only felt more persuaded that on the Protestant side there was nothing to be said. I believe he, too, felt he had at least the worst of the argument, for he evidently had no intention to return; but gave it as his farewell advice, that I should leave Italy, and go home to my relatives, evidently insinuating that a love affair, or something else equally culpable, was leading me astray. He dared only to hint this, however, but it wounded me to the quick at a moment when I felt I was probably about to sacrifice everything I held dear on earth, and for the first time I lost my equanimity, and whilst my eyes filled with tears I exclaimed, 'I know what you think; but God is my witness that I have no worldly motive whatever to induce me to become a Catholic—on the contrary, all are against it.' I asked him to return, but he never did so; and some time after, I wrote to solicit a second visit; but he did not even condescend to reply till I wrote a second time, and then he sent a formal note saying he would answer me either by letter or in person. He did call once at an appointed hour, but from a blunder of the servant he did not gain admittance, and he never returned, though he had promised to do so. We did not again meet, I believe, for six or seven weeks, when he was on the point of leaving Rome; and that evening he began to attack me, though in a hidden way, in the midst of a party where all my country people except myself were sound Protestants. I thought this very ungenerous, as I had offered him so many opportunities of conversing with me in private. However, seeing he seemed determined to force me to speak on the subject, I began to press him on the subject of church authority. He denied it explicitly, and would acknowledge no other arbiter in disputed points than the Scriptures. Having drawn from him a clear statement of his sentiments on this head, I said to him, 'This is very different doctrine from what *you preach*;—do you remember a sermon you gave the Sunday before Christmas?' (in which he had most decidedly disclaimed the sufficiency of Scripture alone, in cases of dispute, and said a living judge was necessary, that God had left that power to His Church). He appeared rather confused at my reminding him of this passage in his sermon, as he was obliged to acknowledge the correctness of my memory, and he only tried to excuse himself by making some undefinable limit to absolute authority. He afterwards discussed several other points with much the same results as the former, and at midnight we found ourselves *tête-à-tête*, the whole party having withdrawn one by one: he wished me good-bye, saying I would wander about for a time and then return to them; which I thought very unlikely.

"From the beginning of March, when I had my first conversation with Mr. Burgess, I had no rest night or day; my change of sentiments having become public, I was harassed by visits from various zealous Protestants, some friends, some not even acquaintances, who used all the arguments they were masters of, to turn me from my purpose. The inconsistencies into which I found every Protestant run to defend their cause, convinced me more than anything that their cause was untenable. Yet their visits agitated and sometimes perplexed me, by starting difficulties which cost me at least some trouble to solve; but I was determined to listen to all they could say, both for my own satisfaction and that of my friends, who, I knew well, would think I had been led astray by some artful priest, without having had it in my power to hear anything on the opposite side. But Providence seemed to have provided against this objection by the process of my conversion, as I owed it not to any one individual, but gained something from each; and I think still more from books, reflection, and prayer.

"During March I set apart two weeks for more especial prayer to God, to grant me by the end of that time light to discern His true Church; and I entreated various persons, both Catholics and Protestants, to pray for me, without specifying my request to any of them. I was then reading Milner's 'End of Religious Controversy,' and his arguments on the Authority of the Church struck me so forcibly, that I fell down on my knees with the exclamation of the philosopher of old—'I have found it! I have found it!' I could not but feel it was in answer to my prayer, and the time was still not expired. I wrote instantly to the Bishop and acknowledged I was convinced, and had the intention of making an open confession of my faith before him and the Protestant clergyman, for which end I did all I could to get them to meet. But this design was frustrated; and meanwhile the Bishop's leaving Rome for a time, and some further difficulties occurring to my mind, prevented me from taking any steps towards a public profession of the Faith.

"Meanwhile, however, I wrote home, and communicated to my parents the convictions of my mind, and expressed plainly my design of becoming a Catholic. I had not done so at an earlier period, solely to avoid giving them pain, and with a view of having my own judgment more unbiassed. The shock, I knew, to them would be dreadful, and I think I would have given my life to avoid inflicting such a wound on those I loved so dearly, and by whom I was equally beloved. In reply, two letters were sent to me within a few days, beseeching me to do nothing, to return home, and take another year for consideration. But to this I could not yield; my convictions were too strong, and had I resisted them, I should have felt unworthy of the light God had given me. I resolved, therefore, with as little delay as possible, to make my Abjuration, though my heart was nearly broken by the struggle between natural affection and duty to my God. Yet how thankful do I now feel, that deeply as I suffered, I can say before God I never cast a backward thought. But I would not endure what I then did, for thousands of worlds. My own heart bleeding at every pore was not enough—there were those who came constantly to cast salt on my wounds. I recall one evening particularly, when almost worn out I had thrown myself on my bed, when a visitor was announced: a gentleman who the winter before had made proposals to me, which I had rejected. I guessed the cause of his visit, and sent to say I was gone to bed—no matter, he must either return, or see me then. I chose the latter, and rose. After tormenting me for a full hour, to find out whether the rumours he had heard about me were true, and I refusing to give him any satisfaction, he at length began to feign to feel only for my relatives, and represented the affliction it would cause my poor father. Ah, what it then cost me to assume indifference! which I was obliged to do, as I was determined not to acquaint him with my intentions, he having told me he had another question to put which depended on my reply. What the nature of that was, I knew pretty well, and my own mind on that head had been long made up; you also know my sentiments too well not to believe I was quite satisfied he should not propose it. At length, finding all means in vain to make me declare myself, he went away. I think it was the same night, though I am not sure, that I was hardly asleep, when a friend broke in upon my rest, to entreat me to call in the morning on certain nobleman, noted for his Protestant zeal, and who was most anxious to see me before leaving Rome. I went, and, believe me, I spent six hours with him and his lady in constant disputation on the subject; during which time I had to swallow several insulting things, such as being told I was only fit for a madhouse, &c., but God gave me patience and undisturbed equanimity, and courage to express my sentiments fully, and we took leave in mutual charity, I more than ever convinced, but ready to drop from exhaustion both of mind and body.

"That God stood by me in these encounters I cannot doubt; for though naturally of a quick temper, I never felt even internally ruffled, and do not recollect ever having made use of an expression to any of them, for which I afterwards felt regret; indeed it was always my most earnest prayer, before entering into discussion with any one, that God would enable me to meet them in the spirit of a follower of the meek and lowly Saviour; and I hope, and do think, *He* granted my request, for most of my Protestant opponents acknowledged, even to myself, that if I was erring in judgment, my spirit was at least that of a Christian. Some of their acknowledgments were curious enough. One bid me farewell, saying he was very sorry I was taking such a view of things, but he had no fear for my soul.

"Another, who had carried with him a ponderous volume, by way of bringing me *light*, after hearing me relate the progress of my convictions, and the process I was following to attain truth, took up his book and walked away, saying, 'I shall leave you to your Heavenly Father, for if there be a God who hears and answers prayer *He must lead you right*.' One told me I was going to embrace the Catholic faith from the love of martyrdom. Another came to dissuade me from taking my final step, saying I was carried away. As this was a friend to whom I had opened my mind very freely, who was thoroughly acquainted with my motives, the unexpected accusation threw me into a passion of tears, and clasping my hands together, I exclaimed, 'Are you too turned against me?—by what can I be carried away?' 'By your love to your Saviour,' replied she, 'which I believe would lead you to die for Him.' 'That motive cannot lead me astray,' thought I. How strange and inconsistent!

"I had already made, both to Bishop Baines and Cardinal Odescalchi, a declaration of my intention of entering the Catholic Church, when I received from my father the above-mentioned letter, which almost quite overwhelmed me. Too conscientious himself to ask me to act contrary to my conscience, he only entreated me, by all that he thought would move me most, to wait till I had more ample means of information before I took any decisive step. God knows, and He alone, what it cost me to persevere in my intention of making my Abjuration without delay; but by the help of His grace I did so, well knowing that I had already had abundant means of information; that I had considered the subject deeply and with much earnest prayer, and my judgment was perfectly convinced. To wait therefore till my return home, would only have been to put myself in danger of allowing the decisions of my conscience to be warped by the affections of my heart; and to have exposed myself to great and unceasing trials, without those aids and consolations which religion could afford. The day was accordingly fixed for my making a public profession of my faith; but ere the day arrived, a kind Providence ordered it so, that the very opportunity my parents could have wished, for my having all that could be advanced on the Protestant side, by an able Divine of that communion, was presented to me, by the arrival in Rome of the celebrated Mr. Benson. Having understood from a friend, that sometime previous I had expressed a wish to converse with him, he kindly offered me a visit, which I readily accepted. I was anxious that this meeting should have taken place in the presence of Bishop Baines, but this Mr. Benson positively declined, and therefore, with the entire approval of the Bishop, I received him alone. I endeavoured, of course, to keep the discussion on the main point, the rule of faith; but from this Mr. Benson soon shifted, and ran out into several of the usual Protestant objections, as to the intercession of the saints being in opposition to the one Mediatorship of Christ, &c., but he got into so many perplexities and contradictions, that I remained more deeply convinced than ever; and I believe grateful to perceive that the evidence on the side of *Truth* became only clearer the more it was combated, and that talents and learning were employed against her in vain.

"The 16th of June, to me the most memorable day of my life, at length arrived, and the state of my mind you may better conceive than I can express. I was spending the morning in prayer that God would support me, when the crown was put to my sufferings by my dearest Protestant friend in Rome (who had promised to be present) sending to say she could not come. I nearly sank under this addition to my trial, at the moment I stood most in need of support. But calling to mind that my Saviour in his last tremendous hour was forsaken of all, I threw myself on my knees, saying, 'Lord, if it be Thy will that it should be thus with me too, it is enough—the disciple should be as his Lord—grant me only Thy presence.'

"At the appointed hour I was conducted to the chapel of His Eminence Cardinal Odescalchi, where, in the presence of the Bishop, several other prelates, and persons of high respectability, both English and Italian, I made my Abjuration, and was thus received into the bosom of the Catholic Church, where, notwithstanding the trials and afflictions I have had to endure, I enjoy a peace and tranquillity of mind I would not exchange for any worldly enjoyment.

"I shall now close the recital you asked of me, and which conducts me to the painful yet happy moment when, kneeling by you, I made my first confession. Accept, dear Father in Jesus Christ, my grateful thanks for your kind indulgence towards me then, and for the care you have exercised over my soul, and the sympathy you have expressed in my sorrows ever since. I pray that you may receive an ample recompense in the kingdom of our Saviour; and when I shall no longer have it in my power to consult you as my spiritual guide to that blessed region of peace to which alone my heart aspires, think of sometimes, and pray for your obedient and devoted daughter in Jesus Christ,

"ANNE AGNES TRAIL."

"As it may be an object of interest to some of my friends to know who were the individuals who witnessed my Abjuration of error, and my admission into the one true Church of our Lord and Saviour Jesus Christ, in which I anew subscribe my firm faith, after having had the happiness of being a member of it for nearly five years, I shall add to the above letters, which were written about four years since, a list of the names.

"My Abjuration was received by His Eminence Cardinal Prince Odescalchi, and witnessed by the Right Rev. Peter Augustine Baines, D.D., Bishop of Siga, and Vicar-Apostolic of the Western District of England.

"Monsignor Drummond, Duke of Melford.

"Don Remigio Crescini, the learned and pious Abbot of the great Benedictine Convent of St. Giovanni at Parma, then at Rome to be consecrated Bishop of Parma, and afterwards Cardinal. He furnished the letters to the ecclesiastics at Rome, though I had not then his personal acquaintance.

"B. Vincenzo Beni, Abbot.

"Monsignor Zacchia.

"Rev. Anthony Magee, Friar of the SS. Apostoli, mentioned above.

"Rev. Don Lorenzo Lucidi, since created Prelate and private chamberlain to His Holiness Gregory XVI.

"The two chaplains of Cardinal Odescalchi.

"The Chevalier Novone and his lady.

"Lady Arundell.

"Miss Mendoza di Reas.

"Madame Chaupegros.

"The Marchesa Testoli, sister to Cardinal Odescalchi, and two daughters.

"The Countess Van Millingen and her daughter, lady of honour to H.R.H. the Duchess of Lucca.

"A Jewish convert.

"Mr. Cook, an American gentlemen and Protestant."

CHAPTER III.

PORTRAIT OF CARDINAL ODESCALCHI—MISS TRAIL LEAVES ROME—HER RESIDENCE AT HAMMERSMITH—INTRODUCTION TO THE REV. JAMES GILLIS—CORRESPONDENCE WITH HIM—HER VOCATION—NOVICIATE AT CHAVAGNES—AND RETURN TO SCOTLAND.

THUS far our readers have followed Miss Trail's narrative as she has herself left it to us. It only remains now to supplement her own words by a brief account of her life as a Catholic, and finally as a Religious.

After her reception into the true Fold, she experienced much kindness from the leading English Catholics residing in Rome, among whom Lord and Lady Arundell of Wardour, and Lord and Lady Clifford, were always foremost in every good and charitable work; and they showed the utmost cordiality to the new and fervent convert, making her welcome to their houses, and aiding her in acquiring the instruction she required, to become familiar with Catholic practice as well as doctrine.

She received Confirmation from the hands of

Cardinal Odescalchi, who administered this sacrament to her in his private chapel.

Miss Trail was as assiduous as ever in the use of her pencil, and her art enabled her to carry away valuable souvenirs of her friends. Thus she took a likeness of Bishop Baines; and having accomplished this, she ventured to ask Cardinal Odescalchi for a sitting. His Eminence refused the request; but Miss Trail returned to the charge, till, at last, the Cardinal repeated his refusal so positively, that she felt it useless to urge him further; and made up her mind to think no more about the matter.

Not so the Cardinal. He was already preparing to exchange the purple for the humble garb of a son of St. Ignatius;—he was already practising the counsels of that great saint. While Miss Trail was sitting alone at dinner that same day, the Cardinal's man-servant was announced; he came, carrying his master's robes, and saying that his Eminence would follow shortly.

By-and-bye the good Cardinal arrived. Miss Trail expressed her pleasure and surprise at so unexpected a visit, and he replied, that when making his mid-day examination of conscience, he felt that he had spoken to her with some hastiness, and therefore, by way of penance, he had come to accede to her request. The portrait was painted accordingly, and is now at St. Margaret's Convent, a precious remembrance of this saintly prince of the Church.

A few pleasant weeks were spent at Subiaco in the summer of 1828; then followed another winter and spring in Rome; and having received the blessing of the Holy Father, and bade adieu to the many friends to whom she had become much attached, and by whom she was sincerely regretted, Miss Trail left Italy on the 6th June 1829, and reached her home at Panbride at the end of August.

Of course it was a trial both to her family and herself to meet again under circumstances so different to what they had formerly been; but the strong conviction that she had acted from conscientious motives had its due weight with Mr. Trail, and his affection for his daughter never changed; while she devoted herself to the task of softening the prejudice of her family and giving them an insight into Catholic doctrine whenever an opportunity for doing so presented itself.

She was not destined to remain long at home.

Her eyes had been overstrained by close application to miniature painting; she was obliged to lay down her pencil, and at last was recommended to go to London to consult an eminent oculist. She left Scotland in October 1830, little thinking on the future which was in store for her.

By a providential arrangement Miss Trail went to reside at the Benedictine Convent at Hammersmith, where a limited number of lady boarders were received, and here she remained for the three following years. Cardinal Weld, who had resided at the Convent, and had just been summoned to Rome to be invested with the purple, left all his store of artist's materials to Miss Trail, who was well known to him through Lord and Lady Clifford. The Cardinal's paint-box, palettes, colours, &c., were highly prized by her, and many of these things are still at St. Margaret's Convent.

Lord Arundell of Wardour invited Miss Trail to his Castle of Wardour, where she passed some months from January till the Easter of 1832; then followed other visits, and in autumn she made some stay in Somersetshire.

Her friends began to wonder where she would ultimately settle. The Convent at Hammersmith was her residence when at home, but she did not regard it as a permanent abode. It was suggested to her to enter a religious Community; the Countess de Senfft-Pilsach wished her to go to the newly-founded Society of the Sacred Heart, others urged the Benedictines of the Perpetual Adoration, or the Third Order of St. Francis at Taunton. Though full of love and esteem for these holy orders, they did not entirely satisfy her desires, which turned to her native land; and she waited on, in the hope that her way might be made plain to her.

Having returned to Hammersmith in the summer of 1832, she was introduced to a young Scotch priest, the Rev. James Gillis, who being acquainted with the chaplain of the Convent had been invited to dine with him. The conversation naturally turned on Scotland, and Miss Trail was much interested in all she heard; more especially, when Mr. Gillis mentioned his earnest wish to found a religious Community for the instruction of young girls in Edinburgh. He was then on his way to Spain, and she hoped to have the opportunity of meeting him on his return; but this not occurring, she wrote to him, asking if his project were likely to be realised, and requesting some details respecting the general plan of the proposed establishment, as she says, "I have some thoughts of entering the religious state, and for many reasons I should prefer a convent in my native land, were it an order of which I could become a member, with the hope of being useful."

Mr. Gillis answered this letter, by saying that his plans had been delayed by the lapse of time before the nomination of a bishop, to succeed Bishop Paterson, but he gave her the desired information respecting the Congregation of the

Ursulines of Jesus, and expressed his belief that if it were the will of God that Miss Trail should become a member of the proposed Community, she would certainly be a very useful addition. He adds, "I certainly think before God, that it is the duty of every Catholic in these countries, to devote their *all* to the good of religion *at home*, in preference to other countries, unless Providence evidently wills and disposes it otherwise. There is a wide field opened here just now: God grant that it may be well cultivated; and here I dismiss the subject, as I would not wish to influence you in the least, to one way more than the other."

Some months were still to elapse before any decision was made respecting the proposed establishment.

Miss Trail wrote to Mr. Gillis on the 5th February 1833, being anxious to fix her future mode of life, and, above all, desirous of devoting herself to Scotland. She asks, "What prospects of success have you, in your interesting project of establishing a convent in our Northern capital? My heart longs to see such a glorious work begun, and I have now full permission to offer my poor services if they will be acceptable. . . .

. . . . . .

I fully enter into your ideas of its being our duty, unless Providence clearly shows it otherwise, to devote our services in the first instance to our own country. This has made me decline a most kind offer from the noble Count and Countess de Senfft-Pilsach to enter a foreign convent, and still makes me hesitate in accepting an equally generous offer in the West of England; but it appears to me that I cannot do so much longer without thwarting the designs of Providence in my regard; and, therefore, I must beg, if possible, an immediate answer to this. I wish my intention to be kept quiet till the consent of my parents has been obtained, and till all is settled for my retirement from a scene which my heart has long regarded as a desert, and to which I shall willingly bid adieu."

She soon received a satisfactory reply to this letter. Mr. Gillis says, "I am now, I hope, on the eve of seeing this most desirable institution commenced, and I am more and more convinced every day that the real difficulties in works of this kind do not lie in the want of financial resources, nor in the opposition which they may chance to meet with from the world, but in the unworthiness of those who undertake them, and *that obstacle* alone do I fear in the present instance. I speak not of others, but of myself. Pray that God may make *me* more worthy of serving the interests of His Church, and Edinburgh will soon be blessed with the proposed establishment."

On the 17th April 1833, he writes again to say that he has the "Bishop's *full consent* to the establishment of the Convent, and the exclusive management of the means whereby to carry it into effect. You may therefore look upon the thing now as entirely settled, and to be set about without delay."

Mr. Gillis started, in company with Bishop Scott of Glasgow, for London and Paris, in the course of the week following the date of the last letter. From Paris he wrote again (14th June), giving Miss Trail directions as to her journey to France. He tells her that Miss Clapperton will join her in London, and that on arriving in Paris they will be hospitably received at the Convent of the *Dames du St. Sacrement, Rue des Postes.* He recommends her to take some English books to Chavagnes, as it is of importance that she should teach as much English as possible, to the French Sisters who are to return to Scotland with her.

The last arrangements were now quickly made. Mr. Gillis requested Miss Clapperton to be in London if possible by the 31st July, and there she met Miss Trail for the first time, and in due course they left London for Paris, as has been already narrated in the early pages of this work. We have also seen that she and her companion received the Religious Habit at Chavagnes on Rosary Sunday,

1833, from the hands of Mr. Gillis. He had intended prolonging his stay in Paris, but was suddenly called home to Fochabers by the illness of his father. Miss Trail, whom we shall henceforth call by her religious name, Sister Agnes Xavier, wrote him a letter of condolence, and at the same time gave interesting details of her life at Chavagnes, in preparation for the foundation at Edinburgh.

The two Scotch Novices were very highly esteemed at the Mother House, and the whole enterprise excited so much enthusiasm, that the number of volunteers for the Scotch foundation far exceeded what was required for the occasion. During her novitiate Sister Agnes Xavier gave lessons, not only in English, but in painting; and she herself obtained a much-valued portrait of the venerable founder of the Congregation, the Abbé Louis Marie Baudouin. He had often been asked to allow his likeness to be taken, but he would never consent. His spiritual children were most anxious to obtain a resemblance of his much-loved and revered features, and this was accomplished, under difficulties it must be owned, by Sister Agnes Xavier.

It was the custom of Père Baudouin to give religious instruction to the Novices on certain fixed days. He took his place at the upper end of the large novitiate and the Sisters sat in rows before him. It was during these instructions, and unknown to the venerable Priest, that Sister Agnes Xavier painted an excellent likeness of him. She placed herself where she could see him perfectly and yet be unnoticed by him. She narrowly escaped detection on one occasion when the instruction was concluded more quickly than usual. Every one rose suddenly, and the poor artist had barely an instant to gather her brushes, &c., together, and conceal her work from view. Père Baudouin never knew what had been done till the colony had left Chavagnes for Scotland, and then a letter from a lithographer in Paris, charged with copying the miniature by lithography, fell into his hands, and revealed the secret. He was much annoyed, but the congregation rejoiced over the success of the little plot. The original miniature was brought to St. Margaret's. Sister Agnes Xavier left a copy at the Mother House, and it is from this likeness that the small engravings and medals of the venerable father have been taken.

The time spent at Chavagnes passed quickly and profitably to the fervent Novices, whose sole desire was to fit themselves for their future career, and to render themselves worthy labourers in the field that was whitening for the harvest.

When the time came for the little band of Sisters

to leave Chavagnes and turn their faces northwards, we may well imagine how joyfully the two Scotch Novices set forth on their journey *home*. The generosity with which the French Religious entered upon the new foundation, with all the sacrifices it entailed, softened the trial of separation from their country, and filled them likewise with that happiness which the world can neither give nor take away.

Sister Agnes Xavier's brother—Captain Anthony Trail—was most helpful to the travellers in London; and the Benedictine Community at Hammersmith, where Sister Agnes Xavier had so long resided, now once more welcomed her back with her companions for a few days' rest, *en route* for Edinburgh.

The long journey came to an end at last, and with thankful hearts the little band of zealous, devoted Sisters reached the temporary abode that kind friends had provided for them, till the Convent should be ready to receive its inmates.

CHAPTER IV.

SISTER AGNES XAVIER AT ST. MARGARET'S—HER ZEAL AND RELIGIOUS VIRTUES—HER ILLNESS AND DEATH—LETTER OF MISS O'NEIL DAUNT.

WHEN crossing the threshold of St. Margaret's on St. Stephen's Day, 1834, Sister Agnes Xavier may well have echoed the words of the Royal Psalmist, "This is my rest for ever: here will I dwell, for I have chosen it." During the many years that she lived, never, for one day, was she absent from the Convent.

She devoted herself to a Religious life, its duties and work, with all the energy of her nature and all the love of her heart.

Having entered religion at a more advanced period of life than is usual for embracing a new career, it may be imagined that many little trials were inevitable to her. She had hitherto been so completely her own mistress, that the mere fact of being constantly submissive to others might be supposed to have caused her much difficulty. But it was not so. She was as humble and docile as a child, and her example was a constant source of admiration and edification to the whole Community. Her cheerful spirit enabled her to accept every sacrifice, and, indeed, she counted it "all joy" when she could offer a holocaust of thanksgiving to God, for all that He had done for her soul.

Her life was henceforth externally uneventful, but it was surely precious in the sight of God. She had her share of teaching in the school, and for years conducted the classes of Christian doctrine and sacred history, while her artistic talent naturally placed her at the head of the drawing-class.

She continued the exercise of her own pencil, and was frequently requested to execute work by those who remembered her skill. To her the Community is indebted for miniatures of Bishop Gillis, Mr. Menzies, Mrs. Colonel Hutchison, and others: besides the paintings which she had finished in Italy, and which she brought to St. Margaret's.

But more than all her other occupations for the good of others, did she value the opportunities given her of helping souls to see and embrace the true faith. She never lost an occasion of saying a timely word, offering an instructive book, or suggesting a prayer for the gift of faith. Her genuine frankness and kindly manner won all hearts, and though she spoke very plainly, she never gave offence. How many now live to bless her memory, and thank God for the first visit to the Convent, which led to an acquaintance with her.

Her own relatives frequently visited her, and the affectionate intercourse with her family was never interrupted. The younger generation of nephews and nieces were much attached to "Aunt Ann;" and the following lines written by her nephew, Mr. David Trail Christie, will express the feelings of the family :—

"How vivid must ever remain my recollections of her bright, affectionate and genial spirit, her quick and sympathetic intelligence, and what—though differing, I could always appreciate and admire—her ardent devotion to the life she had embraced, and her earnest desire that all her kindred should be led to see truth from the standpoint she had realised and made her own.

"Speaking as for those of my family on the Trail side—now, alas! no more—I can say how sincere was the brotherly and sisterly interest and affection with which, notwithstanding divergence of views, she was ever regarded. No less fully can I testify to the warmth with which this feeling was reciprocated on her part, a proof that strength of opposite convictions is not incompatible with that charity that 'hopeth all things.'

"Though the days of my more frequent visits to the Convent are receding into the background as the years pass by, the bright and pleasant picture of her presence will ever remain fresh in my memory."

Another nephew of Sister Agnes Xavier (now Colonel David Henry Trail, R.E.) obtained permission, only granted as a very rare exception, to take a photograph of his aunt. His successful likeness of her is highly valued by her family and by the Community, and is reproduced in this volume.

One of her special characteristics was her devotion to the Holy See. She had imbibed this truly Catholic instinct at the fountainhead, and it increased with years, and in proportion to the sorrows of the Holy Father, which grieved her as much as if they had affected her personally. On the other hand, any good news from Rome, intelligence about conversions, elections favourable to the cause of religion and good order, were to her causes of heartfelt rejoicing. She had a large number of friends in England and on the Continent, who kept her informed of such public events as they knew would interest her, and enlist her sympathy and prayers. She entered warmly into the union of prayer for the conversion of England, instituted by her old friend the Hon. and Rev. Father Spencer; and it was with unflagging interest that she read accounts of missions, retreats, foundations of new churches or convents, or indeed anything that proved the increase of Catholicity in England and Scotland.

Time passed swiftly away, and, as Father Faber says, "Years rob us as they go," and so it was that many old friends were taken, one by one, and Sister Agnes Xavier more and more turned her face heavenward. The death of Bishop Gillis was an inexpressible sorrow to her, and it was not long after his decease that her own health began to decline, and by degrees she relinquished her more active duties in the Community.

A slight shock of paralysis occurred a few years before her death, and this still more obliged her to withdraw from outward occupations. Though bodily strength declined, her warm heart retained its loving nature, and nothing pleased her more than to see old friends and relatives, and to join the Community whenever her health permitted.

She never omitted her religious exercises, which were daily performed with the greatest fervour, and when unable to read, her rosary was her constant companion.

On the 22d November 1872, she was taken suddenly ill, and the following day she received the last sacraments from the hands of Father Williams, S.J. During the remaining days of her life, the Bishop called frequently to see her. Father O'Donnell came over from Falkirk, to her great joy; and other friends were assiduous in their kind inquiries. She survived till the 3rd December, the Feast of her beloved Patron, St. Francis Xavier, when she calmly breathed her last, a little after nine P.M., surrounded by her Sisters; who, while grieving over their own loss, rejoiced at her great gain. They had the consolation of knowing that her last days had been perfectly peaceful; and indeed the expression of her countenance before death, was as if the joys of heaven were already hers. Her brother, the Rev. Dr. Trail, and Mrs. Trail, with some other members of the family, assisted at the funeral, which was attended by a considerable number of the clergy.

Sister Agnes Xavier could never be forgotten by any one who had ever known her. She preserved her own strong individuality throughout life, and was thoroughly original, so true-hearted and sincere in all her ways, so perfectly reliable as a friend and adviser! All the Community felt her loss; and though her declining state had in a measure separated her from the Sisters, still, when the end came, every one felt that the blank could never be filled up

This chapter may be appropriately concluded by a letter from Miss O'Neil Daunt, who contributes some of her own reminiscences of her school days, thus recalling the beloved names of

Sister Agnes Xavier and Mother Mary Angela (so long associated together in the memory of all old pupils of St. Margaret's), and giving some anecdotes of both, which may be interesting to our readers :—

"KILCASCAN CASTLE, BALLYNEEN,
"*April* 1886.

"MY DEAR MOTHER M—— S——.—It delighted me to hear that you intend publishing a memoir of St. Margaret's at an early date; and my pleasure, you may be sure, will be shared by all who have spent their school-days within the dear old Convent walls. Now that you are about to celebrate the jubilee year of its foundation, one rejoices that so many of the old Religious still survive; but one thinks all the more sadly and regretfully of those who have passed away.

"It is thirty-one years since I went first to school at St. Margaret's, although I can remember every circumstance attending my entrance as if it were but yesterday.

"It was just about the time that an alteration in what may be called the management of the Convent had been effected. The French Sisters had returned to their own country, and dear Mother Mary Angela had been nominated Superioress. I recollect so well Bishop Gillis conducting her to the school to receive our congratulations. She was crying, and quite nervous at the idea of the great responsibility placed upon her shoulders. I particularly remember dear old Sister Agnes Xavier's face on that occasion. It was beaming with satisfaction, and even then I felt struck by the humility and child-like simplicity which seemed to characterise all her dealings with her "Mother." The word fell quaintly from her lips, considering the great advantage which she had in age, over her young Superior.

"Sister Agnes Xavier at this period of my reminiscences, always presided over the class of Christian doctrine, and to us little ones, the half hour of Catechism was rather a formidable affair. We all understood that, as drawing-mistress, her eyes were especially precious to her, and to defend those eyes from the glare of the school-room fire, a chair, with a green cloth thrown over it, had always to be placed at a specified distance from the place where she sat. If this chair was not at the precise angle required, we had invariably to undergo a lecture on distance and perspective.

"As a convert from Protestantism, you know how perfectly conversant she was with the Bible. How clear and well-defined her explanations of the Christian doctrine were, we can all remember. Long after I had left school, on re-visiting St. Margaret's, I happened to spend some time in conversation with her. She told me, with such evident pleasure, that an old pupil of hers had become a Catholic, principally by means of her religious instruction, which had made an ineffaceable impression on her mind.

"She was full of faith;—a faith that seemed to *touch* and *taste*. Do you remember her at Mass and Benediction? Sometimes we caught a glimpse of her face at these times. Her eyes used to be fixed on the altar, and her lips moved, while her smile and her whole expression showed that she was really speaking to our Lord, as a friend might speak to a dear and trusted friend. We used to remark to each other, 'Did you notice Sister Agnes Xavier's face? How sweet and child-like she looked!'

"But, with all her kindness and simplicity, she could be very decided on certain occasions. I remember once, when she was conducting a party of Protestant visitors through the house, she omitted, for some good reason, to take them to the schoolroom—the old schoolroom in those days, with its large bay window abutting on the garden. On seeing the window from the outside, one of the ladies exclaimed in an aggrieved tone, 'Why, here is a room you have not shown us. I hate underhand proceedings!' 'For making that remark,' rejoined Sister Agnes Xavier, quietly, 'you shall not see anything further to-day,' and she marshalled the discomfited party to the gate. I think it served them very right, for even in a convent, persons of another faith should remember their good breeding, and be convinced that under the disguise of habit and veil, there are many whose feet neither Protestant nor Catholic is worthy to kiss.

"I do not think she had a particle of human respect. She always said and did what appeared to her to be right. Even as a girl she told me how she exasperated her uncle, a dignitary of the Irish Protestant Church,[1] by espousing the cause of the then down-trodden Catholic population, and by her avowed admiration of the political principles of Daniel O'Connell.

"She was a devoted daughter of the Holy See. In former days a prolonged residence in Rome had made her personally acquainted with more than one Pontiff. She always expressed the utmost distrust of the tortuous policy of the third Napoleon; and she had, on the contrary, the utmost respect for the late Comte de Chambord and all his house. These political opinions had been formed partly in Vendée, which is the cradle of Legitimacy in France.

[1] The Right Reverend James Trail, D.D., Bishop of Down and Connor.

Then, to descend to lesser matters, can we not all recall the interest she took in her museum, and in the Community library? Her whole heart seemed to be in whatever she undertook; and, as a consequence, such things as were under her charge, flourished. At stated periods she used to take some of us school girls to assist in dusting out the books. When each one was intrusted with a hare's foot, a bird's wing, a duster, and a book to operate upon, we felt a solemn sense of responsibility settle upon our spirits; and knew that, with Sister Agnes Xavier's eye upon us, our task must needs be conscientiously performed. To reward us she would often make a descent to the kitchen and return with tart, or other sweet thing, to revive our fainting energies.

"Of course, her chief employment was that of drawing mistress; and she, who was a thorough artist, knew well how to develop the talent which lay in the minds and fingers of her pupils. In the French octavo life of the Venerable M. L. Baudouin, one meets with several references to our dear old Sister Agnes Xavier, to her genius for miniature painting, and to the favourable impression which her humility (above all other virtues) and talents, had made on the minds of the nuns of the Mother House of the Order in Chavagnes.

"How I have run on in my reminiscences of

her! Time would fail me to write as I ought either of her, or of Mother Mary Angela and others, whose names occur to me now.

"What old pupil of St. Margaret's can forget Mother Mary Angela? With what loving care did she not watch over each one of us! She was so tender, so like a mother with us, each and all.

"But beyond everything else her religious instructions dwell with me. She seemed on fire when she spoke of God, or the truths of faith, and her thoughts often seemed to flow too rapidly for utterance. While I was at school, it was always her province to prepare the children for their first communion. I am very sure that not one who had the privilege of being her pupil on those occasions, can ever forget the fervour and strength of her instructions. If we are not all saints in heaven one day, it certainly will not have been her fault!

"I should never cease were I to recount all the instances I remember of her humility, her patience, her love of the poor, her self-denial. And then, she was so simple, and so child-like!

"Do you remember once in 1859 or 1860, an excursion we made to the Pentland Hills? It was a lovely summer morning, and we set out at four o'clock, taking only a small bit of bread in our pockets, as the baskets containing provisions were to follow later. We arrived at the hills, and saw the sun rise. We had eaten our bread, and looked forward to the arrival of the baskets. Vain hope! They did not come. Some of the little ones became very hungry, and then Mother Mary Angela—Reverend Mother—took out of her pocket her untasted bread, and divided it among the hungriest. She had eaten nothing herself. Later on, some of us girls accompanied one or two of the Sisters on a quest for bread and milk. On our return we found Reverend Mother seated in a plantation, with the rest of the children, devouring hotch potch, out of basins with great horn spoons, greatly to Mother Mary Angela's delight; for in negotiations about the hotch potch, she had been mistaken for a beggar by a good woman at a farm-house. It was the Presbyterian fast-day, and all the family were at the kirk but the mistress of the house, who bestowed a quantity of the good broth and oatmeal bannocks in charity. Late in the evening, I am glad to say, the strayed baskets arrived, and we revenged ourselves on their contents.

"I do not think you could give Reverend Mother greater delight than by giving her something for the poor. Her face used to flush with pleasure. All her actions were full of thoughtfulness for others. Even when suffering herself, she would strive to repress all outward signs of pain, and busy herself about the comfort of those around her.

"But, as I said before, I should never come to an end were I to go over all the incidents of school life. You see how they, and the actors in them, are embalmed in my memory.

"The last whom you have lost, Sister Mary Stanislaus, I made my first acquaintance with thirty-two years ago. During my school life, and at subsequent periods, I never remember to have seen her impatient, or even ruffled. She was always so sweet-tempered, kind, and sympathetic!

"I hope that the dear old mistresses of our school days will unite from heaven with the Jubilee of the Convent that was their home on earth; and that they will not forget to pray for us, who love their memories.

"To sum up, dear Mother M—— S——, I really do not think that there is elsewhere a convent like our Alma Mater, nor any other women who can look back, as we do, with equal joy and thankfulness to the days spent under its sheltering roof. At least, I have never met any one who appeared to entertain for the convent where she was educated, the same feelings with which we regard St. Margaret's.—Yours very affectionately,

"ISMENE O'NEIL DAUNT."

CHAPTER V.

THE GOLDEN JUBILEE.

"Quid retribuam Domino pro omnibus quæ retribuit mihi?" These words best express the feelings of every Sister at St. Margaret's, when the Reverend Mother made known that his Grace the Archbishop had decided that the celebration of the Golden Jubilee should take place on St. Margaret's Day, 10th June 1886.

In a preceding chapter of this book, our readers have seen that the anniversary of the foundation of the Convent had been privately commemorated on St. Stephen's Day—26th December 1884—the public festivities being deferred, till the mourning church of St. Andrews and Edinburgh should again possess an Archbishop, who would preside over and bless the proceedings connected with the Jubilee. The Archbishop having been consecrated, and the more pressing calls of his time and attention being satisfied, the Reverend Mother suggested that the Feast of St. Margaret would be an appropriate and auspicious day for the Jubilee celebration. His

Grace acquiesced in the plan, and from that time every one took an active part in the preparations for the event.

Nor was it in any selfish spirit that this festival was kept. It was looked upon as a thank-offering to Almighty God for the numberless graces of the last fifty years—graces bestowed not only on the Religious of St. Margaret's Convent, but on the whole country, by the progress of religion, the foundation of the numerous monastic and conventual establishments now existing, and the incalculable good done by Religious of both sexes according to their holy Institutes. Who can tell what advantage souls have received by the ministry of the Fathers of the Society of Jesus, the Oblates of Mary, the Redemptorists, and others devoted to missionary labours? while the sons and daughters of St. Benedict, in the retirement of their cloisters, implore the blessing of God on the labours of those who toil in the vineyard of the Lord. Since the foundation of St. Margaret's, how many convents have arisen where children are rescued from ignorance and vicious surroundings; where the sick are lovingly tended; where the erring are reclaimed, and where innocence is guarded from even a breath of evil! Surely in all this there is much cause for deep gratitude, and the Sisters of St. Margaret's desired, while celebrating their Jubilee, to give expression to the joy which is naturally elicited, by such retrospect of the past half century.

The first thing, then, to be done, was to give glory to God;—and, to ensure a grand act of thanksgiving throughout the length and breadth of the land, letters were sent to many other Religious Communities announcing the Jubilee celebration, and begging that a "Te Deum" might be sung in union with St. Margaret's on the 10th June. Most kind replies were received to these appeals, and sweet union of sisterly charity was never more clearly shown than by the cordial manner in which the Superiors of Communities responded, with affectionate congratulations and promises of prayers and thanksgivings. These valued letters will be carefully preserved as treasured souvenirs of the Jubilee in the archives of the Convent.

The next duty calling for attention was the honour to be paid to St. Margaret, the holy and beneficent Queen whose gentle sway brought so many blessings to Scotland, and whose prayers are daily procuring fresh graces for the land she loved so well and ruled so wisely.

The Relic of the Saint, brought by Bishop Gillis from the Escurial in 1863, still remained under his seal in the cedar box in which he had placed it. This sacred Relic was now to be enshrined in a suitable Reliquary. Dr. Gillis had himself selected

RELIQUARY, WITH RELIC OF ST. MARGARET.

the design, and it has been followed as nearly as possible and with consummate skill by Mr. Westren of Frederick Street, Edinburgh, to whom the task of making the Reliquary was confided. The relic is enclosed in a crystal cylinder, and is surrounded by clusters of Gothic pinnacles surmounted by a statue of St. Margaret. The base of the Reliquary is provided with a receptacle for the documents attesting the authenticity of the Relic.

On the 8th June his Grace the Archbishop placed the Relic in its crystal case in readiness for the procession which was to inaugurate the celebration.

The taste and energy of the Sacristans were now called into requisition in their special department. In the adornment of the chapel we may suppose that the crypt was not overlooked. The resting-places of all who repose within its precincts were marked by wreaths of evergreens and immortelles. The escutcheons of Bishop Gillis and Mr. Menzies of Pitfodels were prominently placed, and a scroll with the versicle, "Requiem æternum dona eis Domine," was suspended above the altar, which was draped with black velvet, and furnished with a large crucifix and candles.

In the chapel, the window behind the altar was partially screened, and, conspicuous in the centre, was a large statue of St. Margaret surrounded with palms and flowers. The altar was brilliant with lights and flowers—a throne for the Archbishop was placed on the epistle side of the sanctuary, and a prie-dieu for Archbishop Eyre on the gospel side. The sanctuaries of the side altars were furnished with seats for the clergy. The choir was filled with the Sisters and resident Pupils. The south aisle was partly occupied by the orchestra and singers, and the remaining space in the chapel was devoted to the invited guests, who were all to be admitted by ticket.

The house was carefully arranged and tastefully ornamented with plants. The class-rooms were used as sacristies for the accommodation of the numerous body of clergy who were expected. The Archbishop kindly lent his finest vestments for the occasion.

At length the last preparations were completed, and at five o'clock P.M. on the 9th of June, the Archbishop was announced, and the first service of the Jubilee began. The Sisters intoned a joyful chorus in honour of St. Margaret, the clergy entered the chapel, and then the Archbishop carried the Relic in solemn procession through the chapel and garden, and, returning, placed the Reliquary on a side altar especially prepared for its reception. Benediction of the Blessed Sacrament followed.

The Archbishop, clergy, and a select party of friends then adjourned to the schoolroom, where they were entertained by the young ladies with music, vocal and instrumental, and by recitations. A chorus, composed for the occasion, was sung; a trio of violins and a charming violin solo, played by Madame Woycke, delighted the company. Miss Grace Kyan recited a poem, which had been composed by Dr. Horsley on the occasion of Mother Margaret Teresa's Jubilee, and which was perfectly appropriate to the present festival. The composition and the manner in which it was rendered, elicited well-merited applause.

The company then assembled for refreshments in the refectory.

The eventful, long-looked-for 10th of June at length arrived, unfortunately shrouded in mist and rain; but if the material sun hid his face, there was so much bright sunshine in every heart, that the weather was scarcely heeded. After the morning masses and breakfast were concluded, the company began to arrive, and before eleven o'clock the chapel was full, every available space being occupied. The Sisters and Pupils took their places, and as a voluntary pealed forth from the organ, the procession slowly defiled from the Convent buildings, crossing the garden, and entering the chapel by the great door. It was a beautiful and impressive sight to see the long line of Acolytes and Clergy as they walked up the chapel and took their allotted station.

Pontifical High Mass was sung by His Grace the Archbishop of St. Andrews and Edinburgh. The Very Rev. Provost M'Kerrell was the assistant Priest; Very Rev. Canon Grady, V.G., and Canon Hannan were Deacons at the Throne; and Brother Oswald Hunter Blair and Father M'Anaa, Deacon and Sub-Deacon of the Mass. Canon Donlevy acted as Master of Ceremonies. Besides those already named, there were in the Sanctuary the Most Rev. Archbishop Eyre, attended by Canon Macguire and Father M'Lachlan of Glasgow, Canon Macmanus, Canon Grogan, Canon Goldie, Canon Meagher, Very Rev. William Dean Clapperton, Very Rev. Robert Dean Clapperton, Father Gordon, Father Morris, Father Malcolm, Father Turner, Father Griffin, Father Whyte, S.J.; Father Selby, S.J.; Father Pittar, S.J.; Father Stevenson, S.J.; Father Gray, S.J.; Father Charles Gordon, S.J.; Father Kenny, S.J.; the Very Rev. Prior Vaughan, O.S.B.; Father O'Carroll, O.M.I., &c.

After the Gospel of the Mass had been chanted by the Deacon, Archbishop Eyre delivered a discourse from Leviticus xxv. 10 and 11, "And thou shalt sanctify the fiftieth year, and shalt proclaim remission to all the inhabitants of thy land . . . because it is the jubilee and the fiftieth year." His Grace referred to the long-established custom of celebrating the anniversaries of joyful events in the family circle; and instanced the twenty-fifth anniversary of a wedding being called the "silver jubilee." When the fiftieth anniversary is reached, it is celebrated with still greater rejoicing, and is called the "golden jubilee;" and he said that this was the cause of so many friends of St. Margaret's being assembled together on this day, because "it is the jubilee, and the fiftieth year." He then briefly sketched the history of the foundation of the establishment by the late Bishop Gillis, aided by the generosity of Mr. Menzies of Pitfodels, the vocation of its two first members, and the entrance of the Community to the Convent on the Feast of St. Stephen, 26th December 1834.

His Grace remarked that the Feast of the First Martyr was a singularly appropriate day on which to enter on such an undertaking as the foundation of a convent. St. Stephen, when led before the council that was to condemn him to death, looked steadfastly to heaven, and there saw the Son of Man, standing at the right hand of God. The first object of Religious life is to look steadfastly to heaven, and there to see Jesus Christ at the right hand of God; in other words, the first work of Religious is their own sanctification, their second work is the sanctification of others. In France the Ursulines of Jesus are also known by the name of Sisters of the Incarnation, because this mystery is the chief object of their devotion; and the whole aim of their life is the imitation of the Incarnate Word of God, by the practice of poverty, chastity, obedience and teaching. "This is the work that has been going on here for the last fifty years, and you will rejoice with the Sisters because it is their jubilee: to-day there is joy in Edinburgh, joy in Scotland, joy in this house, and joy also in heaven. There is the late Bishop Gillis, whose memory is still fragrant, and who must take great interest in the proceedings of this day. There is St. Margaret, that jewel of Scotland, who herself wished to be a nun, and could only with difficulty be dissuaded from carrying her desire into effect, and whose marriage procured such happy results for Scotland. St. Margaret, patroness of Scotland, will rejoice to-day; and let St. Margaret be your model and your pattern in dealing with children. My dear Sisters, all I could wish to say, is to encourage you in the good work in which you are engaged, and in the life you are leading. Persevere in the piety you practise in the cloister, as this is one of the greatest gifts of the Holy Ghost. You, my dear children, persevere in humility, docility, and purity. All my other friends, you will strive to persevere in godliness, for, as St. Paul tells us, Godliness is profitable, as it promises blessings in the life that now is, and eternal happiness in the life that is to come."

At the conclusion of the Mass, the Very Rev. Provost M'Kerrell announced that special indulgences had been granted by the Holy Father, on the usual conditions, to all who assisted at the Jubilee celebration in the Convent chapel, and that the Papal blessing and plenary indulgence would now be imparted by his Grace the Archbishop of St. Andrews and Edinburgh. The confiteor was chanted by the Deacon of the Mass, and the absolution and benediction given by the Archbishop, who then intoned the "Te Deum." This magnificent expression of joy and thanksgiving was sung on a Gregorian tone, alternately by the choir and the whole body of the clergy and the congregation, and all present felt that it rose to the Throne of God from the hearts of all at St. Margaret's, together with those angelic voices that are for ever singing "Sanctus, Sanctus, Sanctus."

The music of the Mass was Haydn's No. 6, with Mozart's motetto "Splendente, &c.," at the offertory. The "Tannhaüser March" was played as the clergy defiled out of the church.

The service lasted till about half-past one, and

at its conclusion, the guests adjourned to the Convent refectory for refreshments.

It had been arranged that a photograph should be taken of the Archbishops, clergy, guests, Community and Pupils;—and Mr. Shaw attended for the purpose. The unfavourable state of the weather, however, rendered the attempt impossible, much to the disappointment of the whole party; as such a photograph would have been a valuable memorial of the occasion.

The clergy were now invited to go to the Community room, where a number of useful gifts were drawn by a lottery—the articles consisted of altar linen, vestments, and things likely to be of service in small missions.

The plans by Mr. Macpherson, architect, Edinburgh, for the enlargement of the Convent and chapel, were also exhibited.

At three o'clock the bell summoned the company to the chapel, where Benediction of the Most Blessed Sacrament was given by his Grace the Archbishop. The music was again most beautifully performed, the selection being Girschner's "Ave Maris Stella," "O Salutaris," by Gounod; Litany (specially arranged), and Verdussen's "Tantum Ergo." Handel's Hallelujah Chorus was given as the clergy left the Chapel.

The ceremonial was under the direction of Canon

Donlevy; and having said this, it is unnecessary to add that everything was carried out with the most perfect order and decorum. It was by no means easy to arrange for so large a gathering of clergy in the limited space of the Convent chapel, but difficulties vanished under the practised eye and hand of Canon Donlevy, who undertook the charge in the kindest manner possible.

The music was under the leadership of Father Gray, S.J., to whom the Community are indebted for the skill with which this very essential part of the services was carried out, as well as for the beautiful selection of the pieces performed. The sound of orchestral music, and a full choir of trained singers is a very rare treat in a Convent chapel, and it is all the more highly appreciated when, on some extraordinary occasion, it does occur.

At six o'clock the Archbishops, clergy, and a few old friends of the Convent were entertained at dinner, at Aitchison's Rooms, 75 Queen Street. The chair was taken by his Grace the Archbishop of St. Andrews and Edinburgh, on whose right hand was Archbishop Eyre. Almost all the clergy before named were present at the dinner; the other gentlemen present were A. V. Smith Sligo, Esq., of Inzievar; J. Stuart, Esq. of Ballechin; J. Monteith, Esq. of Carstairs; Colonel Gordon, Dr. Moir

Dr. Horsley, Gregory O'Neil, Esq., A. Macpherson, Esq., F. S. Carragher, Esq., D. M. Maguire, Esq. It was intimated that apologies regretting their inability to be present at the Golden Jubilee celebration, had been received from Bishop Macdonald, Aberdeen; Bishop Rigg, Dunkeld; Bishop Angus Macdonald, Argyll and the Isles; Bishop M'Lachlan, Dumfries; Bishop Bewick, Hexham and Newcastle; the Right Rev. the Abbot of Mount St. Bernard's, Leicester; the Right Rev. Monsignor Canon Thomson, Hexham; Canon O'Neill, Dublin; the Very Rev. J. Bennett, C.SS.R.; F. Pinet, O. M. J. F. Gleeson, C.M; Rev. F. Kirsopp; Rev. James Clapperton, Rev. John Sutherland, &c., &c.

The first toast proposed from the chair was that of the Pope. As a gentleman, a peacemaker, a scholar, and a diplomatist, the Archbishop said that Leo XIII. was the admiration of all the world. It was the most marvellous sight in the world to see the man of blood and iron, who swore that *he* would never go to Canossa, now bowing low before the Pontiff, and not only asking him to act as arbiter in a dispute between Spain and Germany, but respectfully accepting the decision, though unfavourable to himself, and then proclaiming to the world his respect for Leo XIII. It was because he joined together the strength of the lion with the meekness of the lamb, that the Pope had conquered Prince Bismarck.

In next proposing "the Queen" the Archbishop spoke of the virtues by which her Majesty had endeared herself to her subjects, and expressed a hope that her jubilee next year would be celebrated in a manner worthy of the loyalty and devotion of her subjects.

The Very Reverend Provost M'Kerrell, of Innerleithen, proposed the health of the Archbishop of St. Andrews and Edinburgh. They had formerly known him, he said, as a simple missionary Priest, fulfilling the important and arduous duties of his charge in a quiet and unostentatious way. Yet, at the same time, all knew the high qualities hidden under that humble exterior; and it was only true to say that not only the Archdiocese of St. Andrews and Edinburgh, but the whole Church in Scotland had reason to be proud of its spiritual adviser. The imposing ceremonies of that day might be taken as a happy inauguration of blessings awaiting the Church in Scotland.

The Archbishop briefly returned thanks for the kind manner in which his health had been proposed, and then gave the toast of the evening, "Prosperity to St Margaret's Convent." "It is," said he, "a red letter day for the ladies who keep the fiftieth year of their foundation, and a happy day for Scotland. I need not enlarge on the claims St. Margaret's has upon us. The Sisters have had their share in the increase of Catholicism in Scotland within these last fifty years. I need not especially refer to the vast number of churches and schools established during that space of time, carried on successfully, and in which the Sisters have had a share. A branch of St. Margaret's has for many years been doing good work at Perth, not only in attending to the poor prisoners at the penitentiary there, but also in educational labours in the city. We have every reason to be proud of the good work begun by Bishop Gillis fifty years ago. There were in the company at the Jubilee celebrations to-day, some ladies and gentlemen who were present at the opening of the Convent, and I trust that they will see the diamond Jubilee of St. Margaret's."

Mr. Smith Sligo, of Inzievar, in the name of the ladies of St. Margaret's Convent, returned thanks for the way in which the toast had been honoured. He was one of those present at the opening ceremony, and as for his brother (the chairman), he was a little acolyte at the altar. Mr. Smith Sligo then contrasted the state of religion fifty years ago, with that which they saw at the present day, and referred much of the progress which had been made to the good work and influence of religious orders.

The Rev. Father Whyte, S.J., proposed "the Guests," naming especially Archbishop Eyre and Mr. Monteith, who both returned thanks, Mr. Monteith recalling the fact that his mother had been received into the Church at St. Margaret's.

Father Whyte, who acted as Guest-master, said that the dinner at which they were assembled was remarkable in one particular,—in that all present were the guests of invisible hostesses. The Sisters had begged him to express their thanks to all who had assisted in the festivities of the day, and especially to Canon Donlevy for the trouble he had taken in his arduous labours as Master of Ceremonies. Canon Donlevy, in reply, said it gave him great pleasure to do anything for St. Margaret's; and he called attention to the perfect manner in which the choir had acquitted themselves of the beautiful music that had accompanied the services. Father Gray said he was sure the choir were happy to render service to the Sisters of St. Margaret's.

The Vicar-General, the Very Rev. W. Grady, proposed the health of Father Whyte, who briefly replied, and the company shortly after dispersed, several of the clergy having to leave Edinburgh by train that evening.

The poor could not be forgotten on such a day

and indeed they had been the subject of much thought for many months past. Large quantities of clothing had been made up; and, to insure the distribution of these articles to the deserving and really necessitous, a division was made, and a portion sent to the Brotherhood of St. Vincent of Paul, of the three Conferences of St. Mary's, St. Patrick's, and the Sacred Heart. The Presidents of the Conferences sent their thanks to the Reverend Mother for these donations.

The aged poor, under the care of the Little Sisters, were also to have a share in the Feast. A substantial dinner was provided for them, and, doubtless, was fully appreciated.

The Children of the Poor Schools in Perth had a special entertainment; so that all who had any claim on St. Margaret's were united in one joyous Festival.

At St. Margaret's the day was happily closed in company with some Religious from the other convents in Edinburgh, by a few hours spent with the Pupils, who entertained the visitors with music and recitations.

On the following day the Pupils from St. Ann's passed the afternoon at the Convent, when several groups were photographed. The Rev. Charles Gordon, S.J., gave Benediction, at which the "Te

Deum" was sung by a choir formed of former Pupils of the school, who volunteered their services in honour of the occasion.

The relic of St. Margaret remained exposed during the Octave, at the close of which it was venerated by the Community and children; and thus the celebration of the Jubilee terminated.

If the anticipation of a happy event is in itself a joy, surely the remembrance of past happiness is no less an abiding source of delight. The preparations for the Jubilee were full of pleasure to all the Community; and now that the celebration is over, and the usual quiet routine of convent life again reigns at St. Margaret's, the Sisters feel thankful for the blessing which fell upon their Festival, the happiness that pervaded the whole, and for the kindness they received from all their friends.

Many were the Masses offered on St. Margaret's Day for her Convent in Edinburgh by holy Bishops and Priests; many were the fervent prayers that rose to heaven from religious communities throughout the United Kingdom, and in far distant countries, that God's blessing may still rest upon His work, and that the coming years may bring with them a yet greater abundance of the Divine grace and aid, increased opportunities for promoting God's glory and His reign in souls, and a fuller knowledge and love of the Word Incarnate.

Such are the petitions that were offered up for St. Margaret's on the Jubilee Day, and they are echoed in the heart of every Sister of the Community.

The Jubilee has opened a new era for St. Margaret's. Those who have read the foregoing pages of its history, have seen that its career has not been unmixed with trials and sorrows; but whether in prosperity or in adversity, the hand of God has guided and protected the work, and brought it to the close of its first half-century of existence.

May the same Fatherly Hand continue to bless the succeeding years, and may the joyful Festival of the Golden Jubilee be as the foretaste of that everlasting felicity which will be the portion of those who are "faithful unto death."

PRINTED BY BALLANTYNE, HANSON AND CO.
EDINBURGH AND LONDON.

Lightning Source UK Ltd.
Milton Keynes UK
UKHW020842010223
416291UK00007B/924

9 781377 209197